P9-DDB-840

The Crash Course

The Unsustainable Future of Our Economy, Energy, and Environment

CHRIS MARTENSON

WILEY

John Wiley & Sons, Inc.

Published by John Wiley & Sons, Inc., Hoboken, New Jersey.
Published simultaneously in Canada.

For general information on our other products and services or for technical support,
please contact our Customer Care Department within the United States at
(800) 762-2974, outside the United States at (317) 572-3993 or fax (317) 572-4002.

Wiley also publishes its books in a variety of electronic formats. Some content that
appears in print may not be available in electronic books. For more information about
Wiley products, visit our web site at www.wiley.com.

Library of Congress Cataloging-in-Publication Data:

Martenson, Chris, 1962-
   The crash course: the unsustainable future of our economy, energy, and environment/
Chris Martenson.
      p. cm.
   Includes Index.
   ISBN 978-0-470-92764-9 (cloth)
   ISBN 978-1-118-01310-6 (ebk)
   ISBN 978-1-118-01311-3 (ebk)
   ISBN 978-1-118-01312-0 (ebk)
         1. Sustainable development—United States.   2. Economic forecasting—
United States.   3. United States—Economic conditions—2009-   I. Title.
   HC110.E5M375 2011
   338.973'07—dc22   2010039914

Printed in the United States of America

10 9 8 7 6 5 4 3 2 1

CONTENTS

FOREWORD

"If you glance up from this book and scan your surroundings, you'd be challenged to spy a single object that did not somehow, in some way, get there because of oil," Chris opens Chapter 16 (*Peak Oil*) of this book you are now reading.

Sure enough, I was reading this chapter on a train bound for Washington, DC, and we'd just pulled up to the BWI airport rail station. Diesel . . . jet fuel . . . and all the large McMansions packed full of plastic, petroleum-based products . . . that we'd just shot past at 64 miles per hour. Thinking about our economy in this simple way, for just one second, leads to one conclusion: Right now we live like kings of old, but on borrowed money and borrowed time.

According to Chris, a gallon of gasoline performs the equivalent energy of 350 and 500 hours' worth of work. If that's the case, a gallon of gas isn't expensive at $3.09—which is what I paid to fill up the family car today. If I were paying that gas a $15 wage (like I do the babysitter), I'd pay anywhere from $5,250 on up to $7,500. Really, we're reaping what may be a once-in-a-species energy orgy that could end in 20 years or less.

That's the genius behind Chris Martenson's *The Crash Course*—direct and straightforward talk about what the next 20 years could look like. But the reason you should pay attention to what Chris has to say is not simply what he writes. It's what he's done.

I thought it was a big deal when, with my wife and our first child, I moved to Paris to work with Bill Bonner, which led to my role in what grew into Agora Financial. Chris has gone one step further.

He realized in 2002 that something wasn't right in the economy of the United States. The research he began—much of which is in this very book—overwhelmed him so much that he vacated his VP seat at a Fortune 300 company just to get to the bottom of it all.

Once he had, he moved to act.

Brave and ready to side with his gut, he picked up his entire family with his wife Becca and left behind their cozy six-bedroom, five-bath house in Mystic, Connecticut. They moved into a rented house in a western Massachusetts town where farmland thrived and there were about 8,400 people.

I have some experience with that side of New England myself. I know how hard that is at first. The 1973 oil shock forced my father to shut down his building supply company. And we tried out sustainable living—he was an early believer.

We moved into a farmhouse without any running water. We had to use an outhouse—try doing that in the middle of February! And we put living off the land into practice. We grew all our own food, raised chickens, and rented land to a local dairy farmer. Chris talks about all these kinds of moves in Chapter 27 (*What Should I Do?*).

In investing, solid stocks are often the ones where the heads of companies and high levels of staff have a lot of skin in the game. Not options, mind you, but actual stock. Again, Chris goes one step further—he classifies stock wealth as "tertiary wealth" and suggests hard assets: gold, silver, farmland.

Chris helps us realize that in just the short span of 150 years, we've spent our way through our greatest wealth—what he calls *primary wealth* and *secondary wealth*. These kinds of wealth are the ores that come out of the ground, phosphates that keep our soil fertile (in the hope of feeding 9.5 billion mouths by 2050), and the fish in our oceans.

If you stop to count, as Chris does here, it's not only Peak Oil we should be worrying about, but Peak Everything—from phytoplankton to nutrient-rich black soil.

This book doesn't make you feel guilty about the energy-dependent lives we lead right now. It's about thinking how you might shift even one small thing—Chris calls this "Step Zero"—and going ahead with that one change until you can make another.

Some very small things, like turning off the faucet when you brush your teeth, might not amount to much. After all, only 10 percent of the world's water usage comes from what we use in our homes. And that's another thing about Chris. He doesn't shy away from the hard facts of just what we're up against.

Right now, we'd need 1.4 Earths to sustain our way of life at current levels. Of the 54 oil-producing nations out there, 40 are past peak production. That means 14 nations must shoulder our decline burden and the bigger burden: growth. When it comes to debt, my pet subject, Chris does it justice in Chapter 10 (*Debt*).

Total credit debt has doubled five times in the past four decades! That's enabled a generation of bubbles, each more perilous than the last.

Working with documentary filmmakers is old hat to me now, after wrapping up the critically acclaimed documentary *I.O.U.S.A.* Chris is no stranger on this front, either. He produced a three-and-a-half-hour video presentation in five months called the *Crash Course.* In 2008, he did something truly startling: He gave out a downloadable version of the *Crash Course*—his life's work so far—for free. When you do that and then 25,000 pay for the professional DVD anyway, you know you're onto something.

And here's where Chris is different: There are a lot of Peak Oil guys out there. Very few offer solutions on a personal level.

In Part VI (*Convergence*), Chris, like the good economic futurist he is, lays out three possible scenarios that cover a very short period of time: starting now (2011) and taking us clear into 2015 and beyond. He sketches out the impact debt, declining oil production, loss of faith in the U.S. dollar, and war will have. The more profound scenario divides our history into two eras: BO and AO. *Before Oil* and *After Oil.*

And then you realize by Part VII (*What Should I Do?*) that the end of the "1,800-mile Caesar salad" will actually be better than you might think.

Chapter 28 (*The Opportunities*), the most important chapter in the whole book, talks about the opportunities before you, before us. My personal favorite, as executive publisher of Agora Financial, is this: *Invest defensively.*

Like Chris, I have three children. And I care about the world they will inherit. It's why I've made enemies in Congress, put sweat and tears into the book *Empire of Debt*, and took on the extra challenge of making the story of our credit-addicted government and economy into the documentary *I.O.U.S.A.* I salute Chris as a fellow fighter on the battlefield for our future.

One thought of his that you can take to the bank: *"The next 20 years will be completely unlike the last 20 years."*

As you read this book, I say to you, prepare to be surprised.

—Addison Wiggin
Author of *Demise of the Dollar, Empire of Debt*, and
Financial Reckoning Day;
Executive Producer, *I.O.U.S.A.;*
Publisher, Agora Financial, LLC

ACKNOWLEDGMENTS

Where do I begin thanking all the people who helped make this book possible? This book represents the most intellectually rigorous and honest work of my life. Without the persistent efforts of my wife, Becca, who has ever urged me see more, try new things, go deeper, and question the ways in which I might be wrong as well as right, this book and the rest of my work would have been pale shadows rather than my best, if they happened at all.

Our three children, Erica, Simon, and Grace, deserve thanks for their tremendous patience throughout my arduous process of researching and creating both the *Crash Course* video and this book. I apologize for having spent our entire 2010 family vacation in a tent in Maine, working on a laptop instead of playing with them on the beach. My family's unflagging, unconditional love and support sustains everything I do.

I'd like to thank Judy Hyde and Helen Armstrong for their love, early and ardent support, and for trusting my reckless business decision to give away the *Crash Course* video series for free.

I am a storyteller, researcher, and data hound who needs to acknowledge the extent to which this book rests upon the work and ideas of others. I owe Michael Browning for invaluable conversations over the years as my early thoughts took shape, to the folks at ASPO and TheOilDrum.com for helping me to deepen my understanding of Peak Oil, and to the blogosphere in general for bravely exploring essential subjects when the mainstream media wouldn't go there.

I'd like to thank the individuals whose donations over the years have funded the considerable work and research necessary to write this book. Special thanks go to Michael Höhne, Erik Townsend, Arthur Tunnell, Mark Klarich, Melissa Wedig, Carrie Pine, and the many others whose sizable donations have allowed my staff and me to invest our time in this work.

I'd especially like to thank my staff, as each member was instrumental in bringing this book to fruition:

Amanda Witman, for her unparalleled gifts as an editor and her masterfully organized working style, and who helped me hone and housekeep this book to within an inch of its life.

Megan Walsh, for her immense competence, intensive project management, help with research and editing, and coordination in weaving together the multiple components of this book.

Jeanine Dargis, for her diligent work in building the charts and graphics, and her patience in fielding the most irksome requests.

Ron Shimshock, for bringing both incredible technical expertise and a rare business mind to bear on the creation of our web site.

Adam Taggart, for his attention as an early editor and for taking charge as ship's captain, keeping our site and business sailing smoothly when I was absorbed in this project.

Finally, I'd like to thank the www.ChrisMartenson.com community for their passion, enthusiasm, and interest in these ideas, for the intelligent conversation they provide on a daily basis, and for their faithful support of this work. Together we are achieving a tipping point of awareness, which is possible thanks to the early adopters of this mission. My heartfelt thanks to all of you who helped us get here.

INTRODUCTION

Not long ago, I was firmly seated on the American Dream bandwagon. I had done everything that you are supposed to do—and more. In the 1990s, I earned my PhD in Pathology/Toxicology from Duke University and did two years of post-doctoral research with the intention of becoming a full-time professor. But life takes its twists and turns; I went on to get an MBA from Cornell and spent the next 10 years working my way through and up the corporate ladder, ultimately becoming a VP at SAIC, a Fortune 300 company. These details are helpful in understanding three things about me: (1) I bring a scientist's understanding and love of data to my work, (2) I am thoroughly at home with financial concepts, and (3) I gave up a very lucrative and promising career to work on the material that now appears in *The Crash Course*.

I first noticed something was awry in 2002, when my portfolio of hard-earned investments hit a new low. At that time, my wife Becca, my three children, and I lived in a 6-bedroom, 5-bathroom house in Mystic, Connecticut. Our boat was in a slip less than a mile away, we had numerous friends and acquaintances, and our children were tracked into the local elementary school. I recall several increasingly uncomfortable conversations with our broker at the time, not because of the losses *per se*, but because he kept giving me reassurances when I wanted information and context. *How did this downturn compare to prior events? What was driving it? How long did people have to wait to recoup their losses in the past? What sort of time horizon should we be expecting before things recover? What will drive that recovery?* None of these questions was ever answered to my satisfaction, so I set about researching the answers myself. What I found shocked me to my core.

I discovered that my nation, far from being the economic ocean liner of the world, was instead like a leaky rowboat. Our levels of debt were extraordinary by any historical measure. Our entitlement programs alone were quite obviously underfunded enough to sink the ship, or at least put a few holes in the hull at the waterline. Our primary sources of wealth creation, manufacturing jobs, were leaving for distant shores, and I could not fathom how merely shuffling paper, a massive growth industry at the time, created any real or lasting wealth. If our 2003 trade deficit were a nation, it would have had the twentieth largest GDP in the world, indicating that Americans' overconsumption exceeded the entire economic activity of all but the largest countries. I was thoroughly stumped by how these things could possibly go on forever, or even for much longer, and so I began to dig deeper.

My wife calls this the period when I "fell down the rabbit hole" like Alice in Wonderland, but to me it seemed more like an entire interconnecting warren of rabbit holes. There was data everywhere, and some of it did not make any sense to me—or at least I could not understand why I had not heard these important things before. I began to share what I was finding with everyone who would listen, especially my wife.

By 2003, our views of the future had become closely aligned, and we decided to move from Mystic to . . . somewhere, anywhere . . . with more community, ample resources, and a few defining characteristics that we thought would provide a better match to the future we saw coming. By July of that year, we had sold our house, moved into a rental home in semirural western Massachusetts, sold most of our stocks, bought gold and silver, and began living a life that contained far fewer physical possessions but offered more direct control over the things that now mattered most to us. I took over complete control of all of our financial investment decisions (no more broker), we took up gardening again, and we started putting serious time into finding and developing deeper community connections. My passion for learning about the economy and financial matters grew as I read dozens of books and hundreds, maybe even thousands, of articles from magazines, trade journals, and the Internet.

By 2004, my research had expanded to include an appreciation for an idea called "Peak Oil," which describes an eventual cresting of oil production leading to a permanent condition of less and less thereafter. By joining this understanding of energy and its role in our daily lives to my newfound clarity on the role of money and how it is produced and managed, I came to a fairly startling conclusion: Our current system of money was unsustainably designed—and it was destined for failure; I just didn't know when.

I felt urgently enough about this revelation that I developed an entire seminar on the subject and called it *The End of Money*. My presentation began with the history of money itself, then romped through slide upon slide of economic statistics, including debt, savings, derivatives, bubbles, economic and monetary history, and energy.

In July of 2005, I left my position at SAIC on good terms, determined to spend more time pursuing the issues that were consuming me. I took a sabbatical from my corporate responsibilities so that I could spend more time researching, distilling, and communicating what I was learning to others.

Friends and family found less humor in my choice to become what I jokingly called "self-unemployed," wondering what sort of person, at 42 years of age and with three young children, would drop his career to pursue a passion without any thought for how that whim might pay the bills. For the next four years we lived entirely off savings, our dwindling bank account ostensibly proving their skepticism to be well-founded.

But the work felt too important, and I threw myself into it. I gave seminars, lots of seminars. I started a blog, I spent the better part of a year working with a documentary filmmaker, and I continued to read everything relevant that I could get my hands on. After more than a year and a half of full-time development, *The End of Money* had reached maturity.

I recall its impact on audiences throughout 2007. At one venue outside of Hartford, Connecticut, I remember how I kept waiting for someone to stand up and challenge my work. That test never came, not even from audiences that included a former president of a State Street financial firm and a member of the board of directors of a large regional bank. All I ever received were heartfelt congratulations and thank yous.

In late 2007, one audience member, Alejandro Levins, a former owner of a Silicon Valley Internet company, convinced me that my seminar was too important not to be shared on the Internet. I didn't see how this was possible, as the seminar was now a four-part series, requiring over eight hours to deliver and involving hundreds of slides. The idea of condensing it gave me nightmares. Yet the idea of producing eight hours of video material also felt prohibitive. I finally relented and spent nearly the entire spring of 2008 working through various technical formats and other issues while condensing the material. In May of 2008, I uploaded the very first video chapter of what is now called the *Crash Course*. It would take me five more months of intense work to complete what would become an additional 19 chapters, comprising 3½ hours of instructional video material housing the core elements of my thinking and research. On October 23, 2008, the last chapter was finally loaded to the site, and we sat back to see what might happen next.

While I had been successful in shrinking the content down to far less than the original eight hours, I was certain that this online series would appeal to only a very limited audience due to its length and content. But I was wrong. Again I waited for the critiques and rebuttals that seemed sure to follow, but aside from some minor errata found by diligent eyes, my work stood mainly unchallenged. Even more surprisingly, the *Crash Course* became an Internet success, drawing well in excess of a million and a half views in its first year.

Determined to try to seek a tipping point of awareness that I believed could pave the way for positive change on a large scale—or perhaps just to exercise my well-ingrained habit of *not* earning a living—I decided to give away the best work of my life for free the *Crash Course* was made available online in a format that anyone could copy and distribute at no charge. We also produced and sold a professionally produced DVD version, initially offered at cost to maximize its distribution. Twenty-five thousand copies were sold within the first few months of its release.

Accolades began to roll in, and volunteers came forward to put an enormous amount of work into translating the *Crash Course* into other languages, first Spanish, then French, German, Hebrew, Portuguese, and Italian. Donations came in to support the continuation of my work. I amassed a team of four part-time staff members, whose considerable skill in handling administrative and technical tasks enabled me to keep my focus centered at the heart of our work. Our subscription newsletter service began to attract a significant number of enrolled members, who overwhelmingly encouraged us to continue moving forward with our efforts. We devoted ourselves to making the web site, www.ChrisMartenson.com, more robust, useful, and navigable. We developed further seminar materials, which we presented at numerous locations in the United States. We created an online archive of original articles and resources, built online forums where like-minded community members could connect, published support materials for volunteer-run *Crash Course* presentations, and produced podcasts and additional video materials to supplement the *Crash Course*. We connected with thousands of individuals through our web site, seminars, and e-mail, most of whom offered overwhelming thanks and encouragement.

Finally, in 2009, the very first dollar of profit flowed out of these efforts and into my life, slowing the exodus of money out of my savings account. We had done it. We had turned passion into income while simultaneously giving our very best content to the world for free.

At the end of 2009, Becca and I finally bought the house that we had been renting, knowing full well that from a purely economic standpoint, it wasn't the optimal time to buy. We decided that, given the state of the world, we valued time more than money, and we wanted to make use of that time to make prudent improvements to our home and invest ourselves permanently in our community.

In 2009 and 2010, I presented the *Crash Course* or related material to the United Nations, the U.K. Parliament, U.S. State Legislatures, the Audubon Society, the Commonwealth Club, the Association for the Study of Peak Oil and Gas, global corporations such as Yahoo! and Honda, capital management firms, and many other noteworthy organizations, large and small. I regularly appear in or am cited by major media, from cutting-edge econo-blogs to more traditional publications such as *The Wall Street Journal* and *The Washington Post*. My web site, www.ChrisMartenson.com, receives over 100,000 unique visitors every month. Most gratifying, our message is resonating with a wide and diverse audience: The 800-plus sites currently linking in to ChrisMartenson.com are nearly impossible to classify as a whole, as they represent a diverse social, economic, and cultural spectrum. The material that comprises my web site and the contents of this book has been launched from the obscurity of my home office to the highest courts of public opinion. But perhaps the biggest testament to the *Crash Course's* success is the many letters that we receive from people who tell us how happy they are to have come across the *Crash Course*—and the ways in which they have changed their lives because of it.

Deciding to change on your own terms, while frightening at times, can be incredibly rewarding. Even though by traditional measures our family's *standard* of living has been cut in half, our *quality* of life has doubled. We now measure our wealth in things like the depth of our community relationships, our free time, our children's joy and curiosity, and the ways in which we are more self-reliant than before. We are living proof that it is indeed possible to step off the American Dream bandwagon and not only survive, but thrive. I will be honest: There are enormous changes, possibly disruptive ones, ahead for all of us. But I want to assure you that there is much in this story that is still within your control.

So that is my story: from research scientist, to corporate executive, to satisfied and never-been-happier husband, father, and economic futurist. Becca and I took a short detour through some fearful thoughts and big decisions, but we discovered something pleasant and unexpected along the way—a better life. Given the opportunity to go back in time, we would do it all over again. Everything that led to those changes, and what I have learned along the way, is now contained within the pages that follow.

PART I
HOW TO APPROACH THE NEXT TWENTY YEARS

CHAPTER 1

THE COMING STORM

In 2008 and 2009, economic activity in the United States and most other developed nations tumbled off a cliff. At several points there was real panic in the air. Stock markets around the world fell to levels that wiped out more than a decade of gains. Trillions evaporated in the housing market, and global trade plummeted.

Questions remain: *What happened? Where did all our money go? How did 10 years of wealth accumulation evaporate so quickly? More important, when can we expect a recovery?*

In truth, our predicament goes far deeper than even these recent, disquieting economic events might suggest. It's time to face the facts: A dangerous convergence of unsustainable trends in the economy, energy, and the environment will make the "twenty-teens" one of the most challenging decades ever. *The Crash Course* explains this predicament and provides sufficient context to support the idea that it is well past time to begin preparing for a very different future.

The entire developed world is entering this next period of time in a severely weakened financial state. The United States, in particular, is carrying excessive levels of debt and unfunded liabilities and is further burdened by a national failure to save and invest in infrastructure. But the issue is not limited to the United States; every nation will eventually have to face the same realities posed by limited and limiting resources.

As a society, our imagined responses to the future make the implicit assumption that we will always remain within a complex economy that is capable of operating in an effective and orderly manner. *The Crash Course* asks the question, *What if this assumption is untrue?* and provides both data and ideas to support the conclusion that the economic status quo cannot be taken for granted, at least not in the form to which we've become accustomed.

Even if the only task ahead of us were attend to the numerous economic mistakes of the past several decades, we would still find this next incarnation of our economy to be extremely difficult. But there are other factors at work.

The big story is this: The world has physical limits that we are already encountering, but our economy operates as if no physical limits exist. Our economy requires growth. I don't mean that growth is "required" as if it's written in a legal document somewhere, but it is "required" in the sense that our economy only functions well when it's growing. With growth, jobs are created and debts can be serviced. Without growth, jobs, opportunities, and the ability to repay past debts simply and mysteriously disappear, causing economic pain and confusion.

In the near future, humanity as a species will have to grapple with a condition that it has never faced before: Less and less energy will be available each year. In the past, there was always another continent brimming with energy resources to tap; another well that could be drilled; more hydrocarbon wealth that could be brought up from the depths. We have always had access to increased resources when we wanted them, and during that long run of history, we have fashioned an enormously complicated society and global economic model around the idea that there always would be more.

Along the way, we moved from burning wood to burning coal, then to whale oil, and then to petroleum. The unanswered question is this: *After oil, what comes next?* What *is* the next source of energy? Nobody has a truly viable answer for that as we cross the threshold of Peak Oil, a concept that represents the moment after which slightly less and less energy comes up out of the ground for us to use as we wish. Many hold out hopes that technology will ride to the rescue, perhaps in the form of nuclear power, natural gas, or alternative sources of energy. But the issues of time, scale, and cost loom large, because we have taken so long to finally recognize the imminence and severity of the petroleum predicament.

With a peak in energy extraction, a host of environmental issues suddenly come into play. Agricultural soils that were forced to produce higher yields via the continuous application of fertilizers derived from fossil fuels will turn out to have been fundamentally depleted. Minerals of increasingly dilute concentrations that require more and more energy to produce will suddenly cost exponentially more each year to extract and process. Where markets once allocated our energy resources according to ability to pay, true scarcity will soon form the dividing line between economic progress and decline for the world's various nations. How soon will all of this happen? If not this year, then within 20 years, which is a blink of an eye given the scale and scope of the potential disruptions implied by this structural shift.

It is only when we assemble the challenges we find in the economy, energy, and the environment—what I call "the three Es"—into one spot that we can fully appreciate the true dimensions of our predicament. The next 20 years are going to be shaped by fundamental resource scarcity in ways that we have never experienced in history. The developed world is entering this race economically handicapped, with no one to blame but itself.

The primary question is whether we want our future to be shaped by disaster or by design. The set of predicaments and problems that we now face are very different from the conditions of the past 20 years and therefore present a solid challenge to the existing status quo. Those currently wielding power and influence are most likely to defend the status quo, raising the risk that our future will consist more of disaster than design. Further, abrupt changes have the unfortunate tendency of escaping notice by the majority of people, who have been conditioned to expect that the future will resemble the past. This is a perfectly valid assumption for ordinary moments, but it is a liability during extraordinary times.

A lucky few will see the changes coming ahead of time and seize the opportunity to make a more gentle series of adjustments on their own terms, while most will be caught unawares and have a much rougher period of transition. Fortunately, by examining and understanding the ways in which the economy intersects with and depends upon energy and other resources from the environment, it is possible to safely navigate and even predict the coming changes.

That is where *The Crash Course* comes in. I will teach you the system of thinking that I used to foresee the financial difficulties of 2008 and 2009 years in advance. Not only did I survive the great credit crunch of those years, I advanced my wealth handily, beating the meager returns that stocks and bonds would have offered.

Because I am discussing subject matter of a serious nature, I may seem to be delivering a doom-and-gloom message. But truthfully, I consider myself to be a "realistic optimist." The spirit and intent of *The Crash Course* are to help you see the options and opportunities in this story of change. I have created a better life for myself and my family through the insights developed from this work. You can, too.

The mission of this book is larger than helping people build more resilience into their lives and portfolios. At our current pace, we are on track to leave behind more than a few predicaments for our children, as part of a substantially degraded world with fewer opportunities than we ourselves were granted. If we make the right choices from this point forward, we have the opportunity to leave a very different legacy. That is what *The Crash Course* is about—helping us to individually and collectively understand that our choices matter significantly and that the time to make the right choices is running dangerously short.

CHAPTER 2

THE LENS

How to See the Future

I would like to share with you the method of thinking that allowed me to skirt the worst of the financial downturn, illuminate the future, and increase my wealth. It has become the lens through which I view the world, combining the economy, energy, and the environment—which I introduced in Chapter 1 (*The Coming Storm*) as the three Es—into a single, comprehensive whole.

The first E, the **economy**, is founded on a workable understanding of how our money system actually operates, as well as basic economic information about debt, savings, and inflation. Not too much; just enough to allow us to assess the sustainability of our current trajectory. A critical understanding rests on the observation that our economy is predicated on growth. It needs growth the way our bodies needs oxygen. Not just any kind of growth, but *exponential* growth, which is a nonlinear form of growth that begins slowly but compounds with urgency toward the end. If you are interested in peering into the future with the intent of predicting how it will unfold, you *must* learn this concept.

Even if we were to limit ourselves to examining just the **economy** while ignoring energy and the environment, we could make a compelling case that prosperity faces the most daunting structural headwinds seen in generations. As baby boomers transition from being net investors and builders to net sellers and downsizers, this change will put downward pressure on the prices of the stocks, bonds, and real estate they will be selling. Further, we might note that the developed world has doubled its debt load over the past 10 years, which was an important component of our perceived prosperity but which, for a variety of reasons, seems unlikely to happen again. Even more dramatically, we have recently seen an explosive expansion in unmatched pension and entitlement liabilities in a majority of developed nations. Without these increases in debt and unfunded liabilities, global growth over the past decade would have been a great deal less dramatic than it was. How will we fuel the necessary growth now required to service our existing debts, let alone double them again? That's a good question.

However, it's when we bring in the second E, **energy**, that the story quickly compounds in urgency. Our economy is dependent on growth, and petroleum—oil—is the undisputed king of fuels that drive economic expansion. It has no substitutes, no replacements waiting in the wings, and it is depleting. There is growing alignment between various government and private institutions predicting the date when an irreversible peak in oil production will occur. This does not mean "running out of oil"; it just means that despite our best efforts, gradually less and less oil will be available each year—though at increasing extraction costs. Many confuse technology with energy, but I don't and neither should you. Technology is a means of exploiting energy more efficiently and effectively, but it is not a *source* of energy. What is our next source of energy? That is the most important question of our time and it remains unanswered.

Oil is not the only critical resource that will be in shorter-than-hoped-for supply in the future. Literally dozens of essential minerals and other natural resources found in the third E, the **environment** (such as silver, phosphate, and possibly even coal, from a net energy perspective) will peak right alongside oil.

Again, this is not a story of "running out"; this is a story where resource extraction gets just a little bit more challenging and a little bit more expensive. Consequently, fewer and fewer resources come up out of the ground to sustain the economy that we know and love. Will all economic activity cease with the depletion of a few key elements? No, of course not. But neither can our economy continue to operate in precisely the same way that it did when demand alone dictated supply.

And that's my key message here. There is a wealth of data suggesting that a period of profound change is either already upon us or coming soon enough to warrant the attention of every serious long-term investor and prudent adult with an eye on the future. We can no longer constrain our thinking to just one E, the **economy**; we must include the other two Es, **energy** and the **environment**. My background as a scientist forces me to consider all the variables within a system. For far too long, economists have been allowed to behave as if the economy was an independent system all on its own. It is not. It is a subset of the larger world, and I attribute all of my success at predicting the events that have unfolded to the fact that I hold this larger, more complete, and therefore more useful view of the world.

Each of the three Es depends upon the other two. They are utterly intertwined, and that's why we need to consider them together. When we do, we are using what I call "the lens." The critical insight that comes from using this lens brings the understanding that continued economic growth is both absolutely essential and also impossible: Essential because our economic system was designed to grow and performs horribly when it cannot, and impossible because nothing can grow forever. The implications are profound and numerous.

Once I developed this lens, I found myself unable to put it completely aside. It has shaped my thinking and my decisions, and was the primary means by which I made sense of new information as it became available. Although I have constantly sought evidence that this view, this hypothesis, might be wrong, it has only been reinforced over the years as the data continues to pile up.

What would I do if new information came along that proved this lens to be mistaken or misleading? I would change my thinking, of course. But as the information has rolled in over the past several years, the validity of this view has only been confirmed. While I am open to the possibility that I may not have everything exactly right, I will present enough solid, fact-based evidence that a reasonable and prudent adult should at least step back, consider the matter, and not reject it out of hand simply because it might seem to be unthinkable.

If I am right, then the next 20 years are going to be completely unlike the last 20 years, and we will be grateful for the foresight that we can gain through the lens of the three Es.

CHAPTER 3

A WORLD WORTH INHERITING

The reason I have chosen this path in life over others that may have been easier or cushier is to fulfill my one highest goal: I want to create a world worth inheriting. Everything else pales in comparison.

I have three children, and I have every expectation of having grandchildren someday. I fervently wish for them to have the same opportunities that I have enjoyed. But my goal extends well beyond my small clan. I want *your* children and grandchildren to have an abundant world filled with meaningful relationships, activities, and careers where they can use their gifts and talents. I believe that a world in which everyone enjoys some degree of prosperity will enrich life for all of us, our children and grandchildren, and those who come after them.

I am concerned that we are on a path that will deliver the opposite of what I hope for. My worry is that the reflexive response of those in power will be to rather defensively attempt to perpetuate the status quo and that their earnest attempts to conduct business as usual for another decade will unquestionably lead to a world of less prosperity, not more. If we pursue this policy of attempting to sustain the unsustainable, what we face is a future filled with scarcity, conflict, and diminished opportunities. I cannot accept those outcomes.

But how can we change the future? Where do we even start? We must begin by taking an unflinching look at our predicament and facing it squarely. No more kicking the can down the road for the next generation to deal with, and no more pretending that real issues don't exist. The measure of any generation is what it does with what it has. Luckily, we still have abundant natural resources, and we have all the information we need to make a better future. But our window of opportunity is closing rapidly. Solutions are becoming fewer, and options are shrinking. Someday they will disappear entirely, our opportunities to be proactive will have been permanently squandered, and we will be left to choose among an unpleasant palette of reactions to an unfortunate set of circumstances that are mostly out of our control.

To me, a world worth inheriting is one where the inhabitants are living within their economic and natural budgets. It is a stable world where people and businesses can plan for the future because they can trust what will be there when they arrive. It is a world in which the brittle architecture of our just-in-time food systems and businesses is replaced by robust, sustainable, locally focused operations. In this world worth inheriting, communities take on more responsibility for their destinies, and stronger and more fulfilling relationships develop among neighbors.

Right now we cannot even count on our money, the sacred contract that binds us all, to be there for us in any recognizable form in the future. Perhaps it will be worth a lot less; perhaps it will be replaced entirely. These are both possible and even likely outcomes given our current economic trajectory, and both are unacceptable. We can do better, and we deserve better.

But the issues extend well beyond just our money, and the sooner we recognize the dimensions of our predicament, the sooner we can get on with the work of responding intelligently to the numerous challenges that wait.

Step one toward creating a world worth inheriting is to become aware of what the problems and predicaments really are. Step two is to deepen that awareness into what we might call *understanding*. Step three is to craft intelligent responses to the issues as we understand them.

How do we accomplish these things? We begin by changing the stories we tell ourselves. The narratives that we run at the individual, national, and even global levels define the actions we take and what we prioritize.

Here is an example: Up until about 2006, the entire developed world was perpetuating an ongoing story that went like this: *Houses always go up in price.* As we now all know, that tale is not true, but it was a deeply embedded belief that shaped individual decisions and led even the most sophisticated investors in the world astray. That's the power of a story. The right narrative can save the world, while the wrong one can be incredibly destructive. This means that we should take the time to examine our current stories and assess whether they are truly the right ones for our era and our set of circumstances.

Some of the stories that we might want to reevaluate include:

- "Economic growth is essential (and good)."
- "U.S. Treasury bonds are risk free."

- "The rest of the world needs the United States more than the United States needs the rest of the world."
- "Technology will always meet our energy needs."

There is a very strong chance that some or all of these stories (and many more) will prove not only to be wrong, but, like any false narrative, also highly destructive to hopes, dreams, capital, and prosperity.

We are at an absolutely unique time in humanity's history, where a sharp corner lies in the road ahead, the traditional controls that we use to steer ourselves will no longer produce the intended effects, and much of what we believe to be true will be proven false. We need to locate these stories and change them, while at the same time supplanting them with realistic, positive visions that will guide the transformations that we need to see.

In most stories of change, there are winners and losers. I want to give you the opportunity to be among the winners. I also want to set the stage for building a more prosperous future for everyone. I believe it can be done. I don't think we need new technologies, or revolutions, or dramatic breakthroughs in thoughts or ideas; we already have everything we need, save one thing: political will.

But that, too, can be overcome. It begins here between us, in this book, starting with a proper and open assessment of the situation in which we find ourselves. I am confident that together we can indeed create a world worth inheriting.

CHAPTER 4

TRUST YOURSELF

To enhance your use of the lens described in Chapter 2 (*The Lens*), I invite you to adopt another somewhat radical technique: *trusting yourself.*

Rather than waiting for someone else to hand you an "expert" solution, give yourself permission to rely on your own intuition, research, and experience regarding what is best for you and your family. Go with what you just know to be right. If something doesn't seem right, however you arrive at that conclusion, it probably isn't. If you wait for authorities, even trusted professionals, to offer a clear signal that it's time to take different actions and make different decisions, you will almost certainly be disappointed with the results. It may not sound easy, but if you learn to trust yourself first and foremost, it will greatly improve your chances of future success.

It took me a while to come to this realization, but I finally figured out that my interests were only accidentally and occasionally aligned with those of Wall Street and the numerous purveyors of their products. Conflicts of interest abound in this area and are mostly hidden, so when a downturn comes along and there's not enough money both for Wall Street to pay itself and for your portfolio to gain in value, it pays to not follow the advice from Wall Street.

In fact, distressingly, it often pays to do the exact opposite of what Wall Street recommends. But Wall Street is just doing its job: making a profit . . . for itself. That's all it cares about, that's all it does, and it does it really well. Similarly, politicians deal in a form of profits, too, but their currency is power. It took me a while to see the game for what it was, but I now know that waiting for the political class to inform us about any issues of real or pressing urgency is not wise, especially when the issues do not have any clear political advantage. Take Peak Oil (discussed in Chapter 16), for example—there's no "win" in that story for any politician in office, which results in nothing being said at all. They simply don't talk about it . . . publicly, anyway.

Where Wall Street has misinformed us and politicians have chosen not to inform us about critical issues, the mainstream media has also dropped the ball, failing to counteract these transgressions by providing essential oversight and context. The media, our "fourth pillar of democracy," has largely failed in its investigative duties, and now mainly provides interesting but generally unhelpful post-mortems on accidents after they've happened.

The way to counteract this conflict of interest is to simply decide for yourself what makes sense and act accordingly. Do not wait to read about a looming issue above the fold of your local newspaper or hear about it on television from a politician, because by then it will be too late to do much about it.

In a nutshell, if something seems wrong, it probably is. I have lost count of the number of people who have told me that they "knew something wasn't right" as their portfolios shed 40 percent or more in 2008 and 2009. Many did not fully trust the placating explanations offered by their stockbrokers, but they didn't act on those feelings, and they subsequently lost money. The critical thing about trusting yourself is that it often means acting on incomplete information, relying on what you might call a "gut hunch" or intuition. I have learned that our bodies will often "know" something is up well before our minds can fully process the situation. In the future that I anticipate, where colliding trends in the economy, energy, and the environment are going to deliver extremely large and fast-paced changes, the ability to make rapid decisions will be essential. This is the sort of landscape where trusting yourself becomes a vital skill.

A second aspect of trusting yourself is that quite often your instincts will lead you to do what very few other people seem to be doing. Surprisingly often, your gut sense will tell you to buck the conventional wisdom, ignore your broker, or override a past decision. I am now extremely glad that I have been able to make decisions that run counter to conventional wisdom and sometimes cut across the social grain. I benefited greatly from trusting gut feelings that led to responses such as buying gold when it was generally reviled as an investment back in 2003, selling my house before the housing collapse, and dumping all of my stocks before the big rundown into 2008. I fought my broker and withstood smirks from knowing friends and even some family members who were sure that they were watching me make enormous mistakes. After all, nobody else seemed to be doing these things, so how could they make any sense? Today these look like genius moves, but they were obvious decisions to make. All that was required to make them was taking a good, hard look at the data and then trusting myself.

To be fair, some of the decisions that I made have led to financial gains, and some led to improvements in my quality of life, but not *all* of them did. The important thing here is that trusting my intuition ensured that I was not paralyzed. There is a time to reflect deeply and accumulate as much information as you can before making a decision, but during less-certain or fast-moving times, you just have to go with what you know to be true on some other level. When events unfold rapidly, the desire to stay ahead of them places a premium on quick decisions. How can you arrive at the best decisions most efficiently? This is the main issue, and it is the primary reason why I promote the idea of trusting yourself. Feeling secure in your intuition is the quickest way to ensure a worthy decision.

I trusted myself enough that when I saw something that didn't make sense, something that just felt wrong, I took actions accordingly. Here is a short list of things that were concerning me in 2003 when I made what my broker, family, and friends assured me were a set of ill-advised decisions:

- It didn't make sense to me that a nation could consume beyond its means and remain wealthy.
- I was stumped by how an economic system predicated on continual expansion of credit could continue on like that forever.
- I didn't understand how people making $50,000 per year could buy $500,000 houses with no money down and have any hope of paying that back.
- The concept of Wall Street somehow transforming subprime loans into higher-grade securities, while extracting money every step of the way, puzzled me deeply.
- It didn't seem possible to me that money and debt could continue to expand faster than the economy without some sort of inflationary outcome or eventual financial crisis.

While I readily admit to rooting around in masses of complicated data during this period, this habit was neither the key to my recent investing success nor to my other life-altering decisions. Instead, I found that asking a few very simple questions provided the answers I needed. Questions such as:

- *Is this sustainable?*
- *If it can't go on forever, what impact would I experience if it stopped?*

- *How much do I trust the authorities here to either tell me the truth or to do the right thing?*
- *Are there any conflicts of interest that might be clouding the experts' message?*

The most important lesson that I have learned is that you should trust yourself and act accordingly. If you have significant doubts about the sustainability of your country's current trajectory, or the stock market, or where food comes from, then those doubts are worth observing and acting upon. There is a time to trust professionals, and there is a time to trust yourself. Now is the time to trust yourself.

We are about to embark on a series of chapters where I will present evidence indicating numerous current but unsustainable trends that will not only someday stop (as all unsustainable things must do) but will potentially even collide, magnifying their individual impact into something greater than their individual parts. These trends are complex, nonlinear, and intertwined. But they can be understood, and should be, because that understanding is the best way of illuminating the future.

Just as we don't have to understand molecular biology in order to "know" about the process of aging, we can assess the trends in the economy, energy, and environment without having to know every detail. Much of what I am going to present is really just a common-sense connection of dots, combined with a researcher's ability to extract relevant information and an educator's desire to make it all interesting.

As we step through the material in the next chapters, I am going to invite you to recall the simple questions above, particularly *Is this sustainable?* At the end of it all, if you find you agree with me that we are collectively on a highly unsustainable path, then the decisions you need to make will become clear. All you need to do is trust yourself.

PART II
FOUNDATION

CHAPTER 5

DANGEROUS EXPONENTIALS

In this book we will explore a few key foundational concepts that will help you gain a better understanding of what lies ahead. None of them is more important than exponential growth. **Exponential growth** holds the honorary position as the "fourth E" in this story. Understanding the ways in which our lives are surrounded and shaped by exponential growth is a necessary part of our ability to effectively anticipate and proactively prepare for our future.

When the president comes on television and says that our highest priority is "returning the economy to a path of growth," what he is really saying is that our top priority is returning the economy to a path of *exponential* growth. Exponential growth is the only type of growth that is expected and required by our economy.

Examples of exponential growth in your life extend well beyond the economy. We are literally surrounded by examples of exponential growth. The human population has been growing exponentially for thousands of years; consequently, so has humans' use of resources. This decade there will be exponentially more retail outlets, reams of paper produced, cars on the road, units of energy burned, money created, and food consumed than last decade.

Exponential growth dominates and defines everything that is happening—and that will happen—regarding the economy, energy, and resources of all kinds, which is why you should pay particular attention to this chapter. As soon as you understand exponential growth and can connect it to the other three Es, then you, too, will appreciate why the future will be radically different from the past.

If exponential growth is so ubiquitous and surrounds us at every turn, why is it not completely obvious to everyone? Why do we need to discuss it at all? The reason is that we're all accustomed to thinking linearly, and exponential growth is nonlinear. We think in straight lines, but exponentials are curved.

Here is an example: Suppose I gave you two chalkboard erasers, and asked you to hold them at arm's length and then move them together at a constant (linear) rate of speed. You would do pretty well at this task, as would most people.

Now let's repeat the same experiment, but this time we'll replace the erasers with two powerful magnets. As you move them together, the first part of the journey will progress in a nice, constant fashion, just like with the erasers. But at a certain point—BANG!—the magnets will suddenly draw themselves together and wreck your deliberately even speed. (Let's hope your fingers were out of the way.)

We could run this experiment a hundred times, and you would never be able to get your body to achieve the same linear control with the magnets as with the erasers. That is because our brains and bodies are wired to process linear forces, and magnets do not exert constant (or linear) force over distance because their force of attraction increases exponentially as they get closer.

Despite our natural affinity for straight lines and constant forces, we *can* still achieve a useful understanding of exponential growth and why it is important. That is what we're going to do in this chapter.

Exponential growth is not unnatural, but the idea of *perpetual* exponential growth is. We have no models of perpetual exponential growth in the physical world to which we can turn for observation and study. For example, microorganisms in a culture will increase exponentially, but only until an essential nutrient is exhausted, and at that point, the population crashes. Viruses will reproduce and then spread exponentially throughout a population, but they will eventually burn out as their hosts either develop immunity or die off. Nuclear chain reactions caused by neutrons cascading through fissile material are exponential, at least until the resulting explosion forces the material too far apart for the reaction to be sustained.

One thing that we lack here on earth, however, is an example of something growing exponentially *forever*. Exponential growth is always self-limiting and is usually relatively short in duration. Nothing can grow forever, yet somehow that's exactly what we expect *and* require of our economy. But we will explore more about why that's the case in a bit.

THE CONCEPT OF EXPONENTIAL GROWTH

What do we mean when we say that something is "growing exponentially"?

To begin with, let's define "growth." When we say that something is growing, we're saying that it's getting larger. Children grow by eating and adding mass, equities grow in price, and the economy grows by producing and consuming more goods. Ponds get deeper, trees grow taller, and profits expand. Within these examples of growth, we can identify two types.

The first type is what we would call "linear growth." *Linear* means adding (or subtracting) the same amount each time. The sequence 1, 2, 3, 4, 5, 6, 7 is an example of linear (or arithmetic) growth in which the same number is reliably added to the series at every step. If we add one each time, or five, or forty-two, or even a million, it won't change the fact that this kind of growth is linear. If the amount being added is constant, then it represents linear growth.

The other type of growth is known as "geometric" or exponential growth, and it is notable for constantly *increasing* the amount of whatever is being added each time to the series. One example is the sequence 1, 2, 4, 8, 16, 32, 64, in which the last number in the series is multiplied by two (or increased by 100 percent) at every step. The amount that gets added in each period is both dependent upon and a little bit larger than the prior amount. In the sequence example given, we see a case where the growth rate is 100 percent. So 2 becomes 4, and 4 becomes 8, and so on. But it doesn't have to grow by 100 percent to be exponential; it could be any other constant percentage and it would still fit the definition.

Figure 5.1
Linear Growth Compared to Exponential Growth

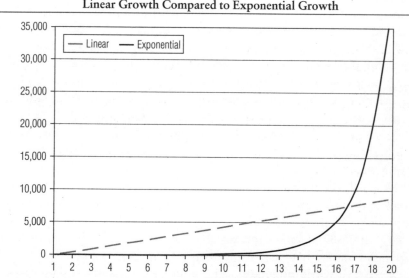

Linear growth is the dotted line; exponential growth is the solid line. The units on both axes are arbitrary; amount is on the vertical (or Y) axis and time is on the horizontal (or X) axis.

Now let's take a closer look at exponential growth so that we can all be clear about what it is and how it relates to our collective future. The chart below illustrates exponential growth—a chart pattern that is often called a "hockey stick."

In Figure 5.1, we're graphing an amount of something over time. It could be the number of yeast grown in a flask of freshly squeezed grape juice every 10 minutes, or it could be the number of McDonald's hamburgers sold each year. It doesn't really matter what it is or what's driving the growth; all that is required to create a line on a graph that looks like the curve seen in Figure 5.1 is that whatever is being measured must grow by some percentage over each increment of time. That's it. Any percentage will do: 50 percent, 25 percent, 10 percent, or even 1 percent. It doesn't matter: 10 percent more yeast per hour, 5 percent more hamburgers per year, and 0.25 percent interest on your savings account will all result in a line on a chart that looks like a hockey stick.

Looking at the figure a bit more closely, we observe that the curved line on the chart begins on the left with a flat part, seems to turn a corner (at what we might call the elbow), and then has a steep part.

A more subtle interpretation of Figure 5.1 reveals that once an exponential function turns the corner, even though the *percentage rate* of growth might remain constant (and low!), the *amounts* do not. They pile up faster and faster. For example, imagine that a long-ago ancestor of yours put a single penny into an interest-bearing bank account for you some 2,000 years ago and it earned just 2 percent interest the whole time. The difference in your account balance between years 0 and 1 would be just two one-hundredths of a cent. Two thousand years later, your account balance would have grown to more than $1.5 quadrillion dollars (more than 20 times all the money in the world in 2010) and the difference in your account between the years 1999 and 2000 alone would have been more than $31 trillion dollars. Where the amount added was two one-hundredths of a cent at the beginning, it was roughly equivalent to half of all the money in the entire world at the end. That's a rather dramatic demonstration of how the amounts vary over time, but it gets the point across.

Now let's look at an exponential chart of something with which you are intimately familiar that has historically grown at roughly 1 percent per year. It is a chart of world population; the solid part is historical data and the dotted line is the most recent UN projection of population growth for just the next 42 years.[1]

Figure 5.2
World Population

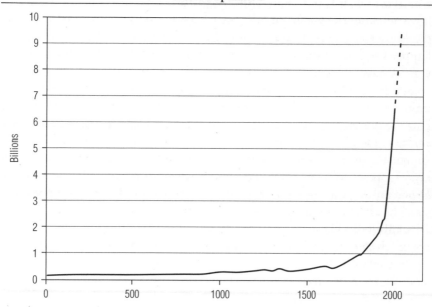

The solid line is historical; the dotted line represents the UN projection.
Source: U.S. Census Bureau Historical Estimates[2] & U.N. 2004 Projections.[3]

Again I want to draw your attention to the fact that the chart has a flat part, then a corner that gets turned, and then a steep part. By now, it is quite possible that any mathematicians reading this are hopping up and down because of what they might view to be an enormous error on my part.

A first point of departure is that where mathematicians have been trained to define exponential growth in terms of the *rate* of change, we're going to concentrate here on the *amount* of change. Both are valid, it's just that *rates* are easier to express as a formula and *amounts* are easier for most people to intuitively grasp. So we're going to focus on amounts, even though this is not where classical mathematicians would train their logical eyes.

Unlike the *rate* of change, the *amount* of change is not constant in exponential growth; it grows larger and larger with every passing unit of time. For our purposes, it is more important that we appreciate what exponential growth demands in terms of physical amounts than whatever intellectual gems are contained within the rate of growth.

A second point of contention that I expect most mathematicians would vigorously dispute is the idea that there's a turn-the-corner stage in an exponential chart. In fact, they're right. It turns out that the point where an exponential chart appears to turn the corner is an artifact of how we draw the left-hand scale. An exponential chart is indeed turning the corner at any and every point along its trajectory. Where that point happens to *appear* on our charts is simply a function of how we scale the vertical axis.

For example, if we take our population chart above, and instead of setting the left axis at 10 billion we set it at one billion (Figure 5.3), we see that the line disappears entirely off the chart somewhere around 1850. We can't see the part after that because it is now way above the top of the chart frame, but in this version of the chart we note that the turn-the-corner event appears to happen around 1900. Instead of having this conversation about turning the corner with population growth right now, it appears as though we really should have had it back in 1900.

Similarly, if we scale our left axis to, say, one trillion (Figure 5.4), the corner disappears entirely and the entire line becomes flat. We can't see its curve anymore. But it is still there; it has just been suppressed by our management of the left axis. No more population problem! Right?

Figure 5.3
World Population

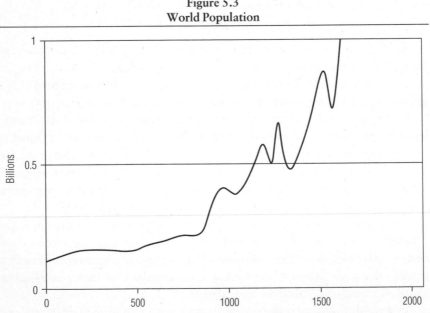

Same world population chart as Figure 5.2, but with left axis set at one billion.
Source: U.S. Census Bureau Historical Estimates.

Figure 5.4
World Population

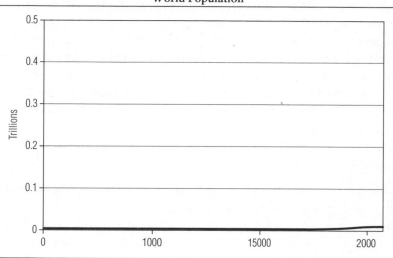

Same world population chart as Figure 5.2, but expressed in trillions.
Source: U.S. Census Bureau Historical Estimates.

So the turn-the-corner moment is really just a product of how we draw our chart. Does it mean that the turn-the-corner stage is a worthless artifact and that we can forget all about it? No, far from it. It is very real and vitally important. Let me explain why.

Where the turn-the-corner stage becomes enormously meaningful and important is when you can reasonably set a boundary—that is, *fix* the left axis to a defined limit—because you know how much of something you have. When you do this, the shape of the chart tells you important things about how much time you have left and what the future will hold. For example, if we were studying yeast growth, we might start with a flask that holds one liter of grape juice, a quantity that we already know can only support so many yeast cells. With this defined limit, we can accurately calculate when an introduced population of yeast will crest and then crash.

Similarly, if we happen to know the carrying capacity of the earth for human beings, then we can "fix the left axis" and make some important observations about what the future might bring and how much time remains to stabilize things. Without fossil fuels to assist with agricultural production, the total carrying capacity of the earth for humans is thought to be somewhat less than the current 6.8 billion and possibly as low as one billion.[4]

Even if these carrying-capacity calculations prove to be pessimistic and we could set the left axis for sustainable human population at 10 billion (although I've not read any scientific analyses that would support such a number), we would still discover that population has turned the corner and that we're no longer on the flat portion of the curve but the steep portion. This means that you and I happen to live in a very different world with entirely different challenges and opportunities than the people who came before us. We live at a time when most people alive will hopefully witness the transition of human population from exponentially expanding to "not growing." I say hopefully, because the alternative is to overshoot and collapse, just like our friends, the yeast in the flask.

SPEEDING UP

A critical concept that I want you to take away from this discussion about exponential growth is that of "speeding up."

It doesn't matter how you prefer to approach this concept. You can either think of speeding up in terms of how the amounts accelerate in size over each unit of time, *or* you can think about how the amount of time shrinks between each fixed amount that is added. It's more stuff with each unit of time or less time between each unit of stuff. Either way you prefer to think of it, you'll come away with a sense of speeding up.

To illustrate this idea using population, if we started with one million people on the planet and set their growth rate to a relatively tame rate of 1 percent per year (it is actually higher than that), we would find that it would take 694 years for world population to grow from one million to one billion people.

Figure 5.5
Population Growth Example

Population Growth
Start: *1 million*
Growth Rate: *1% per year*

Time between each additional billion	
694 years = 1 billion	*Speeding Up*
70 years = 2 billion	
41 years = 3 billion	↓
29 years = 4 billion	
22 years = 5 billion	
18 years = 6 billion	
12 years = 7 billion	

Note how time "speeds up" by shrinking between each new billion people added to the total population.

But we would reach a world population of 2 billion people after only 100 more years, while the third billion would require just 41 more years. Then 29 years, then 22, and then finally only 18 years, to bring us to a total of 6 billion people. Each additional billion-people mark on our graph took a shorter and shorter amount of time to achieve. The time between each billion shrank each time, meaning that each billion came sooner and sooner, faster and faster. That's what I mean by speeding up.

Speeding up is a critical feature of exponential growth—things just go faster and faster, especially toward the end.

Making It Real

Using an example loosely adapted from a magnificent paper by Dr. Albert Bartlett,[5] let me illustrate the power of compounding for you.

Suppose I had a magic eye dropper and I placed a single drop of water in the middle of your left hand. The magic part is that this drop of water will double in size every minute. At first nothing seems to be happening, but by the end of a minute, that tiny drop is now the size of two tiny drops. After another minute, you now have a little pool of water sitting in your hand that is slightly smaller in diameter than a dime. After six minutes, you have a blob of water that would fill a thimble.

Now imagine that you're in the largest stadium you've ever seen or been in—perhaps Fenway Park, the Astrodome, or Wembley Stadium. Suppose we take our magic eye dropper to that enormous structure, and right at 12:00 PM in the afternoon, we place a magic drop way down in the middle of the field.

To make this even more interesting, suppose that the park is watertight and that you're handcuffed to one of the very highest bleacher seats. My question to you is this: *How long do you have to escape from the handcuffs?* When would the park be completely filled? Do you have days? Weeks? Months? Years? How long before the park is overflowing?

The answer is this: You have until exactly 12:50 PM *on that same day*— just 50 minutes—to figure out how you're going to escape from your handcuffs. In only 50 minutes, our modest little drop of water has managed to completely fill the stadium. But wait, you say, how can I be sure which stadium you picked? Perhaps the one you picked is 100 percent larger than the one I used to calculate this example (Fenway Park). Wouldn't that completely change the answer? Yes, it would—by one minute. Every minute, our magic water doubles, so even if your selected stadium happens to be 100 percent larger or 50 percent smaller than the one I used to calculate these answers, the outcome only shifts by a single minute.

Now let me ask you a far more important question: *At what time of the day would your stadium still be 97 percent empty space (and how many of you would realize the severity of your predicament)?* Take a guess.

The answer is that at 12:45 PM—only five minutes earlier—your park is only 3 percent full of water and 97 percent remains free of water. If at 12:45, you were still handcuffed to your bleacher seat patiently waiting for help to arrive, confident that plenty of time remained because the field was only covered with about 5 feet of water, you would actually have been in a very dire situation.

And that right there illustrates one of the key features of compound growth and one of the principal things that I want you take away from this chapter. With exponential growth in a fixed container, events progress much more rapidly toward the end than they do at the beginning. We sat in our seats for 45 minutes and nothing much seemed to be happening. But then, over the course of five minutes—whoosh!—the whole place was full of water. Forty-five minutes to fill 3 percent; only five more minutes to fill the remaining 97 percent. It took every year of human history from the dawn of time until 1960 to reach a world population of 3 billion people, and only 40 additional years to add the next 3 billion people.

With this understanding, you will begin to understand the urgency I feel—there's simply not a lot of maneuvering room once you hop on the vertical portion of a compound graph. Time gets short.

SURROUNDED BY EXPONENTIALS

Dr. Albert Bartlett once said that ". . . the greatest shortcoming of the human race is the inability to understand the exponential function."[6] He is absolutely right. We are literally surrounded by examples of exponential growth that we have created for ourselves, yet very few people recognize this or understand the implications. You now know one implication: speeding up.

Figure 5.6 shows total global energy consumption over the past 200 years. It is plainly obvious that energy use has been growing nonlinearly; the line on the chart looks like one of our hockey sticks. Can energy consumption grow exponentially forever, or is there some sort of a limit, a defined capacity to the energy stadium, that would cause us to fix the left axis on this chart?

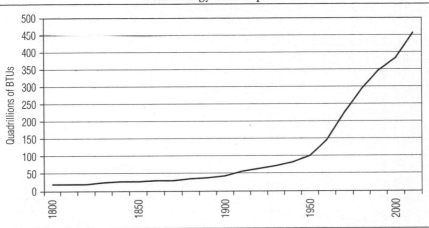

Figure 5.6
Total Energy Consumption

This chart includes energy from all sources: hydrocarbons, nuclear, biomass, and hydroelectric.

Source: Vaclav Smil, Energy Transitions.

On the following page is another exponential chart—the U.S. money supply, which has been compounding at incredible rates ranging between 5 and 18 percent per year (Figure 5.7).

These are just a few examples. We could review hundreds of separate charts of things as diverse as the length of paved roads in the world, species loss, water use, retail outlets, miles traveled, or widgets sold, and we'd see the same sorts of charts with lines that curve sharply up from left to right.

The point here is that you are literally surrounded by examples of exponential growth found in the realms of the economy, energy, and the environment. Far from being a rare exception, they are the norm, and because they dominate your experience and will shape the future, you need to pay attention to them.

THE RULE OF 70

As I said before, anything that is growing by some percentage is growing exponentially. Another handy way to think about this is to be able to quickly calculate how long it will take for something to double in size. For example, if you are earning 5 percent on an investment, the question would be, *How long will it be before a $1,000 investment has doubled in size to*

Figure 5.7
Total Money Stock (M3)

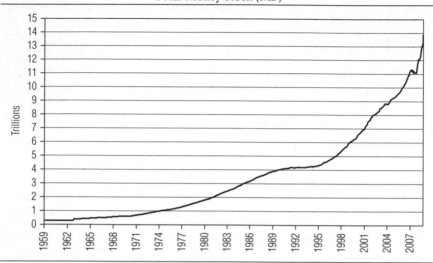

This was the widest measure of money before its reporting was discontinued by the Federal Reserve. M3 money included cash, checking and savings accounts, time deposits, and Eurodollars.

Source: Federal Reserve.

$2,000? The answer is surprisingly easy to determine using something called the "Rule of 70."*

To calculate how long it will be before something doubles, all we need to do is divide the percentage rate of growth into the number 70. So if our investment were growing at 5 percent *per year*, then it would double in 14 years (70 divided by 5 equals 14). Similarly if something is growing by 5 percent *per month*, then it will double in 14 months.

How long before something growing at 10 percent per year will double? Easy; 70 divided by 10 is 7, so the answer is 7 years.

Here's a trick question: *Suppose something has been growing at 10 percent per year for 28 years. How much has it grown?* Some people intuitively guess eight times larger (2 + 2 + 2 + 2 = 8), or four separate doublings over each of the four 7 year periods in the example, but the answer is sixteen, because each doubling builds off of the last (2 → 4 → 8 → 16). Two doubles to four, which doubles to eight, which doubles to sixteen, which is twice as large as intuition might suggest.

---

* Some use "the Rule of 72," which is more accurate in some circumstances, but less easy to calculate in our heads, so we'll stick to 70 for now, as it is perfectly accurate for our purposes.

Here's where we might use that knowledge in real life. You might have read about the fact that China's energy consumption grew at a rate of slightly more than 8 percent between 2000 and 2009, which perhaps sounds somewhat tame. Using the Rule of 70, however, we discover that China is doubling the amount of energy it uses roughly every 9 years, as was confirmed by the International Energy Agency (IEA) in 2010.[7] After 9 years of 8 percent growth, you're not using just a little bit more energy, but 100 percent more. If a country has 500 coal-fired electricity plants today, after 9 years of 8 percent growth it will need 1000 such plants.

If this seems rather dramatic and nontrivial to you, you're right. Time for another trick question about doublings: *Which is larger in size, the amount of energy China used over just the past 9 years (its most recent doubling time), or the amount of energy China has used throughout all of history?* The intuitive answer is that the total amount of energy consumed throughout China's thousands of years of history is far larger than the amount consumed over the past 9 years, but the correct answer is that the most recent doubling is larger than all the prior doublings put together.[8]

This is a general truth about doublings, not China in particular, and applies to anything and everything that has gone through a doubling cycle. To make sense of this preposterous claim, let's use the legend of the mathematician who invented the game of chess for a king. So pleased was the king with this invention that he asked the mathematician to name his reward. The mathematician made a request that seemed modest: to be given a single grain of rice for the first square on the board, two grains for the second square, four grains for the third square, and so on. The king agreed, and foolishly committed to a sum of rice that was approximately 750 times larger than the entire annual worldwide harvest of rice in 2009. That's what 64 doublings will get you.

Note that the first square had one grain of rice placed upon it, while the next square, the first doubling, got two grains. Here on the very first doubling, we can observe that more rice was placed upon the board than was already on the board; two compared to one. That is, the doubling was larger in size than all of the grains that had come before it. And on the next doubling, when we place four grains upon the board, we see that these four grains of rice are more numerous than the three grains $(1 + 2)$ already upon the board from all the prior doublings. And at the next doubling we place eight grains on the board, which is a larger total than the seven that are already upon it $(1 + 2 + 4)$. And so on. In every doubling, we'll find that the most recent doubling is larger in size than all of the prior doublings put together. That's one of the less intuitive but more important features of doublings. Each doubling is larger than all the ones that came before *put together*.

So if your town administrators are targeting, say, 5 percent growth, what they're really saying is that in 14 years time they want to have more than twice as much of everything in the town than it currently has. More than twice as many people, sewage treatment plants, schools, congestion, electrical and water demand, and everything else that a town needs. Not a few more, but *more than twice as many*.

Your Exponential World

The reason we took this departure into discussing exponential growth and doubling times is that you happen to be completely surrounded by examples of exponential growth. And your future, like it or not, will be heavily shaped by their presence.

As you read the rest of this book, it will be helpful to continue to recall these three concepts related to exponential growth and doublings:

1. *Speeding up*. Time really gets compressed toward the end of the exponential phase of growth.
2. *Turning the corner*. This is a very real and extremely important event in systems with limits.
3. *More than double*. Each doubling equals more than all of the prior ones combined.

This information is going to be especially critical when we talk about the idea that our economy, our money system, and all of our associated institutions are fundamentally predicated on exponential growth. As we'll see, it's not just any type of growth that our money system requires, but *exponential* growth.

Up until recently, that has been a fine and workable model, but once we introduce the idea of resource limits into our collective story of growth (in other words, once we know just how big is the stadium in which we're all sitting), we quickly discover some serious flaws in our current narrative. It turns out that the economy does not exist in a vacuum, and it does not have the power to create reality. The economy is really just a reflection of our access to abundant energy and other concentrated resources that we can transform into useful products and services. As long as those resources can continue to be extracted from the earth in ever-increasing quantities, then our economic model is safe and sound. And that is where the trouble in this story begins.

CHAPTER 6

AN INCONVENIENT LIE

The Truth about Growth

All truth passes through three stages. First, it is ridiculed. Second, it is violently opposed. Third, it is accepted as being self-evident.

—Arthur Schopenhauer (1788–1860)

Unless we are careful, we might accidentally pursue growth when what we really are seeking is prosperity. The problem is that prosperity has so often accompanied growth that it has become easy to confuse the two.

Growth appears to solve many problems. Growth creates jobs and adds new money to strained government coffers. At the same time that growth occurs, new opportunities often arise. Growth is so central to our economic models and thinking that many economists will, with completely straight faces, refer to recessions as periods of "negative growth." If that doesn't reveal a bias toward growth, I don't know what does. It's impossible to listen to a presidential press conference on the economy without hearing about growth and how important it is that we create more of it. Economic growth is unquestionably assumed to be desirable, and that's pretty much all there is to the story.

Anybody who believes exponential growth can go on forever in a finite world is either a madman or an economist.

—Kenneth Boulding (1910–1993)[1]

35

The type of growth upon which our economy depends, exponential growth, is completely unsustainable and will therefore someday stop. Nothing can grow forever, at least nothing that consumes finite resources to fuel its growth. It is my view that this shift to no growth or even negative growth (to use that odd economic term) will happen within the next 20 years, although a transition could happen much sooner, if it didn't already begin in 2008. Whenever it happens to occur, it will be destructive to wealth and unpleasant for most people. This means that the paradigm of economic growth, along with its presumed necessity and even desirability, needs to be hauled out into the bright light of day and carefully examined.

The imperative for growth is only very rarely questioned, and it's usually reported in the news as though it were just another necessary component of life. So few people ever question the importance of economic growth that it has become culturally elevated to the same top tier of the winner's podium as other "essentials" such as supermarkets and gasoline stations. From this, we might be led to conclude that economic growth is truly an essential feature of our economic landscape.

To give you a good example of this assumption, look at how embedded the concept of growth is in this short passage in a 2010 *New York Times* editorial by Treasury Secretary Timothy Geithner:

The process of repair means economic *growth* will come slower than we would like. But despite these challenges, there is good news to report:

- Exports are booming because American companies are very competitive and lead the world in many high-tech industries.
- Private job *growth* has returned—not as fast as we would like, but at an earlier stage of this recovery than in the last two recoveries. Manufacturing has generated 136,000 new jobs in the past six months.
- Businesses have repaired their balance sheets and are now in a strong financial position to reinvest and *grow*.
- Major banks, forced by the stress tests to raise capital and open their books, are stronger and more competitive. Now, as businesses expand again, our banks are better positioned to finance *growth*.

By taking aggressive action to fix the financial system, reduce *growth* in health care costs and improve education, we have put the American economy on a firmer foundation for future *growth*.[2]

The word *growth* appears six times in eight sentences, while the words *expand* and *booming* have cameo roles. The message is clear: Growth is what we are after.

Businesses constantly seek to grow, local municipalities have growth targets, states and provinces covet high growth, and the federal government seeks to promote economic growth. Meanwhile, the Federal Reserve ("the Fed") has full employment as one of its core mandates: Since the population is constantly growing and new jobs come from an expanding economy, economic growth is a logical mandate of the central bank. The Fed also has a minimum inflation target of roughly 2 percent, which means that growth of the money supply is a central bank target. But wait a minute . . . since the inflation target is expressed as a percentage, it means that exponential monetary growth is an express goal of the Federal Reserve. How did economic growth come to be so deeply embedded in our language, ideas, and philosophies?

For a long time, longer than anyone reading this has been alive, economic growth has been synonymous with increasing prosperity. By prosperity, I mean a higher standard of living defined by more of everything, easier access to all of the conveniences, luxuries, products, and services that define modern life, and plentiful and varied jobs and opportunities.

The Industrial Revolution brought an explosion of both growth and prosperity. When you read today about how many people live below the poverty line, it's helpful to realize that nearly every citizen of any developed country today lives at a level of prosperity and comfort that is equivalent to a level enjoyed only by the wealthy in the not-too-distant past. If growth delivered this prosperity, then it is easy to understand why growth would be revered and sought. If growth brings prosperity, then let's have growth! From there, it's just a hop, skip, and a jump to the measurement and pursuit of economic growth as an end all its own, and that is where we find ourselves today.

But is it actually true that growth equals prosperity? What if it doesn't?

Thought about one way, we might conclude that growth is actually a consequence of and dependent on the presence of surplus. For example, our bodies will only grow if they have a surplus of food. With an exact match between calories consumed and calories burned, a body will neither gain nor lose weight. A pond will only grow deeper if more water is flowing in than flowing out. With a deficit of food or water, growth of bodies and ponds will cease and then reverse. Growth in these examples is dependent on surplus.

But exactly what sort of a "surplus" is economic growth dependent upon? It's not a surplus of money, or labor, or ideas, although each of those can be an important contributing factor. All economic growth is dependent on what economist Julian Simon called "the master resource"—energy.[3]

We'll have much more to say about that later on, but for now we'll just make the claim that without energy nothing else is possible.

Prosperity is also dependent on surplus. Here is an example: Imagine a family of four with a yearly income of $40,000 that is sufficient to precisely cover life's necessities. For this family, there is a perfect balance between income and outflow. Now suppose that good fortune befalls them and they receive a 10 percent boost to their household income. This windfall will allow them to *either* afford to have one more child (i.e., grow) *or* to shower a little bit more spending on each person (i.e., economic prosperity), but they can't do both. There's only enough surplus money in this example to do one of those things, so they have to choose between additional growth and more prosperity. When the amount of surplus is limited, either growth *or* prosperity can be increased, but not both at once. "Funding" both growth and prosperity at the same time can only happen during periods when there's enough surplus to fund both.

From this simple example, we can tease out a very basic but profound concept: *Growth does not equal prosperity*. For the past few hundred years, we've been lulled into linking the two concepts, because there was always sufficient surplus energy that we could have both growth *and* prosperity at the same time. But that was largely an artifact of a fossil fuel bonanza, not an intrinsic attribute of growth.

If growth in structures and population could bring prosperity, then Quito, Ecuador, and Calcutta, India, would be among the most prosperous places on earth. But they're not. If growth in a nation's money supply brought prosperity, then Zimbabwe would have been the wealthiest country on the planet in 2010. But clearly it wasn't. Growth alone does not bring prosperity, and, worse, growth can steal from prosperity if there aren't enough resources to support both.

In wealthier countries where an energy and resource bonanza can provide enough surplus for both growth and prosperity, we see both. In poorer countries that can only afford to fund one or the other, we only see (population) growth. For the past 200 years, the developed world has not had to choose between growth and prosperity—it could have both, and it did.

As long as energy supplies can continue to grow forever, there is no conflict between growth and prosperity, and we'll never have to choose between the two. But someday total energy will decline, and the world will discover that a dogged insistence on growth will diminish its prosperity. Unless we're careful, there will come a time when 100 percent of our surplus money or energy will be used to simply grow, and the result will be stagnant and then declining prosperity.

The inconvenient truth about growth, then, is that it only really serves us if there is sufficient surplus to fund both growth *and* prosperity. Once there is not enough surplus for both, it becomes a contest between the two. The risk is that our slavish, unexamined devotion to growth, so deeply embedded within our language and customs that it rarely surfaces for examination, will dictate that growth is what we seek, rather than the prosperity that we actually desire. For politicians and others who are fully invested in the status quo, seeking economic growth is on par with supporting motherhood and apple pie. For them, it's the path of least resistance, but for the rest of us, it's now the path with the highest risk because it may very well lead to a future of vastly reduced prosperity.

The most important decision of our time concerns where we direct our remaining energy and other natural surpluses. Choices must be made. We can either spend our surplus resources toward trying to figure out how to simply grow, or we can spend them toward increasing and enhancing our prosperity. We're rapidly approaching the time when we will no longer be able to do both, if that time has not already arrived. My strongest preference would be to see continued progress in energy efficiency, medical technology, and other significant advancement opportunities that modern society can offer. These are a few of the things that we place at risk if we allow ourselves to do what is easy—that is, to take the path of least resistance and simply grow—instead of doing what is right, which would be to intelligently dedicate our remaining energy surplus to a more prosperous future.

CHAPTER 7

OUR MONEY SYSTEM

Before we begin our tour through the economy, energy, and the environment, we need to share a common understanding of this thing called *money*. Money is something that we live with so intimately on a daily basis that it has probably escaped our close attention, much like the distinction between growth and prosperity.

Money is an essential feature of our lives. Were all of our paper money to disappear, a new form of money would rapidly and necessarily arise to take its place. People in practically every culture ever studied, in every region of the world, have used money in some form or another, which indicates without a doubt that money is a very common attribute of civilization. More precisely, trading, greatly facilitated and enhanced by money, is the essential human activity that gives money its meaning.

By way of example, in Federal correctional facilities in the United States, prisoners pay each other with "money" in the form of plastic-and-foil pouches of mackerel, which they call "macks."[1] Prisoners use "macks" to pay for haircuts, get their clothes pressed, and settle gambling debts. The "macks" work because they are inexpensive (they cost about $1 each), but few inmates actually want to eat them, so they remain reliably in circulation. Their use arose shortly after cigarettes were prohibited in federal facilities in 2004, dethroning the former currency of choice.

In the great economic crisis of 1999–2001 in Argentina, circulating dollars evaporated practically overnight and people were left with rapidly depreciating pesos. Many businesses closed and imported products became virtually impossible to buy. Within a relatively short period of time, farmers began using soybeans to trade for new vehicles and individual provinces rapidly issued their own forms of paper money.[2]

Money is essential, especially to complex societies. Without money, the rich tapestry of job specializations enjoyed today would not exist, because barter is too cumbersome and constraining to support a lot of complexity.

Money must possess three characteristics. The first is that it must be a *store of value*. Gold and silver historically filled this role perfectly, because they were rare, took a lot of human energy to mine, and did not corrode or rust. The "macks" in federal prison use fit the bill because they last a long time without degrading, so they have staying power. Just as gold and silver stick around because they don't rust, "macks" stick around because nobody wants to eat them. These forms of currency represent excellent stores of value.

A second feature is that money needs to be accepted as a *medium of exchange*, meaning that it's widely accepted within and across a population as an intermediary for all economic transactions. Here again, "macks" work as a currency because everybody has agreed they do. In the rest of modern culture, paper currencies obtain their value by fiat, or by law, and so they're termed "fiat currencies." Governments declare that these pieces of paper (and their electronic equivalents) are legal tender, that you have to accept them in settlement for debts, and that taxes can only be paid with them and nothing else. The "medium of exchange" feature is enforced by government decree for fiat money, whereas the "macks" are legitimized by a form of cultural consent. But in all cases, money is an agreement between people. We agree that *these* bits of paper, but not *those*, have value. The prisoners agreed that foil pouches of mackerel are valuable, but not gym socks. If you think of money as simply an agreement between people, then you understand the essence of money.

The third feature of money is that it needs to be a *unit of account*, meaning that each unit must be equivalent to any other unit. Along with this idea comes the characteristic that money should be divisible, meaning that you can make it into smaller parts, which can then be recombined without harming the value.

The "unit of account" in the United States is the dollar. Each dollar has exactly the same utility and value as the next, and you can take a dollar and exchange it into four quarters and then back again without losing value. Diamonds have a very high value, but they're not good at being money because they are individually varied and are therefore not perfectly equivalent to each other. Diamonds fail at being a set unit of account, and dividing them causes them to lose value. "Macks," on the other hand, are all exactly the same, so they score high in that category, but presumably they don't divide very well, so they're not as useful for transactions that cost less than one "mack" or require a partial "mack." So "macks" are reasonably good at being money, but they're not perfect. But, hey, this is federal prison we're talking about, so close enough is apparently good enough.

So what is money, really? I believe in a very simple definition: *Money is a claim on wealth*.

As we will see in Chapter 9 (*What Is Wealth?*), primary wealth represents the abundance of the earth. If you move some electronic digits from your bank account to another person's account and gain an oil field in the process, you have just used your *claim on wealth* to secure some *actual wealth*. Now it's up to the recipient of your money to decide where and when they'd like to claim some wealth of their own, too. This idea of money merely representing a claim is important, especially when we consider that these claims have historically been growing exponentially, which we'll discuss in more depth later on.

FULL FAITH AND CREDIT

Literally anything can fulfill the role of money in a given culture: Cows, bread, shells, beads, and tobacco have all served as forms of money in the past. Once upon a time in U.S. history, a dollar was backed by a known weight of silver or gold of intrinsic value and came directly from the U.S. Treasury. Of course, those days are long gone. Now dollars are the liability of the Federal Reserve, a private entity entrusted to manage the U.S. money supply and empowered by the Federal Reserve Act of 1913 to perform this function.

If you pull out a physical U.S. dollar and read it carefully as though it were a contract (which it is), you'll notice that modern dollars no longer have any language on them entitling the bearer to anything. Dollars are no longer backed by any tangible substance sitting in a vault, warehouse, or silo. You can't demand something from the Federal Reserve or the U.S. Treasury in exchange for a dollar, other than a replacement dollar. Rather, the "value" of the dollar comes from the language on the front, which reads *Legal tender for all debts public and private*, which means that it's illegal to refuse to accept dollars for debt settlements and that you can't pay taxes in anything else. Dollars have value because they're backed by the "full faith and credit" of the U.S. government, but what this really means is that they can legally be exchanged for wealth created by its citizens.

It is therefore vitally important that a nation's money supply be well-managed (particularly if it's fiat money), because if it's not carefully administered, the monetary unit can be rapidly destroyed by inflation. Thousands of paper currencies have come and gone throughout history and now no longer exist. A few examples from the United States include Confederate money, colonial scrip, and the infamous greenbacks issued during the Civil War, which still lend their nickname to modern money despite having lost all of their monetary value long ago. The value of some currencies simply erodes slowly over time until they're no longer useful, and then they're replaced. But a smaller yet noteworthy number suddenly lose all of their value in dramatic, hyperinflationary episodes.

How Hyperinflation Happens

A relatively recent example of hyperinflation comes from Yugoslavia between the years 1988 and 1995. Pre-1990, the Yugoslavian dinar had measurable value—you could actually buy something with a single dinar. However, throughout the 1980s, the Yugoslavian government ran persistent budget deficits and printed money to make up the shortfall. By the early 1990s, the government had used up all of its own hard currency reserves, and turned next to the private accounts of citizens as a source of funds. As the dinar slowly and then more rapidly began to lose value to the process of inflation, successively larger and larger bills had to be printed, finally culminating in a rather stunning example of the use of zeros on a piece of paper: a 500 billion dinar note.

At its height, inflation in Yugoslavia was running at over 37 percent *per day*. This means that prices were doubling roughly every two days, which is hard to even imagine. But we can try. Suppose that on January 1 of this year you had a single U.S. penny and could buy something with it. Inflation running at 37 percent per day means that by April 3 of this same year, you'd need a billion dollars to purchase the very same item. Using the same example, but in reverse, if you had a billion dollars on January 1, by April 3 you would only have a penny's worth of purchasing power.

Clearly, if you had attempted to store your wealth in the form of Yugoslavian dinars during the early 1990s, you would have lost it all, which is how inflation punishes savers. It literally steals value from their saved wealth while their money sits in storage. Inflationary regimes promote rapid spending by people concerned about using their money while it has the most value, and increase the amounts wagered on speculation in order to at least try to keep pace with inflation. Of course, investing and speculating involve risks, so we can broaden this statement to make the claim that inflationary monetary systems require the citizens living within them to subject their hard-earned savings to risk. There's really no escape. You either opt out of the game by holding onto your money and lose for sure, or you play the game by speculating on stocks and bonds and risk losing it in the markets.

Even more important, since history shows how common it is for currencies to be mismanaged, we need to keep a careful eye on the stewards of our money to make sure that they're not being irresponsible by creating too much money out of thin air and thereby destroying our savings, culture, and institutions by the process of inflation.

MONEY CREATION

What do we mean by "creating money out of thin air," and how exactly is it that money is created?

John Kenneth Galbraith, the famous Harvard University economics professor, was active in politics and served in the administrations of Franklin D. Roosevelt, Harry S. Truman, John F. Kennedy (under whom he served as the United States Ambassador to India), and Lyndon B. Johnson. He was one of only a few two-time recipients of the Presidential Medal of Freedom.

Clearly, Galbraith was a pretty accomplished kind of guy, one whom you would correctly suppose was a rather calm and collected fellow who wasn't given to hyperbole. He once famously remarked about money: "The process by which money is created is so simple that the mind is repelled."[3]

What he meant by this is that the gulf that exists between the effort required to obtain money by working for it and the ease of creating money by creating it out of thin air is too enormous for most people to fully accept on the first go. Some find it just too unfair to believe.

To begin with, let's look at how money is created by banks.

Suppose a person walks into town with $1,000, and lo and behold, a brand new bank with no deposits has just opened up. This is lucky for the town, because prior to this person arriving, there was no money anywhere in the town. The $1,000 is deposited in the bank, so now the depositor has a $1,000 asset (the bank account) and the bank has a $1,000 liability (that very same bank account).

There's a rule on the books, a federal rule, which permits banks to loan out a proportion—a fraction—of the money deposited with them to other people who wish to borrow some money. In theory, that amount is 90 percent, although, as we'll see later, banks often loan out much closer to 100 percent of their deposits than 90 percent. As the thinking goes, it is very unlikely that all of the bank's depositors would demand all of their money back at the same time, so most of it can safely be lent out under the assumption that only a fraction will be demanded by depositors at any one time. Because banks retain only a fraction of their deposits in reserve (10 percent), the term for this institutional practice is "fractional reserve banking."

Back to our example. We now have a bank with $1,000 on deposit, which it is itching to loan out. After all, banks don't make money by holding on to it; they make their living by paying a lower rate of interest to depositors while lending to borrowers at a higher rate. Banks live on the "spread" between these two rates.

Because federal rules permit our bank to loan out up to 90 percent of deposits, our bank seeks out and finds an individual who wishes to borrow $900. This borrower then spends that $900, perhaps by giving it to their accountant, who, in turn, deposits it in a bank. It doesn't matter which bank; it could be the same bank or a different bank. All that matters is that the money goes back into the banking system, which all money eventually does. For now, to keep things simple, suppose the accountant deposits this money at the very same (the only) bank in town.

With this new deposit, the bank now has a fresh $900 deposit against which it can loan out 90 percent, which works out to $810. So it gets busy finding somebody who wants to borrow $810 and loans them the money, which then gets spent and (surprise!) redeposited in the same bank. So now another fresh deposit of $810 is available to create a loan of $729 (which is 90 percent of $810), and so on, until we finally discover that the original $1,000 deposit has mushroomed into a total of $10,000 in various bank accounts. This is how fractional reserve banking can, and does, turn $1,000 into $10,000.

Is this all real money? You bet it is, especially if it's in *your* bank account. But if you were paying close attention, you would realize that there's more than just money in those bank accounts. The bank records the existence of $10,000 in various accounts, but it also has the notes to $9,000 in debts, which must be paid back. The *original* $1,000 is now entirely held in reserve by the bank, but every *new* dollar in the town, all $9,000, was merely loaned into existence and is now "backed" only by an equivalent amount of debt. How is your mind doing? Is it repelled yet?

You might also notice here that if everybody who had money at the bank, all $10,000 dollars of it, tried to take the money out at once, the bank would not be able to pay it out because . . . well, they wouldn't have it. The bank would only have $1,000 sitting in reserve. Period. You might also notice that this mechanism of creating new money out of new deposits works great as long as nobody defaults on a loan. If and when that happens, things get tricky. But that's another story for another time.

For now, I want you to understand that money is loaned into existence. When loans are made, money appears as if by magic. Conversely, when loans are paid back, money disappears, as the debts and the money cancel each other out when the loans are paid back. This is how money is created. I invite you to verify this for yourself. One place you can do that is the

Federal Reserve, which has published all of this information in handy comic book form, which you can order from them for free.[4]

You may have noticed that I left out something very important in the course of this story: interest. Where does the money come from to pay the interest on all the loans? If all the loans are paid back without interest, we can undo the entire string of transactions, but when we factor in interest, suddenly there's not enough money to pay back all the loans.[*]

So where does the money come from to pay back the interest? And where did that original $1,000 come from? We can clear up both mysteries by traveling to the headwaters of the money river.

THE FED

Even though you might have gotten a loan from Bank of America, creating money in the process, the dollars you received don't say "Bank of America Note" on them; they say "Federal Reserve Note." To find out where all money originally comes from, we need to spend a little time understanding how the Federal Reserve creates money.

Chartered by Congress in 1913 to manage the nation's money supply, the Federal Reserve (a.k.a. "the Fed") has complete and unilateral discretion to decide when and how much money is made available to the banking system, and by extension the entire economy.

But the Fed doesn't just print up a bunch of money and send it out in trucks; it *lends* the money into existence. After all, it is a bank. The process works like this: Suppose the U.S. government wishes to spend more money than it has. Perhaps it has done something really historically foolish, like cutting taxes while conducting two wars at the same time, and finds itself short of money.

---

[*] Some argue that there is enough money to pay back all of the loans, but this is only true under highly unrealistic conditions, where every loan creates goods or services that are bought by the bank or bank shareholders, who buy them with interest payments that are perfectly recycled to the very same people who took out the loans. I call this the "theory of perfect interest flows." While theoretically possible, it is not at all realistic and is therefore something of an intellectual parlor trick. Under this model, nobody can ever take out a purely consumptive loan, undertake a failed business venture, or save money without spending it. As soon as any of these three things happens (and they happen all the time in real life), there's not enough money to pay off all the loans. Suffice it to say that this vision of "immaculate interest flows" is an interesting thought experiment, but it is not at all useful in understanding how the system operates in practice and is therefore not terribly helpful as a way of understanding the current situation or future risks.

Now, having abdicated its monetary responsibilities to a third party (the Fed), the U.S. government can't create any money, so the request for additional spending money by Congress gets routed through the Treasury Department, which, it turns out, rarely has more than a couple of weeks of cash on hand (if that) already earmarked for spending that was put into motion months or even years ago.

So in order to raise the desired cash, the Treasury Department will print up a stack of Treasury bonds (or bills or notes, which are essentially all the same things with different maturities). A bond has a "face value," which is the amount that it will be sold for, and it has a stated rate of interest that it will pay the holder. So if you bought a bond with a $100 face value that pays a rate of interest of 5 percent, then you would pay $100 for this bond but get $105 back in a year, representing your original $100 plus $5 in interest.

Treasury bonds, bills, and notes are sold in regularly scheduled auctions and are mainly purchased by banks, other large financial institutions, or the central banks of other countries. So if a batch of bonds with a face value of $1 billion is sold at auction, then that $1 billion lands in the Treasury's coffers, where it is then available to the U.S. government to spend. Assuming these are Treasury Notes with a one year maturity, in a year the Treasury Department will return all $1 billion to the purchasers of those bonds, plus an amount equal to whatever the rate of interest happened to be.

So far no new money has yet been created. Treasury bonds are bought with money that already exists. The question remains, *Where does new money come from?*

New money, a.k.a. "hot money," comes into being when the Federal Reserve buys a Treasury bond from a bank. When the Fed does this, it simply transfers money in the amount of the bond to the other bank and takes possession of the bond. The bond is swapped for money.

But where did *that* money come from? It was created out of thin air, as the Fed literally creates money when it "buys" this debt.

Don't believe me? Here's a quote from a Federal Reserve publication titled "Putting it Simply":

> When you or I write a check, there must be sufficient funds in our account to cover the check, but when the Federal Reserve writes a check, there is no bank deposit on which that check is drawn. When the Federal Reserve writes a check, it is creating money.[5]

Now *that* is an extraordinary power. Whereas you or I need to work (i.e., expend human labor) to obtain money, and then place it at risk to have it grow, the Federal Reserve simply prints up as much as it deems prudent and then loans it out, with interest.

The answer to how money originally comes into existence is very simple: It's loaned out of thin air by the Fed.

Is your mind repelled yet?

TWO KINDS OF MONEY—ONE EXPONENTIAL SYSTEM

So now we know that there are two kinds of money out there. The first is bank credit, which is money that is loaned into existence, as we saw in the first bank example. Bank credit comes with an equal and offsetting amount of debt associated with it, consisting of a principal balance and a rate of interest that must be paid on that balance. Because this money, which is also created out of thin air, accumulates interest charges, it promotes the growth of the money supply, even though the principal balance must be paid back. The interest represents money that accumulates over time, and as long as everything is working according to plan, it does so exponentially because it accumulates on a percentage basis.

The second type of money is also printed out of thin air, but it is created by the Fed, and it forms what is known as the "base money supply" of the nation. If you're thinking of "base" as in a solid foundation, as in permanent, then you have the right mental image. This money forms the base of all other loans, which, as we saw earlier, can be multiplied fantastically due to the miracle of fractional reserve banking. Base money, too, is loaned into existence, and a quick glance at the Federal Reserve's balance sheet reveals nothing but various types and forms of debts that it has swapped for thin air money. Together these two forms of money (base and credit) conspire to create a money system that will expand exponentially. Loaning money into existence, at a rate of interest, virtually assures this outcome.[†]

The very mechanisms of our money system promote and even demand the exponential growth of money and debt. If the deconstructed workings of the lending and interest cycle are not enough to make the case, then perhaps some empirical data will do the trick.

[†] I know that I have skipped over a number of details, some of them quite important for the sake of accuracy, but we've covered enough of the process for the purposes of this book. For more complete explanations please see the *Crash Course* at www.chrismartenson.com/crashcourse.

Figure 7.1
Total Credit Market Debt

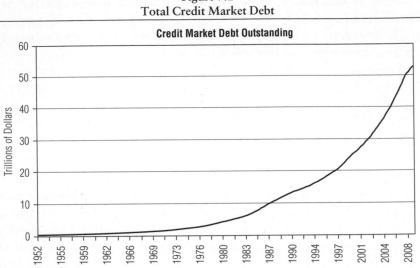

All forms of debt are represented here: federal, state, municipal, corporate, and household.

Source: Federal Reserve.

In Figure 7.1, we see a chart of the total credit market debt in the United States from 1952 to 2008.[‡]

Here again, we see a nearly perfect hockey stick, but this example is of debt. Even without knowing all of the details that underlie money creation and policy, we could simply observe the exponential features of this chart and readily form a quite strong hypothesis that we're studying an exponential system.

The fact that our money/debt system is growing exponentially is an exceptionally important observation, and one that has enormous bearing on how claims on wealth will be settled in the future. Remember, money is simply a claim on wealth. When money is exponentially accumulating (growing), it carries both an implicit and explicit wager that the economy will be exponentially larger in the future. After all, if the economic future turns out to be smaller, but there is exponentially more money and debt floating around, then all of those monetary claims will be chasing a smaller

---

[‡] This chart uses the M3 data series from the Fed up until March of 2008, when it was discontinued. No further M3 data is available from the Fed, although a number of private firms still construct and follow this data series. Using their data to continue the graph does not alter the conclusions; the money series displays nearly perfect exponential behavior.

stack of goods, which means they will be worth less than they currently are. Therefore, when we see money and debt growing exponentially, our very first task should be to assess whether the economy is growing similarly. If not, then we might rationally question whether paper claims against wealth are the best way to store wealth. Perhaps it might make more sense to hold wealth itself, not claims against it. We will go into more detail about wealth in Chapter 9 (*What Is Wealth?*).

What we've just learned about money allows us to formulate two more extremely important concepts. The first is that all dollars are backed by debt. At the level of the local bank, all new money is loaned into existence. At the Federal Reserve level, money is simply manufactured out of thin air and then exchanged for interest-paying government debt. In both cases, the money is backed by debt—debt that pays interest.

Because our debt-based money system is always continually growing by some percentage, it is an exponential system by its very design. A corollary of this is that the amount of debt in the system will always exceed the amount of money.[§]

I'm not going to cast judgment on this system and say whether it's good or bad. It simply is what it is. By understanding its design, though, you'll be better equipped to understand that the potential range of future outcomes for our economy are not limitless; rather, they are bounded by the rules of the system.

All of which leads us to another concept, the idea that perpetual expansion is a *requirement* of modern banking. Without a continuous expansion of the money supply (via credit expansion), all sorts of trouble emerges within the modern banking system, including debt defaults, which are the Achilles heel of a leveraged, debt-based money system.

Just to be clear, I'm not saying that this requirement to expand is written down somewhere, neither etched in legal stone in the basement of the world's centers of power nor forever enshrined in Google's search cloud. Instead, I use the word "requirement" in the same way that your body requires oxygen. Yes, the system can operate for brief periods without it, but it's a lot happier and more productive with it.

By understanding the requirement for continual expansion, we are in a position to illuminate the future and make informed decisions about what is likely to transpire.

[§] Again, for those who prefer data over theory, consider that in the United States at the end of 2009, there were more than $52 trillion of total credit market debt, but only approximately $14 trillion of money (and money equivalents). This means that we now have far more debt than money.

CHAPTER 8

PROBLEMS AND PREDICAMENTS

John Michael Greer makes a very important distinction between two common but critical words: "problems" and "predicaments."[1] This terminology is important, especially in an urgent situation, because knowing whether you're facing a problem or a predicament is integral to shaping your understanding of and response to the situation.

The distinction boils down to this: Problems have solutions; predicaments have outcomes. A solution to a problem fixes it, returning all to its original condition. Flat tires get fixed, revenues recover, and bones mend. Once a suitable solution can be found and made to work, a problem can be solved.

A predicament, by contrast, has no solution. Faced with a predicament, people can develop responses, but not solutions. Those responses may succeed, they may fail, or they may fall somewhere in between, but no response can erase a predicament. Predicaments have outcomes that can be managed, but circumstances cannot be returned to their original state.

Greer framed this distinction in terms of the enormous changes wrought by the rise of industrialization and English wars of conquest upon a prosperous English farming village in 1700. For many villagers, the transformations of that era were wrenching and fatal. What those English villagers faced in the years after 1700 constituted a predicament, not a problem, because change was inevitable and the consequences were unavoidable.

If you have a problem on your hands, then spending time searching for a solution is a perfectly good use of your resources, because by definition, a solution exists. Seeking solutions to a predicament, on the other hand, is a waste of time because none exist; all you will find are outcomes that must be managed as intelligently as possible. Growing older, depleting a finite resource, and developing Type I diabetes are all examples of predicaments. The historical search for the fountain of youth was a perfect example of an attempt to solve the predicament of aging—a very attractive proposition, if a fountain could ever be found—by treating it as a problem with a potential solution (the fountain). But sadly, those efforts were a complete waste of time.

Let us first explore the essence of having a problem. Look at the two gentlemen in Figure 8.1. They have a problem on their hands.

I admit that this is an extreme example, as no prudent climbers would ever put themselves in this situation, but it illustrates my point. There are a number of solutions to this problem that would return both climbers to

Figure 8.1
A Problem at the Cliff

Photo: Greg Epperson

their original condition of relative safety. Perhaps a big mattress could be placed under them, a rope could be lowered, or the climber hanging by a toe could even reach the rock face and climb down all on his own. Any of these solutions could result in both climbers returning to the ground safe and sound. Solutions exist that potentially allow both participants to return to their previous, presumably unimpeded state.

The gentleman in Figure 8.2, however, has a predicament on his hands.

No matter how fast or how hard he pinwheels his arms backward, he isn't going to fly back to the top of the cliff. He is going to get wet; that outcome is certain. And he needs to carefully manage his current situation to secure the safest outcome that he can, by trying to hit the water feet first instead of belly flopping.

What if the gentleman plummeting toward the water spends his time busily thinking of clever ways to fly back to the top of the cliff, instead of

Figure 8.2
A Predicament at the Cliff

Photo: Brady Jones

focusing on how he will land in the water? First, he won't succeed, because no feasible solution exists there. Second, he'll waste time and divert critical mental resources away from the all-important task of managing the best landing possible, and with this approach he will be placing himself at greater risk of injury, or worse. When faced with a predicament, seeking a solution isn't just a useless thing to do; it is the wrong thing to do. Critical time and resources should be devoted to managing the outcome, not trying to do the impossible.

In this book, we are going to review reams of data collectively pointing to the fact that we're facing a very large predicament made up of a series of smaller, nested predicaments. The ongoing depletion of energy, the frivolous but deadly serious mountains of debt that we have accumulated, the advancing age of baby boomers, and depleting minerals are just some examples of the predicaments we face.

Yet many people and most politicians spend nearly all of their time treating these predicaments as if they were problems. Solutions are sought, promised, and counted upon where none really exist, because predicaments have been confused with problems. Even as we face dozens of outcomes that are far more dire than a painful belly flop, we find our leadership either gazing elsewhere or promising what can't be delivered.

By failing to appreciate the nature of our collective predicament, we place ourselves at greater risk, because the longer we dither, less time and fewer options remain. As you read this book, it will be helpful for you to be on the lookout for predicaments and problems, and to recall the important distinction between the two.

CHAPTER 9

WHAT IS WEALTH?

(Hint: It's Not Money)

When Becca and I first decided to move away from our suburban location in Mystic, Connecticut, we drove around southern New Hampshire, Vermont, and central Massachusetts looking for a place to settle. Our list of criteria included typical things such as a nice neighborhood and proximity to culture and shopping, but I had one additional thing on my personal list: good soil. Knowing that I wanted to have a big garden, and knowing that it's much easier to start with good soil than to build it up from scratch, I had good soil in the "non-negotiable column" on my mental list.

As we drove around, I kept a trained eye on the types of trees and plants in each area, looking for the plant-based clues that would let me know if the soil underneath was good quality or not. I knew that an excess of pine trees often indicate that weak, sandy, and acidic soils are underneath, while maple trees suggest rich, sweet soils.

After passing through a succession of small towns, each established 150 or more years ago, a relationship suddenly became apparent to me. In the towns surrounded by pine trees, the historic churches were small, modest affairs, generally without steeples. The churches looked poor. But in the towns with maple trees, the churches were invariably grander, with large, ornate steeples attached. Small, modest churches in the poorer soil communities; large, ornate churches in the wealthier soil communities. All at once, the saying "dirt poor" took on new meaning to me.

The phrase originally dates from the Great Depression and may well have meant "poor as dirt," but to me, from that trip on, it could only convey that one is as rich as one's soil. It must have been axiomatic to our ancestors, whose lives and livelihoods depended on agriculture, that if your dirt was poor, you were poor, too. They knew, in a way that most of us have either forgotten or never learned, that wealth comes from the ground. If two people work just as hard as each other, but one enjoys fine, rich soil and the other struggles with poor dirt, they will reap very different rewards for their efforts. One will be wealthy and the other poor; one is dirt poor and the other is dirt rich. Very simply, all wealth originates with resources from the earth.

We have lost sight of this connection in recent decades because we have been bestowed with the most amazing abundance of magical, wealth-producing stuff ever pulled out of the ground: petroleum. It has masked the previous direct relationship between wealth and land-based resources, which has been a central part of true wealth for every generation except for the most recent ones. It's unlikely that the nature of this relationship can remain hidden for much longer.

A HIERARCHY OF WEALTH

Let's begin by describing what we mean by "wealth." We can think of wealth as coming in three layers, like a pyramid of sorts. At the bottom of the pyramid sits primary wealth, then secondary wealth, and finally tertiary wealth.

Rich soils, concentrated ores, thick seams of coal, gushing oil, fresh water, and abundant fisheries are all examples of *primary wealth*. The foundation of the wealth pyramid comprises these concentrated resources. Today we might call this our "natural resource base," but once upon a time your access to these things (or lack thereof) meant the physical difference between a life of ease and a life of hardship.

Secondary wealth is what we make from primary wealth. Ore becomes steel, abundant fisheries lead to dinner on the table, soil becomes food in the store, and trees turn into lumber. The richer, closer, and more concentrated your primary wealth, the easier the task of creating secondary wealth and the more likely you were, in the past, to be wealthy, or rich. If your soil was "dirt poor," then you had a weak source of primary wealth, and no matter how devotedly or intelligently you worked, you could never achieve the same level of productivity (or wealth) that would be possible if you were working rich soil.

The landed gentry of antiquity were as wealthy as their lands were productive and their holdings expansive. Before the Industrial Revolution (in other words, not all that long ago), this very basic connection was not only well understood, it formed the basis for societal hierarchies. There were wealthy people who owned land, and then there was everybody else. The same is true for weak grades of mineral ores as compared to high grades, or an overharvested fishing ground as compared to a healthy one. Poor primary wealth translates into poor secondary wealth.

We can transform primary wealth into secondary wealth more intelligently, quickly, and cost-effectively with every passing year as we evolve continued improvements in technology and processes. But no matter how good we get at making these transformations, there can be no secondary wealth unless there is primary wealth to begin with. Unless there are trees to mill, there's no lumber; no oil means no gas; without ores we can't refine new metals; and plants will not grow if they don't have the nutrients and water they need. Without primary wealth there cannot be secondary wealth. The second depends on the first; it's a requirement.

The final layer, *tertiary wealth*, consists of all of the paper abstractions that we layer upon the first two sources of wealth. Derivatives, stocks, bonds, and every other paper vehicle you can think of comprise forms of tertiary wealth. Such "wealth" is a claim on the other two forms, but it is not wealth itself. If you grow wheat, you can always eat it if circumstances require, but good luck obtaining any sustenance from your (paper or electronic) wheat futures contracts. To repeat, third-order wealth is a *claim* on sources of wealth, and not a *source* of wealth itself. The distinction is vital.

Without the prior two forms of wealth, third-order wealth has no value and no meaning at all. For example, imagine that we hold stock in a mining company. One day the stock has lots of value, perhaps billions of dollars' worth. But if the next day the mine collapses, dragging the refinery and all of the capital stock of the entire company down into its hole, which then irrevocably floods. Our stock shares in the mining company—our tertiary claims on that mining wealth—become totally worthless. The reason for this is simple: The earth is the source of primary wealth. The long chain from primary wealth to tertiary wealth begins with the abundance of the earth and ends with some impressively complicated paper-based abstractions that even the brightest Wall Street minds sometimes have trouble deciphering.

As you read this book, it will be helpful to recall that what most people call "wealth" isn't actually an independent *source* of wealth, but is instead a dependent *claim* on wealth. In a world of limitless natural resources (primary wealth), the distinction between independent and dependent wealth is irrelevant. We can ignore it, concentrating instead on playing the game of accumulating as much wealth of all kinds as we can while it's our turn to be in our prime. But in a world of *limited* resources—soon to be *limiting* resources—the distinction is vital, especially when the claims on that wealth are literally manufactured out of thin air.

For many of us, tertiary wealth is all that we know; it seems very real, and we base many of our future expectations and dreams on how much of it we hold. Stocks and bonds have been tangible, useful vehicles for storing and growing our collective wealth for such a long period of time that it's easy to see why they've assumed such a superior position in most people's minds.

It bears repeating, however, that all wealth begins with primary wealth; without it, there is nothing. Today, when there is more abundant luxury available to more people than at any point in history, much of it traveling from very far away to arrive in our lives as if by magic, it has been easy to lose sight of this fact, but it remains as true today as ever before.

MONEY AND WEALTH

What about money—how does it factor into the wealth story? Money can and should be a store of wealth, but it's not wealth itself. It's a way for us to conveniently measure and transfer ownership of true wealth from one entity to another, but just like a stock, bond, derivative, or any other financial product, money is simply a claim on wealth. It also happens to be an exceedingly important social contract that we collectively uphold, a vehicle in which we've invested the enormous power to shape lives, nations, and destinies. Ultimately, though, what we call "money" is either a piece of paper (indistinct from any other except for the ink patterns on it) or it's an ephemeral collection of numbers that exist as a series of ones and zeros on a computer hard drive somewhere.

Money has value because, and only because, we collectively agree that it can be exchanged for something. If we go far enough backward or forward in any line of transactions, that "something" is always some form of primary or secondary wealth. Perhaps we exchange money for a college education; this might seem to be quite different and less tangible than the examples of primary or secondary wealth that I've already described. But if we keep following the path of money in that exchange, we'll eventually find the money in the pocket of a college professor who will use it to buy food, or clothing, or a house, or some other form of primary or secondary wealth.

The point of money is to help us secure those things that we need, beginning at the very bottom of Maslow's hierarchy of needs.* We start with food, shelter, warmth, and security, and then progress higher if and only if the base needs have first been satisfied. It's vitally important, then, that money be stable and trustworthy, because if it's not, and people begin to suspect that money might fail to enable them to meet their basic needs, the entire social contract that money fulfills will begin to fray. As long as money exists in a balance with actual primary and secondary *sources* of wealth, then it will retain its perceived value and perform an important function. However, when the supply of money gets out of balance with resources, money's value can begin to gyrate wildly. We call this process *inflation* or *deflation*, depending on whether the gyration goes down or up.

THE NATURE OF WEALTH

The idea that monetary wealth originates with the wealth of the earth is hardly new, but abundant primary wealth, as described here, has been such an assured feature of the landscape of the last few centuries that it seems to be almost entirely taken for granted. Over two hundred years ago, the great economic thinker and observer Adam Smith took great pains to describe how wealth came about, but given that he lived during a time of natural primary abundance and poorly formed tertiary paper-based wealth abstractions, he focused mainly on the role of labor in creating wealth. He turned his considerable attention to secondary wealth and did a most credible job of isolating the essential features by which better-organized labor led to greater wealth. Here he essentially discounts the importance of "soil, climate, and territory" compared to the number of people laboring productively:

> [T]his proportion [between production and consumption] must in every nation be regulated by two different circumstances; first by the skill, dexterity, and judgment with which its labour is generally applied; and, secondly, by the proportion between the number of those who are employed in useful labour,

---

*Maslow was a psychologist who proposed that humans have many needs existing in a hierarchical structure in which the higher levels will not be sought and met until the lower ones are met. At the bottom of his pyramid are the physiological needs of breathing, being fed, obtaining water, sleeping, and excreting. The next layer up covers our safety and security, and self-actualization resides at the very top of the pyramid.

and that of those who are not so employed. Whatever be the soil, climate, or extent of territory of any particular nation, the abundance or scantiness of its annual supply must, in that particular situation, depend upon those two circumstances.[1]

This was a fair view of wealth in the late eighteenth century. Given the limitless natural abundance of the time, those who could transform primary into secondary wealth faster and more productively created wealth the quickest.

We live under very different circumstances than Smith, but the question of how we create wealth remains as relevant today as it was in his day. There are thousands of books to help you navigate tertiary wealth, virtually all of them assuming that the future will resemble the present, only bigger. But here we take a very different stance, recalling that all wealth starts from the bottom of the wealth pyramid with primary wealth and observing that the creation of secondary wealth, without exception, requires energy, which seems the least likely candidate to continue its exponential trend of the past 300 years for very much longer.

By swiveling our gaze to a long-forgotten and dusty intellectual realm, we have the chance to rediscover some basic truths and stake out our positions in relative quiet before the masses arrive like so many wild-eyed land-rush speculators bent on grabbing their share while they still can. The basic truth is this: Our money, debts, stocks, and bonds have a high value in a world of constant economic growth—and a much, much lower value in a world without economic growth. Constant economic growth requires constant inputs of primary resources, especially energy, and someday those will undoubtedly fail to expand any further.

The question is, when?

PART III
ECONOMY

CHAPTER 10

DEBT

If something cannot go on forever, it will stop.
—Herbert Stein, Economist (1916–1999)[1]

The United States and much of the developed world suffer from a condition that I call "too much debt." We could spend an entire book just on the subject of debt, because debt by itself has the capacity to initiate a chaotic and diminished future. But we're only going to spend just enough time on debt to get to my main conclusion: Debt markets are making an enormous collective bet that the future economy will be exponentially larger than the present. It is a dangerous wager, and one which, if it doesn't pan out, places the collective wealth of entire nations at risk.

When debt markets have been disappointed in the past, standards of living have suffered, governments have been tossed, currencies have been destroyed, and/or countries have fallen. We therefore care very deeply about whether our debt markets are at risk of being disappointed, and, if so, what the source of their disappointment might be.

WHAT IS DEBT?

In Chapter 7 (*Our Money System*), we learned that all money is loaned into existence. The other side of the loaned money is the loan itself. We now need to spend some time looking at the nature and quantity of those "loans," which are also sometimes referred to as "credit" or "debt." All three terms are interchangeable, and sometimes we'll switch back and forth between them to follow established conventions. For example, government debt and some consumer loans trade on and are part of the credit markets.

To really mix it all together, we'll examine a data series called "total credit market debt." If at any time you find the use of a term confusing, feel free to mentally insert whichever word you prefer—loan, credit, or debt—they're essentially the same thing, and their minor differences aren't relevant to our discussion.

So what exactly is a "debt" (or "loan")? A debt is simply a legally binding, contractual financial obligation to repay a specific amount of borrowed money, at some point in the future, at a defined rate of interest—in other words, an IOU. An example would be an auto loan of $10,000 at an 8.75 percent rate of interest.

An auto loan is a debt, a credit card balance is debt, and mortgages, Treasury bonds, home equity loans, corporate bonds, and municipal bonds are all examples of debts. In every case there is a piece of paper (or its electronic equivalent) that identifies an amount borrowed, a maturity date, and a rate of interest.

Auto loans and mortgage debt are known as "secured" because there is a recoverable asset attached to those kinds of debts. Credit card debt is known as "unsecured" because no specific asset can be directly seized in the event of a default, although other remedies exist.

Because a debt is a legal obligation, if repayment fails to happen on schedule, all sorts of prescribed legal remedies exist for the lender to pursue, ranging from asset seizure, to liens, to legal judgments.

Debts are distinct from *liabilities*, and it's important to remain acutely aware of the difference between them. A liability is a form of financial obligation, but it's not the same thing as a debt. Someone who has a young child may think of their potential future college expenditure for that child as a liability, but it's not a legally binding obligation, and therefore it's not a debt. Debts represent known quantities and fixed amounts, whereas liabilities are imprecise and prone to fluctuations. Many things can change between today's perceived liability and the actual future payout. The child in question may decide not to go to college after all, allowing the parent to evade the entire amount, or he or she may decide to go to the most expensive college in the country, drastically boosting the final cost of the liability. However, if the parent decides not to pay for college, no legal remedy exists for the child, because the obligation wasn't a debt.

At the national level, the entitlement programs in the United States (e.g., Social Security, Medicare/Medicaid, and so on) are *liabilities* of the U.S. government. Though they may be vast, huge, enormous liabilities, they aren't debts. At any point along the way, the U.S. government could, by way of an act of Congress, completely change the terms of the obligation, perhaps by raising the retirement age to 100 or slashing benefits by 80 percent, and no legal remedy for any of the affected recipients would be available. We might consider such actions to be a moral default on the part of Congress, but they would not be a legal default.

With regard to the nation's debts, however, Congress could not pass an act which would reduce the principal repayment of Treasury bonds without triggering a legal default. Once a default happens, all sorts of legal machinery kicks into high gear. That's the difference between a debt and a liability: Debts are legal obligations, while liabilities are, at best, moral obligations.

There are only two ways to settle a debt: pay it off or default on it. Until one of those two things happen, the debt remains "on the books." Sometimes you'll hear of debts being "restructured," as with Greece in 2010, but that's just a fancy way of saying that the debt has either been delayed (i.e., had its payment schedule extended) or reduced in some way, which constitutes a partial default, but a default nonetheless. In this regard, debts are simple beasts—they can either be paid off, or they can be defaulted upon. Those are the only two options for making them go away.

However, if you happen to have a printing press, as many governments do, there's an alternative way to "pay off" a debt—simply print up the money to pay it off. Because such printing seems to work for a while and offers the least amount of immediate political pain, it has been a very common feature of economic history. A long time ago this involved physically debasing hard coinage, either by shrinking the precious metal content of each coin or by doing what was known as "clipping," which involved making each coin slightly smaller in size so that a greater quantity could be minted from the same amount of precious metal. Later on, printing money involved actual printing presses churning out paper currency by the wagonload.

These days we have the means to create money electronically without involving paper or coins at all. A few keystrokes on a computer are all that's required. Debasing and/or clipping coins was difficult (as you had to recall them first); paper printing was easier, but you still had to physically print and then distribute the money. Electronic printing is virtually instant and practically free, representing the easiest, fastest, and surest method of them all.

Such printing efforts have never worked for very long because the inevitable result has nearly always been ruinous inflation. In this sense, printing up money to pay off sovereign debts is nothing more than a poorly disguised form of taxation, since it forcefully removes value from all existing money and transfers that value to the debt holders, who otherwise might never have been paid at all. Some might even consider this a form of partial default, because the bondholders, too, are being paid with money that is worth less.

Of all the things that I track in my research, the variable that I follow most closely is the use of the official printing press to pay for government expenditures, past and present, that cannot otherwise be funded through legitimate means (such as current taxes).

Levels of Debt

The U.S. experience with debt is significant, but most other developed countries are in almost precisely similar straits. Feel free to mentally replace "United States" with the name of some other country, perhaps the United Kingdom or Japan, in the discussion below; the differences are few and have little impact on the final analysis.

The chart of total credit market debt seen in Chapter 7 (*Our Money System*, Figure 7.1) was a beautiful example of exponential growth, and there's quite an interesting story embedded in its data. Roughly speaking, the total amount of debt in the United States doubled over the course of the 1970s. By the early 1980s it doubled again, and by 1990 it doubled once more, and then it doubled again by 2000. Between 2000 and 2010, debt doubled yet again, from $26 trillion dollars to $52 trillion dollars. We can see this all plotted out in the table in Figure 10.1.

Do you see the pattern here? In the United States, total credit market debt has doubled five times in four decades. Everything that most people know about "how the economy works" was learned during a period of time when credit was doubling every 30 quarters on average.

In order for the decade of the twenty-teens to economically resemble any of the past four decades, we might reasonably conclude that credit market

Figure 10.1
Debt Doublings

Start	End	Trillions	Quarters
4/2000	1/2009	52.9	34
1/1990	4/2000	26.2	41
10/1983	1/1999	13.1	25
10/1977	10/1983	6.47	24
1/1971	10/1977	3.29	27

Time between complete doublings of debt in quarters.

Source: Federal Reserve.

debt would have to double once more, from $52 trillion to $104 trillion, or an average of slightly more than $5 trillion per year. While the economy could certainly operate on a slower rate of debt accumulation, it will not operate in precisely the same way that it did while it was doubling so rapidly. On this basis alone we can predict that some change is in store if we conclude that another rapid doubling seems unlikely.

To put the next doubling in perspective, we might note that $5 trillion represents more than a third of 2010 GDP or that all of the mortgages on every residential house in America currently only total a bit over $10 trillion. And if somehow such a staggering amount of debt is achieved, what about the decade after that: the 2020s? Can we envision debt climbing from $104 trillion to $208 trillion for the United States? What kind of an economy is required to support $208 trillion of debt? Without getting too fancy and detailed here, such a level of borrowing doesn't seem at all realistic (even without taking into consideration complicating issues related to energy or the environment, which we'll be doing later on). It seems prudent to have a strategy that will work even if these next debt doublings don't occur. The story of economic growth that has shaped the past four decades, including many of our expectations about "how the economy works," was heavily dependent on and financed with debt. Without the explosive growth in debt seen over the past four decades, economic growth would have been a lot smaller than we experienced (and enjoyed). Our experience of "normal" economic conditions was actually an unsustainable illusion, albeit a very pleasant one.

To understand how debt distorts the picture of economic growth and health, let's reduce the entire economy to a small island occupied by just a single family earning $50,000 per year ("Family A"). Right next to this island nation is a second island nation, also consisting of a single family earning $50,000 ("Family B"). At our first yearly "GDP snapshot" of these two families, we find that the GDP of each island is $50,000; they're exactly equal. But the next year, using a combination of auto loans, credit card balances, student loans, and a home equity line of credit (HELOC), Family B goes out and borrows an additional $50,000, which it uses to purchase various enjoyable goods and services for itself. Family B lives it up. But Family A, representing the first island nation, prudently plunks their year's $50,000 earnings into savings and lives a frugal life, eating homegrown food and making do with last year's clothing, toys, and motor vehicles.

At our second "GDP snapshot" the next year, we see that Family A has not increased its earnings and is still "suffering from" a GDP of only $50,000. Therefore, despite their diligent savings, our conventional economic standards indicate that this family has suffered through a horrible year of zero percent economic growth (ugh, *no growth!*). In contrast, Family B—the family that now effectively owes every penny of last year's income to its debtors—has seemingly undergone an exciting and dramatic 100 percent growth in their economy (yay, *growth!*) and their island is now sporting a GDP of $100,000. Investors the world over cheer the fast growth and preferentially purchase the currency and debt of Family B's more exciting island nation, eschewing the "anemic growth" of Family A's island nation, mired in the deplorable condition of zero percent growth.

But let's be absolutely clear here: The underlying reality is that each family still has exactly the same $50,000 of national income. They're economically identical, except that one nation, Family B, is now saddled with debt equal to 100 percent of its income, while the other, Family A, isn't. And ironically enough, Family B is being lauded, while Family A isn't.

As it happens, the conventional way of measuring GDP (which is how all developed nations happen to measure it) doesn't take into account the impact of debt—it completely ignores the accumulation of most forms of debt as if they do not matter. However, as I hope that our island nation example has made clear, debt is an absolutely critical component of the story, and excluding it paints a quite misleading picture.

This would become more obvious if we were to turn off the credit spigot and observe the fortunes of Family B immediately slamming into reverse. Where Family A would still be plodding along enjoying the very same $50,000 of income year after year, Family B, now deprived of credit, would find its income stream shredded by the amount of its interest payments. Too much prosperity in one period for Family B will be followed by too little in the next.

Debt-to-GDP for the high-borrowing family assures that they'll be living under the strain of paying down those loans for years to come, which will weigh down their disposable income and future standard of living. To state this as a general rule, time spent living beyond one's means necessitates a future period of living below one's means. This is such a universal and often-repeated economic event that it is almost unbelievable to see that it's about to make a "surprise" appearance on the world stage.

Because the conventional GDP measure neglects to factor out the use of credit/debt when measuring "growth," it isn't telling us everything we need to know. This oversight goes a long way toward explaining why the United States, along with every other debt-saturated country, is now in for a very painful adjustment process: Past growth was partially (and unsustainably) bolstered by debt, and future growth will be sapped by it.

Good Debt and Bad Debt

It's time to distinguish between two major types of debt. Not all debt is bad or unproductive. Debt that can best be described as "investment debt" provides the means to pay itself back. An example would be a college loan securing the opportunity to earn a higher wage in the future. Another would be a loan to expand the seating at a successful restaurant. In the parlance of bankers, these are examples of "self-liquidating debt." Because these kinds of loans will boost future revenues by enhancing productivity or increasing output, they self-generate the cash flows that will be used to pay them off in the future.

The other type of loan, however, is purely consumptive in nature, such as debt incurred for a fancier car, a vacation, new granite countertops, or perhaps a war that results in a large quantity of destroyed equipment. These loans don't come with the means to pay themselves back. They are called "non–self-liquidating debts" (a mouthful of a term) because they don't lead to additional future revenue, productivity, or profits. In our island nation example above, if we postulated that Family B had instead borrowed $50,000 for productive (and not consumptive) purposes, perhaps to build a factory which would then triple its income for the next twenty years, the entire story of which nation is in better financial shape? would shift. So not all debts are potentially harmful; only excess "non–self-liquidating" debt becomes a corrosive burden. Between 2000 and 2010, U.S. total credit market debt grew by more than $26 trillion, an unfortunately large proportion of which was of the non–self-liquidating variety. The implication is clear: Just like the island nation that borrowed and spent $50,000 on purely consumptive purchases, much of this debt load will translate into diminished standards of living in the future as it gets paid back out of a finite pool of income.

The key here is not to just look at the total pile of debt relative to income, but to look at how much of the debt has been spent on non–self-liquidating consumption, as opposed to investments boosting productivity and income.

THE CRISIS EXPLAINED IN ONE CHART

Long before the economic crises of 2008 onward, I knew that such events were coming. While I admit to wallowing around in massive quantities of base data—I'm a scientist at heart, so data is a kind of like catnip for me—I found certainty about the trouble ahead in a single piece of evidence. The chart below, all on its own, led me to conclude that the next 20 years are going to be completely unlike the last 20 years.

Figure 10.2
Credit Market Debt to GDP

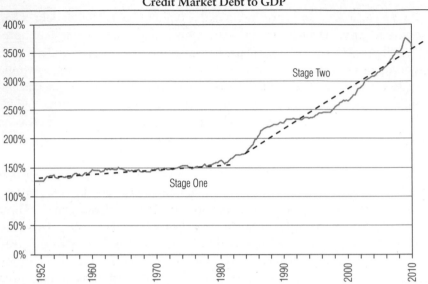

Compares total credit market debt in the United States to GDP (Gross Domestic Product) on a percentage basis. Current total credit-market debt stands at more than 360 percent of total GDP. Notably, this chart excludes all liabilities of the nation. No pension or entitlement shortfalls appear here, as they aren't technically "debt."

Sources: Federal Reserve & Bureau of Economic Analysis.

The dotted line in Figure 10.2, covering the period from the 1950s to the early 1980s ("Stage One" in the chart), was very nearly flat over those three decades but then adopted an entirely new and steeper trajectory beginning in the early 1980s ("Stage Two"). It is in Stage Two where we can detect the underlying cause of the economic predicament that first revealed itself in 2008. Whether you are talking about an individual, a municipality, a state, or a nation, there must be some reasonable proportionality between one's debts and one's income. Stage Two illuminates when, for how long, and to what extent the United States lost its footing.

But that's the past; what about the future? In order for the four decades that will come after 2010 to economically resemble the four decades that came before, the slope of line in Stage Two must not change. If it flattens out a bit, or, more ominously, returns to the anemic slope seen in Stage One, then the next four decades will have weaker growth, fewer opportunities, and be marked by less wanton indulgence and more cautious purchasing habits. In short, they will not resemble the prior four decades, at all.

A key question you might ask yourself here would be, *How likely is another doubling of debt over the next decade?* My current prediction is *not very*, but that is my own personal assessment. If I were to summarize my view here, I would say that anyone who is counting on, requiring, or otherwise hinging their future sense of prosperity on an uninterrupted continuation of the Stage Two line is making a very low-probability bet. Your assessment may well be different, or perhaps not, but no matter where you fall on the spectrum of possibilities, remember to trust yourself.

Back to the main topic. A simple way to interpret Figure 10.2 is to simply note that when the solid line is rising, it means that debt is growing faster than GDP (i.e., income). This is analogous to a credit card balance that steadily grows larger even as the income of the cardholder remains the same. It doesn't take a PhD in economics to understand that sooner or later such a trend will come to a screeching halt. Someday payments on the interest will become too difficult and debt accumulation will cease. The strict math limit to that process occurs when 100 percent of income is required to service the interest payments alone, but thankfully things rarely get that far.

When viewed historically and compared to GDP, the current levels of U.S. debt are unprecedented. There are no maps to guide us in these unknown waters. There's no history, no institutional memory to draw upon, and no experienced leadership prepared to confidently guide us through such a crisis. That's my major point here: Anybody who is counting on the past extending seamlessly into the future is headed for almost certain disappointment, both because there's a very low chance of doubling debts yet again and because there are no experienced leaders with their hands on the wheel.

Of course, with more than a single chart, I can make a far better case that the future will be quite different from the past.

The History of Debt

The first part of this story, historically speaking, always begins with the accumulation of debt. Perhaps there are important wars to fund or an exciting new technology in which to invest (e.g., railroads, Internet, and so on) Or perhaps there's nothing more to show for the debt accumulation than a period of reckless consumption.

The second part of this story involves the psychology of the players who are fully invested in perpetuating the status quo. There are careers to consider, and small matters of legacy here and there, but mostly there's an overwhelming desire by the leaders of each generation to conform and not rock the boat.

The circumstance of "too much debt" has been revisited dozens of times throughout history, and the same exact, perfectly understandable, imperfectly human response has been applied nearly every time: printing money.

This Time Is Different

In their landmark work titled *This Time Is Different*, Kenneth Rogoff and Carmen Reinhart[2] assembled a comprehensive database spanning 800 years of economic data including international debt and banking crises, inflation, currency crashes, and debasements. The one constant throughout history is that many governments, for myriad reasons, have gotten themselves wedged into a situation best described as "too much debt." Throughout history, nearly all governments so stricken by debts have tried to find salvation by wriggling out through the same unworkable portal. In every case, the same rationale has been used as internal justification for official actions: *This time is different*.

Here are a few of the important conclusions from Rogoff and Reinhart's work:

> A recent example of the "this time is different" syndrome is the false belief that domestic debt is a novel feature of the modern financial landscape. We also confirm that crises frequently emanate from the financial centers with transmission through interest rate shocks and commodity price collapses. Thus, the recent U.S. sub-prime financial crisis is hardly unique. Our data also documents other crises that often accompany default: including inflation, exchange rate crashes, banking crises, and currency debasements.

Their work reveals that throughout history, various countries have attempted to live beyond their means and inevitably failed to sustain it for very long. The response has nearly always been to try and squeeze past the difficulties by printing more money in the hopes that somehow things will work themselves out. But it has never quite worked out as hoped; "printing" has only served to deepen the severity of the economic and political pain. Yet it has been tried again and again, as if there's some biologically irrelevant human gene that stimulates the desire to print money while suppressing the ability to learn from history.

The work of Rogoff and Reinhardt demonstrates that historically, some form of default always follows the condition of "too much debt," and currency debasement (known as "money printing" in modern times) is the most common form that this default takes. Along with these defaults, banking crises, exchange-rate volatility, crashes, inflation, and political and social unrest often arise.

The most important finding from the Rogoff and Reinhart study is that periods of relative global financial tranquility have always been followed by waves of defaults and restructurings. Ebb and flow are a normal part of economic history. In this light, we might then view the last four decades of debt accumulation as the calm before the storm, rather than the last few steps of a long march toward a final and lasting equilibrium.

The important points to take away here are these: Country-level debt defaults are historically common and economically painful events that typically arise from the condition of too much debt, and the four most dangerous words in economic history are *this time it's different.*

Too Much Debt

Now that we understand the differences between debts and liabilities, can tell good debt from bad debt, and know that debt has been growing far faster than national income (i.e., GDP), we're ready to dive one layer deeper into the debt data as the final step toward assessing the severity and magnitude of the economic predicament.

The pure debt obligations of the U.S. government as of October 2010 stood at $13.7 trillion.[3] But this is only the debt. Once we add in the liabilities of the U.S. government, chiefly Medicare and Social Security, we get a number somewhere between $100 trillion and $200 trillion dollars, depending on whether you use the Federal Reserve's own estimates or those of Boston University economics professor Laurence J. Kotlikoff, respectively.[4] As mentioned before, these liabilities can be changed at any time with the stroke of a congressional pen, but one thing to remember is that entitlements are a zero sum game. In other words, if the government decides to save money by slashing benefits, the result will be a lower standard of living for the recipients of those monies. The government will see budget savings, to be sure, but retirees will experience a reduction in cash flows and in their living standards. Savings in one place translate into losses elsewhere. That's the essence of "zero sum."

But it's not just the federal government that has underfunded liabilities totaling in the trillions of dollars. States and municipalities are also deeply underwater on their pension promises. Once we add up all the debts and liabilities of the United States, we discover that they are more than 10 times larger than GDP. How many historical examples can we look upon where a country managed to gracefully grow its way out from under such an enormous pile of unfunded paper promises? None. There are zero historical examples to guide us. The world-record holder in this regard is England, which managed to pull itself out of debt during the period from 1820 to 1900, but its debt load was only 2.6 times its GDP and the Industrial Revolution came along to help out. We will discuss this example more in Chapter 12 (*Like a Moth to a Flame*).

Debt's Big Assumption

As troubling as all that is, the story of debt extends well beyond the idea that there is too much of it. To understand why, let's look at the role of debt and how it relates to the future.

Consumptive debt, or debt that's not self-liquidating, provides us with money to spend today. Perhaps we buy a nicer car, and we enjoy that car today. But future auto loan payments will represent money that we've already spent in the past and won't be able to spend in the future. Put simply, debt enables future consumption to be taken today, not tomorrow. In this sense, debt is a claim on future money, and therefore debt is really just a fancy way of pulling money from the future so that we can spend it today.

We learned in Chapter 7 (*Our Money System*) that money can be viewed as a claim on wealth, and we just learned that debt is just a claim on future money. We can put these statements together and arrive at this important conclusion: *Debt is a claim on future wealth*. This implies that a constantly growing level of debt, like the one we have collectively experienced (and participated in) in the decades since 1980, has an enormous and unavoidably gigantic assumption baked right into it.

Ever-Growing Debt's Massive Assumption

Go back and take one more look at the upwardly sloping line that represents debt-to-GDP in Figure 10.2. The critical assumption inherent in that slope is this: The economic future will be—*must be*—exponentially larger than the present.

Logically, if debt represents a claim on the future, then ever-larger amounts of debt represent ever-larger claims on the future. Okay, that sounds easy enough. But let's recall that debt carries with it the expectation of repayment of both the principal and the interest components. If the debt has a principal balance of "X," we must not forget that the interest component is a percentage increase based on "X." How do we describe something that grows by some percentage over time? That's right—we say it's growing exponentially.

Therefore, each incremental expansion of the level of debt is an explicit assumption that the future will be larger than the present. And not just a little bit larger—the future will need to be *exponentially* larger than the present for debts to be fully paid back and not defaulted upon.

Given that U.S. debts now represent over 360 percent of GDP and total liabilities over 1000 percent of GDP, there's an explicit assumption being made by the debt markets that the future GDP of the United States is going to be larger than today's GDP. A *lot* larger. More cars must be sold, more resources consumed, more money earned, more houses built—*every* facet of economic growth and complexity must increase simply to pay back the loans that are already booked. Any continuation of debt expansion will compound these claims on the future. Now think back to that Stage Two line on the Debt-to-GDP chart in Figure 10.2 and ask yourself how likely it seems that the United States will be able to engineer another 20 years of faster-than-income (GDP) debt expansion.

Banks, pension funds, and government solvency, whose futures are intimately tied to the continued exponential expansion of debt, all have an enormous stake in its perpetual growth. This defines the pressure to continue the expansion and explains why our fiscal and monetary authorities seem to talk of nothing but economic growth. Without economic growth, further debt expansion does not make any sense. Without continued debt expansion, large-scale debt defaults emerge and the financial system begins to break down. The tension that stalks the financial and economic markets results from the conflict between (a) the fact that preserving the status quo *requires* (there's that word again) the continuous and uninterrupted growth in debt and (b) the fact that nothing can continue to grow forever. That's the essential conflict. Each of us already knows deep down which side of that conflict will win that battle.

How It Unfolds

But what happens when the debt markets finally figure out that the future cannot grow to infinity? What then? Well, broadly speaking, when that day comes to pass, there can only be one outcome, although it could arrive in either of two different forms. The outcome is simply that a lot of what we think of as wealth simply must vanish, because the claims are too numerous and potential future growth is too little. This destruction of wealth can come about in one of two very opposite ways. The first is by deflation, manifested as a process of debt defaults, and the second is by inflation.

Defaults are easy to explain—the debts don't get repaid and the holders of that debt don't get their money back. Boom—over and done. The claims are diminished. Thus, if the future isn't large enough to pay back the claims, then defaults are simply a way of squaring up past claims with current reality. This path is easy to understand. Perhaps a pension fund holds a billion dollars of General Motors debt, GM goes out of business, GM debt goes into default and becomes worthless, and pensioners in the future have a billion fewer dollars distributed to them, dragging down their standards of living.

However, the inflation route can be confusing. Think of it this way: Imagine that you sold your house to someone, and, to keep it simple, you provided them with a mortgage for $500,000. The terms call for the mortgage to be repaid all at once in 10 years as a single payment of $650,000, providing you with a nice kicker of $150,000, which amounts to something above the prevailing rate of interest. So far, so good. Well, 10 years passes, and, as stipulated, you are paid your $650,000 right on time. But now, due to inflation, that $650,000 will only buy a house half as nice as the one you sold. Yes, you got paid, but your claim on the future was vastly diminished by inflation. In this example, $650,000 in the future buys half as much as $500,000 today.

In the default scenario, your money is still worth something, but you don't get it back, which also diminishes your claim on the future. In the inflation scenario, you do get your money back, but it hardly buys anything, which also diminishes your claim on the future. In both cases you have less wealth in the future, so the impacts are very nearly the same, but the mechanisms by which you lose out are remarkably different.

To make investing simple, the questions you need to ponder for yourself are these:

- *Have too many claims been made on the future?*
- *If so, will we face inflation or defaults as the means of squaring things up?*

You'll arrive at wildly different life decisions depending on whether you answer yes or no to the first question and "inflation" or "defaults" for the second question. I strongly recommend that you spend some time pondering these questions and revisiting them as circumstances shift.*

---

*This is a complicated subject and one that requires constant vigilance, as its ultimate outcome is not mathematically defined, but is the product of unknowable decisions by fiscal and monetary authorities. At www.ChrisMartenson.com, this is one of the most vigorous areas of debate, and our assessment of which outcome is most likely varies considerably. In short: If you expect inflation, you will seek to get rid of your money as fast as possible by spending it on things that have value to you today and which you suspect will cost you even more tomorrow. If you expect deflation, your correct strategy is to hoard your money carefully, as it will be harder to come by and will grow in relative value with every passing day. My own assessment in the closing months of 2010 is that inflation vs. deflation for U.S. citizens has an 80/20 probability.

CHAPTER 11

THE GREAT CREDIT BUBBLE

In order to understand what the future may hold, we need to see the excessive accumulation of debt between the early 1980s and 2010 for what it really was—an enormous and protracted credit bubble. Debt levels doubled, redoubled, and doubled again with uncanny mathematical precision. Within that larger credit bubble, we had several minibubbles—one in stocks and the other in housing—and while these were both financially destructive, they were sideshows on the way to the main act.

Because our hopes and dreams for the future rest upon a well-functioning economy, we need to understand what bubbles are and the financial risks they pose. If my analysis is correct, the main bubble has only just begun to burst. Under the best of circumstances, this will exert profound influences for a long time to come; under less favorable circumstances, it will prove to be a uniquely unfortunate and disruptive period of economic adjustment.

Because this past episode of credit expansion was so ubiquitous (it spanned the globe) and lasted for so long (30 years), it came to be accepted as normal and logical by otherwise bright and intelligent people. Like all credit bubbles, this one was founded on the most enduring of human weaknesses: the desire to get something for nothing.

Before we dive into the Great Credit Bubble, let's spend a bit of time defining what an asset bubble is and examining some of the more common characteristics of bubbles.

WHAT IS A BUBBLE?

Along the continuum of irrational financial behavior, it can be tricky to tell the difference between a bubble, a mania, and a touch of overexuberance. The designation "bubble" is reserved for the height of folly, but unfortunately, history is rich with folly. Throughout the long sweep of history, the bursting of an asset bubble has always been a financially traumatic event and has often precipitated social and political upheavals.

Because they are so culturally and financially painful, bubbles used to be separated by one or more generations because it took time to forget the experience. Bucking this convention, less than 10 years passed between the bursting of the dot-com bubble in 2000 and the housing bubble in 2006—a thoroughly unprecedented event—which calls into question the mindfulness of its participants. However, it is my contention that instead of these being two separate and distinct bubbles, they were merely subbubbles housed within a much larger and more profound credit bubble, which partially (but not entirely) excuses the all-too-close nature of their occurrences.

. The Federal Reserve famously likes to claim that you can't spot an asset bubble until it bursts. This is something of a mystery, because the definition of a bubble is pretty simple: *A bubble exists when asset prices rise beyond what incomes can sustain.* There is nothing especially tricky about that definition, and it provides an easy test that can be founded on solid data.

For example, when houses in Orange County, CA[1] rose to the point that the median house cost more than nine times the median income,[2] housing there was clearly in the grip of a bubble. A more normal ratio for housing would be in the range of roughly three times income, while anything over four times income really begins to stretch things a bit.[3] When you get to eight times income, you've been in a bubble for quite a while, it's completely obvious even to casual observers, and it's going to burst with predictable, economically painful results.

This seems pretty straightforward, but for some reason the Federal Reserve, under Greenspan and then Bernanke, continued to insist that bubbles couldn't be spotted, and even if it *were* possible to spot them, that nothing should be done about them until after they burst. Greenspan and Bernanke hold to the view that it's not the Federal Reserve's job to spot or stop bubbles, only to ride to the rescue and help sweep up the debris after they burst. Given that the Fed is the principal source of the necessary credit and liquidity that are an absolute requirement of bubbles, this is a bit like firefighters claiming there's no point in curbing arsonists' behavior—that it is better to let them set fires so that they can then battle the blazes they've set. Lest you think this is a general defect of central banks and bankers, I should point out that New Zealand's central bank takes the opposite view and sees it as their right and proper job to both spot bubbles early and nip them in the bud.[4]

Bubble History

To better understand what bubbles are, how they form, and why they are economically painful, let's take a look at a few historical examples, beginning with the tulip bulb craze in Holland in the 1630s.

In that period, a virus swept through the tulip farms and had the effect of creating beautiful and unique variants in tulip coloration that were transmissible to succeeding generations. Tulips were already an economically important crop for the country, so while it may seem strange to us now that a bubble could develop around flowers, tulips represented an important element of commerce to the people of Holland. Before long, incredible variants with brilliant streaks and accents were developed, and the more spectacular examples began trading at higher and higher amounts, building a speculative frenzy. Complicated trading routines built up around the products, and before long nearly all trades were conducted using credit.

At the height of the bubble, a single bulb of the most highly sought-after example, the Semper Augustus, which sported red petals and racy white streaks, commanded the same selling price as the finest house on the finest canal.

The tulip bubble could not have occurred were it not for the presence of ample credit. Credit is a necessary fuel for all bubbles; without it, no bubble can develop. After all, if the very definition of an asset bubble is that it grows "larger than incomes can sustain," it means that funds to support the bubble's growth have to come from somewhere besides current cash flows (i.e., current income). True to form, tulip-bulb trading soon outstripped the local money supply, and people began trading on credit.

Records indicate that the tulip craze ended even more suddenly than it began, crashing nearly to the bottom in a single day at the start of the new selling season in February of 1637. When bidding opened on that day, no buyers would bid, and prices rapidly cratered, never to recover. The people holding the last batches of purchased bulbs recorded major losses, creditors went bust, and an enormous amount of wealth evaporated, never to be seen again. Lives were ruined, fortunes were lost, and people promised themselves, *Never again.*

A second example of an early recorded bubble comes from the 1720s and is known as the South Sea Bubble. The South Sea Company was an English company granted a monopoly by the government to trade with South America under a treaty with Spain. The fact that the company was rather ordinary in its profits prior to the granting of the monopoly did not deter people from speculating wildly about its financial potential.

Even more startlingly, people were undeterred in snapping up shares of its stock, despite the fact that the company rather accurately billed itself as "A company for carrying out an undertaking of great advantage, but nobody to know what it is." That's about as clear a scam warning as an investor will ever receive, but bubbles have a way of shutting down critical thinking in the masses.

Sir Isaac Newton, when asked about the continually rising stock price of the South Sea Company, said that he "could not calculate the madness of people." But then he, too, apparently went mad for company stock. He may have invented calculus and described universal gravitation, but he also ended up losing over 20,000 pounds,[5] a massive fortune in those days, to the burst South Sea Bubble, proving that even a truly rare intelligence can be outwitted by a bubble. For some reason, bubbles are extremely hard for most people to spot in advance. A bubble begins when people start relying on hope instead of reason, but a bubble really hits its stride when prudence is replaced by greed.

Bubble Characteristics

History is littered with the wreckage of financial bubbles involving a surprising diversity of assets, with more recent examples involving railroads, swamp land, Internet stocks, and housing. The asset itself, whether land or bulbs or pieces of paper, is irrelevant. What matters is having the right story—usually involving massive riches soon to come—a credulous mob, short-sighted (or greedy) lenders, and an ample supply of credit. If any one of these things is missing, no bubble will result.

What's interesting is that nearly every bubble shares the same common, and therefore predictable, features. Bubbles are self-reinforcing, meaning that on the way up, higher prices become the justification for higher prices. Once the illusion is lifted, the game is suddenly and permanently over, but not instantly, as it takes time for reality to set in. This lends a rough symmetry to the price charts of assets as they rise and then fall over time. In the 1920s a bubble developed in U.S. stocks, and its bursting still echoes even today, because it was immediately followed by the Great Depression.

Figure 11.1 demonstrates two important traits about bubbles. Note that the amount of time it took the Dow Jones to run up to its price peak in 1929 is roughly the same amount of time that it took for prices to fall back to their starting levels. The first characteristic of bubbles is their rough symmetry. They first rise, and then they fall, but not instantly, revealing that bubbles take time to develop and then to unwind. First the psychology

Figure 11.1
Dow Jones Industrial Average, 1922–1935

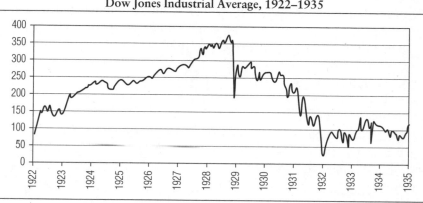

Source: Yahoo! Finance.

has to be built into a frenzy, a mob has to be formed, and then it has to be slowly dismantled, one person at a time. However, despite this apparent symmetry, bubbles usually burst just a little bit faster than they develop.

The second characteristic of bubbles that we see reflected in Figure 11.1 is that asset prices will usually fully retrace to their starting point, if not just a little bit further. Whatever the starting point was for the asset prices in question is a reasonable place to suspect they'll eventually end up at some point in the future.

To reinforce this point, Figure 11.2 shows the stock price of General Motors (in the black line) between the years 1912 and 1922 and Intel (in the shaded line) between 1992 and 2002, periods during which both stocks were swept up in bubbles. Here we might also note that the price data looks very similar for both stocks, despite the fact that one was a car company in the 1920s and the other was a high-tech chip manufacturer trading some 80 years later. Again we might note that they share the two characteristics of bubbles that we've already discussed: a rough symmetry in both time and price. They crescendo, then crash, and end up right where they began.

The fact that bubbles display the same price behaviors over the centuries and decades tells us that they're not artifacts of particular financial arrangements, cultures, or legal systems. Instead, the constant factor is people. Bubbles do not develop as a condition of poor financial engineering or specific financial laws and regulations that happen to be present, nor because of particular cultural practices, but as the by-product of greed, hope, and excessive credit. Wherever these circumstances exist, bubbles will

Figure 11.2
Stock Prices: GM and Intel

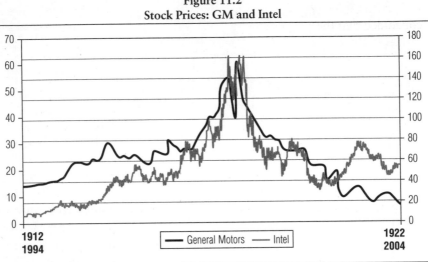

Source: Yahoo! Finance.

eventually develop, which is why investors should hold onto their wallets whenever they spot such conditions.

Asset bubbles, therefore, aren't so much financial phenomena upon which we can conduct meaningful financial post mortems as they are sociological events best understood through the study of human psychology and mob behavior. Perhaps we can even speculate that bubble behavior is wired into our biological software, an evolutionary remnant that was useful in our deep past but is now a profound liability when it comes to making investment choices.

That bubbles happen isn't the surprising part of this story; rather, it's that well-educated people responsible for knowing about such things have apparently never learned that bubbles aren't rare and random events but are very common and predictable features of the economic landscape. In their defense, perhaps these people have learned about bubbles, but then mistakenly overestimate their ability to manage their destructive effects (yes, I am talking about Alan Greenspan here).

By way of illustration, the Federal Reserve entirely missed the opportunity to nip both the 1990s stock and 2000s housing bubbles in the bud, and even devoted considerable internal resources to the task of proving to itself that no housing bubble existed. Even as a number of analysts and commentators (including me) were warning of a housing bubble back in 2004, the

Fed released a study titled "Are Home Prices the Next Bubble?" which concluded that the answer was no.

Here's the main conclusion of that paper:

> Home prices have been rising strongly since the mid-1990s, prompting concerns that a bubble exists in this asset class and that home prices are vulnerable to a collapse that could harm the U.S. economy. A close analysis of the U.S. housing market in recent years, however, finds little basis for such concerns. The marked upturn in home prices is largely attributable to strong market fundamentals. Home prices have essentially moved in line with increases in family income and declines in nominal mortgage interest rates.[6]

All of that sounds perfectly logical, and the paper is stuffed with comforting and supportive data, but it is also completely and hopelessly wrong. Although they should arguably have known better, the Fed's researchers were simply doing what millions of people did; namely, falling prey to the belief that somehow "this time it's different." That's just how bubbles are. People take leave of their senses, using all manner of rationales to justify their positions, but then suddenly one day the illusion lifts, and what was once unassailably true no longer makes any sense at all. Once that tipping point occurs, there's really nothing left to do but track the speed of the bubble's collapse and the damage it will cause.

The Housing Bubble

Let's focus a bit more of our attention on the housing bubble that burst in 2007. It is important to show just how obvious this bubble was. Anyone with a tiny bit of bubble history under their belt and access to some publicly available data can appreciate its clarity.

Because a bubble occurs when asset prices rise beyond what incomes can sustain, I'm not so interested in the actual prices of houses all by themselves, but I am keenly interested in the ratio of house prices to income. Because the amount that people can afford to pay sets an ultimate limit on house prices, it is impossible for median house prices to forever rise faster than median incomes. Sooner or later, when illusions lift, that dynamic comes to a halt, and at that point, the last buyers will be in the same position as the last purchasers of tulip bulbs in 1637.

Figure 11.3 compares median household incomes to median house prices. If what the Fed research paper said was correct and housing prices rose in alignment with incomes, the two lines would overlay each other perfectly

Figure 11.3
Median Income and Housing

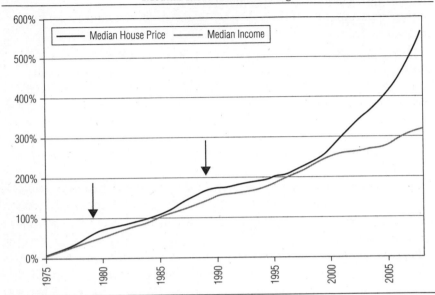

Sources: Census Department (Median Income) and Office of Federal Housing Enterprise Oversight (Housing).

and never depart, but that's not what we see. Instead we observe that even before the year 2000, median house prices elevated away from median incomes and were hopelessly separated by the time the Fed was convincing itself no bubble existed in 2004.

The housing bubbles of 1979 and 1989 (marked with arrows) were quite sedate in comparison to the most recent housing bubble and aren't very dramatic on this graph. The fact that median incomes did not deviate especially far from those prior bubbles' house prices helped to limit the damaging effects of the bursting of those bubbles. Painful though these burstings were, house prices did not have to fall very far before they were once again aligned with incomes.

But look at the enormous gap between house prices and incomes for the most recent housing bubble. There's no historical precedent for the size of that gap, and there were disturbing warning signs as early as 1999 that things were getting off track. It's interesting to ponder how the Federal Reserve had access to this same data but still managed to convince itself that nothing was amiss. In fact, at the time, Greenspan was busy extolling the wonders and virtues of the massive "wealth-creating" effect of housing for the average person, apparently unaware of the wealth-destroying impacts of the future bursting of the bubble he enabled.[7] It was completely obvious that we had a bubble on our hands, and prudent people could have simply looked at this data and then trusted themselves to avoid getting swept up in it.

But back to the story. Based on simple calculations performed on the base data for Figure 11.3, we can predict a minimum 34 percent national decline for house prices from peak to trough. That's what is required to get those income and housing price lines back together again. Given the propensity of bubbles to sometimes overshoot to the downside, we can't discount the possibility that a steeper decline of perhaps 40 percent or even 50 percent is in store. That was my conclusion, published in 2007,[8] and it seems as sound here in 2010 as it did then. Based on Figure 11.3 and the assumption that the housing bubble will burst with the same rough symmetry as prior bubbles, my prediction is that housing prices in the United States will bottom in 2015.

A Bubble Thirty Years in the Making

All of this review of bubbles was meant to get us to the point where we could talk about the biggest and what will almost certainly be the most destructive bubble in history: The Great Credit Bubble.

So far (as of 2010) this bubble, like every serious bubble worthy of mention, has largely escaped attention. Most economic experts are convinced that a credit bubble doesn't exist, and few people think twice about using credit in their daily lives or dwell on the past four decades of debt accumulation. Bubbles that have not yet collapsed are incredibly hard for most people to detect; that's why they exist in the first place.

As mentioned in Chapter 10 (*Debt*), total credit in the United States has doubled five times over the four decades between 1970 and 2010. At the end of 2000, when the stock bubble was bursting, total credit market debt stood at $26 trillion, but by the end of 2008 it stood at an astounding $52 trillion. This $26 trillion increase in borrowing was five times larger than the increase in U.S. Gross Domestic Product (GDP) over the same period of time. As profound as the housing bubble was, it represented only a small piece—only around $5 trillion out of $26 trillion[9]—of this massive surge in debt.

Figure 11.4
Growth in GDP Compared to Total Credit Market Debt

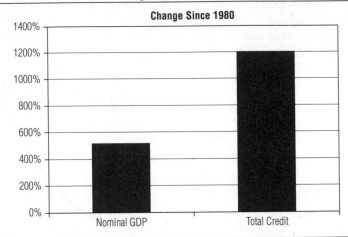

Change Since 1980

1980 to present. Both in nominal dollars. Debt excludes all unfunded liabilities.
Source: Federal Reserve.

If the idea is that debt is meant to be paid back, then over the long term debt cannot rise faster than income. Now let's look at the increase in the size of the United States's debt compared to its GDP over the past 30 years.

Where debts have increased by just over 1200 percent since 1980, GDP has advanced by just under 520 percent. Imagine your credit card bills growing at more than twice the rate of your income for the next 30 years. Sooner or later that has to come to a stop. It is a thoroughly unsustainable proposition.

Recall that the definition of an asset bubble is that it exists when asset prices rise beyond what incomes can sustain. This means that on the other side of every asset bubble lurks an equal-sized credit bubble. Bubbles usually end, not because of any significant shift in the worth of the coveted assets, but because credit runs dry, which reveals the main storyline to be false. Without credit as a fuel, bubbles deflate.

What then should we think of this mountain of debt, or credit, which has been consistently expanding faster than GDP (or income)? Given that this matches the very definition of a bubble, it might be prudent to dedicate some thought to what will happen if—or when—that bubble bursts. When viewed this way, housing becomes a sideshow, instead of being the epicenter of the bubble. It is an eddy in a much larger ocean of debt that has been 40 years in the making.

Figure 11.5
Credit Market Debt Outstanding

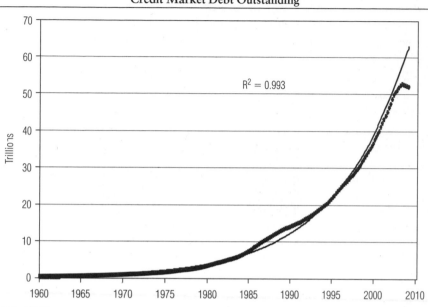

With exponential 'fit' yielding an "R-squared" of 0.99.
Source: Federal Reserve.

EXPONENTIAL DEBT

There are two ways to go about understanding things: One is to build your knowledge from the ground up, piece by piece, and the other is to stand back, look at the big picture, and then work backward to deepen your understanding of the system. If we look at growth in the credit markets over the past several decades, we might note that not only has credit been growing, but it has been growing in a nearly perfect exponential fashion.[*]

---

[*] Mathematicians and other scientists have a means of assessing how accurately an observed event conforms to, and therefore can be explained and even predicted by, a mathematical formula. For example, if you saw the number series 1, 2, 3, 4, 5, and 6, you would instinctively predict that the next number in the series would be 7. The way a mathematician would approach this would be to arrive at the number seven by converting the number series into a formula, $y = x + 1$, and then testing this formula against the number series using a statistical method that calculates the variance between observed and predicted results.

The term for this method is "goodness of fit," which means just what it sounds like: *How close of a fit was there between the measured variables and one's formula?* In this example, the formula perfectly matches the observed number series and

What does it mean that debt has been accumulating in a nearly perfect exponential fashion? What will happen when it someday can't continue to increase exponentially? What will change in terms of how the economy works and how stocks and bonds function as vehicles for storing and accumulating wealth?

We can begin to answer these questions by simply noting that debt has been growing faster than national income, and that such a system is unsustainable. Like any bubble, it will someday pop.

If we accept the premise that this credit expansion does, in fact, fit the definition of a bubble, then we can make the following predictions:

- Credit growth will peak, stall, and then decline, a process that I conclude began in 2008.

---

because it does, it is said to have a perfect "fit," which means it is assigned a value of "1." An utter lack of "fit" would be assigned the value of "zero." By convention, a perfect fit, as in our number example above, is said to have a value of 1.0, while a formula with a no descriptive or predictive power at all would have a "fit" of zero. In my science days investigating messy, real-world biological systems, a fit of 0.80 or better was a very good fit, meaning that a real and predictable (and therefore understandable) process was being studied and the scientists involved would get excited like hounds on a strong scent. But a "fit" of 0.90 or better? Practically unheard of for the systems I studied. Experimental noise and biological complexity conspired against such robust readings.

Now let's imagine another system designed and run by biological creatures with enormous, nonlinear complexity built into it, which we seek to similarly describe and understand by "fitting" it with a mathematical formula. I'm speaking of a system composed of millions of moving parts arising from billions of individual decisions and totaling in the trillions of dollars. The entire system is in constant flux, with many of the parts interacting with each other in a delicate, chaotic symphony of positive and negative feedback loops. From a ground-up perspective, such a massive and complicated bit of machinery would seem to defy easy characterization and offer slim hopes for getting a good "fit." The system I am speaking of is the entire, massive, complex credit market of the United States (although other countries would work equally well in this example), which is composed of every manner of type of debt you can imagine, spanning multiple decades with wars, recessions, booms, and bubbles interspersed along the way. Mortgages, derivatives, federal debt, auto loans, municipal debt, student loans, and dozens of other types of debt are all mashed into one, gigantic market. What's your prediction for how well we can describe the growth in this market over the past 50 years? How good will our "fit" be? Will it be a horrid 0.50 or less, a respectable 0.65, or perhaps something higher? The answer surprised me enormously when I performed the test; our total credit markets are described by an exponential function with a "fit" of 0.9937 (!!). That's as close to perfect as you can get without actually being perfect. It is powerful evidence that our credit markets operate exponentially.

- The bubble will take somewhat less time to deflate than it took to inflate. If we date this to the start of the housing bubble in 1998, then we might expect it to bottom out somewhere around 2015, give or take. If instead we date the bubble to the early 1980s, then we might expect it to truly bottom out somewhere around 2025, +/– 4 years.
- Depending on where we date the start of the bubble (1998 or 1980 or even 1970), somewhere between $20 trillion and $30 trillion of debt in excess of income (GDP) has been piled up and will need to be eliminated in one fashion or another (i.e., by inflation or deflation). This will simply return debt back to the place from which it started, just the same as any other bubble.

Those predictions imply an immense amount of painful adjustment. If they come to pass, then the United States will be a vastly diminished nation in the twenty-teens and twenty-twenties as compared to 2008, with far fewer economic opportunities and less capacity to muscle through any other challenges that might arise.

By itself, exponentially growing credit isn't necessarily a problem, but if it is growing faster than the economy, then it does become a problem.

We have a problem.

WITHERING HEIGHTS

How was it possible to keep such a bubble going for so long? One essential factor was that interest rates constantly fell even as the total amount of credit market debt rose.

Here's why this matters. Imagine that you had a credit card with a most unusual feature, whereby the rate of interest declined as the balance grew. The more you charged, the lower the interest rate became, which had the effect of stabilizing or even reducing the minimum payment due. Clearly such an arrangement would allow more borrowing than if the interest rates had not fallen (let alone risen). It is highly doubtful that the credit bubble would have developed without U.S. interest rates steadily falling over the 30 years between 1980 and 2010 (see Figure 11.6). This was really a perverse development when you think about it; interest rates should *rise* with a rising balance of debt, not *decline*. But there's no law saying that these things have to make sense.

This practice of lowering interest rates to keep the game alive for awhile longer has a natural limit: Rates cannot go below zero. In 2010, we saw the

Figure 11.6
Chart of 30-Year Bonds over Past 30 Years

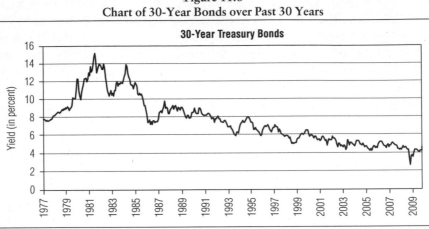

Source: Yahoo! Finance.

Federal Reserve set interest rates for overnight money[†] to between zero percent and 0.25 percent, and we saw the interest rates on two-year Treasury notes go below 0.50 percent. There's really nowhere else for them to go; they are already at zero. In short, interest rates hit bottom in 2010 and were placed there in an effort to keep the credit bubble expanding for a while longer. In my opinion this was an enormously misguided effort, but it happened, and now we need to consider how we're going to manage the outcome(s) that will result.

All good things must come to an end, and if such low interest rates fail to keep the credit bubble on its "double every decade" trajectory, it is unclear what other remedies are available to the Fed that could cover the gap. The only ones I can think of are so "out-of-the-box" that how they might impact our future is impossible to determine. Some of these alternative measures might include complete Fed ownership of all productive assets (bought with thin-air money), a massive repudiation of all debt (just hit the reset button), and/or the Fed purchasing all government debt in an effort to keep things flowing, which has already partly been done with the first rounds of Quantitative Easing (QE).

The alternative would be to admit to ourselves that perhaps doubling debt every decade (far faster than income growth) isn't a sustainable practice and willingly terminate our efforts to continue on that path. If we do, then the

---

[†] Overnight money is also known as the Federal Funds Rate. When you read about the Federal Reserve raising or lowering the interest rate, it is this rate to which they are referring.

economy will have to grow well below its potential for a period, to offset the time when the steroid injections of debt unnaturally swelled its growth.

The Austrian school of economics has a very crisp and historically accurate definition of how a credit bubble ends. According to Ludwig von Mises:

> There is no means of avoiding the final collapse of a boom brought about by credit expansion. The alternative is only whether the crisis should come sooner as a result of a voluntary abandonment of further credit expansion, or later as a final and total catastrophe of the currency system involved.[10]

In plain language, either we willingly end our efforts to continue doubling our debt faster than income, or we risk seeing the dollar collapse. While growing a bit slower than the hectic pace to which we have become accustomed will be *slightly* painful, a currency collapse would be *enormously* painful, not just to the United States but to the world. As a nation, the United States has undertaken desperate measures to avoid abandoning the continuation of its credit expansion, leaving a final catastrophe of its currency as the most likely outcome.

As for the timing? It could hardly be worse. Dealing with a bursting credit bubble is hardly the sort of challenge we need at this particular moment in history, where energy and environmental issues loom large. But here we are. The stewardship and vision displayed by the Federal Reserve and Washington, DC, in shepherding us to this position leaves a lot to be desired.

So, what can we expect from a collapsing credit bubble? Simply put, everything that fed upon and grew as a consequence of too much easy credit will collapse back to its baseline position. Where we lived beyond our means for too long, we will have to live below our means until the excesses are worked off. Living standards will fall, debts will default, and times will be hard. Those are the lessons of history.

But there's more to this story than the simple accumulation of debt, even as serious as that is all by itself. We'll explore more of the story later when we discuss the role of energy in supporting economic growth. For now, let's just hold onto the idea that in order for the next 20 years to resemble the past 20 years, total debt will have to double and then double again. How likely does that seem to you?

CHAPTER 12

LIKE A MOTH TO FLAME

Our Destructive Tendency to Print

The twenty-teens will be marked by the collapse of sovereign debt. When the Great Credit Bubble first began to lurch about unsteadily in 2008 as the consumer withdrew, most governments of developed nations predictably turned to Keynesian stimulus to try and keep the bubble going. What this means is that they racked up enormous and unprecedented levels of debt trying to stabilize the situation, and this debt will someday need to be paid back.

History is quite clear on the subject: Whenever governments or countries have found themselves saturated with too much debt totaling more than could possibly be paid back out of their productive economy, they've nearly always resorted to money printing. As mentioned earlier, in times past this meant physically debasing the coinage of the realm by reducing the purity of the silver or gold in the coins, or by making the coins smaller, or both.

MOTHS

In the fourth century BC, Dionysius of Syracuse became the first recorded ruler to debase his currency in order to pay down his accumulated debt. In the more recent past, this has meant running actual, physical printing presses and churning out wheelbarrow loads of paper cash, as Germany did in the 1920s and Zimbabwe did in the 2000s.

Today "money printing" means using computers to generate electronic entries denoting money. The difference between then and now is that today's debasements are virtually instantaneous and are not as easily observed by the common person. Where it took several decades for the

Roman Empire to debase its coinage (contributing to its downfall), it only took Germany about five years to accomplish the same task in the 1920s using paper printing presses. Today it's possible to create unlimited quantities of money almost instantly with just a few strokes on a keyboard.

Despite these "advances," the core of the matter has not changed one bit over the centuries. In all instances, additional money is created without the benefit of anything else being produced. Once we understand that money is a claim on wealth, but not wealth itself, it becomes obvious why simply printing more of it neither creates wealth nor corrects the problem of having previously consumed more than one has produced. Money is not wealth; therefore printing it does not create wealth or solve the problems of the past that arose due to printing too much money.

The purpose of this chapter isn't to present an exhaustive recounting of economic history, although there are many fascinating tales to be told, but to help us assess what the future might hold. In order to mitigate our economic risks, we have to know what they are. *Which path or outcome is most likely? Will we head down a path of inflation or deflation? Should I hold cash, gold, land, stocks, bonds, or something else?*

FLAMES

Recall from Chapter 10 (*Debt*) that there are only three ways for a government to get rid of its debt:

1. Pay it off.
2. Default on it.
3. Print money.

If we put ourselves in the shoes of the leaders who choose money printing, it's easy to understand why that option is nearly always selected over the other two, both of which are dreary and difficult options.

Because debt is a claim on the productive output of a country, the first option, paying off the debt, is deeply painful because it bleeds off economic growth and directs the nation's productive output into the hands of creditors. In practical terms, "paying off debt" means that the government has to tax its citizens so that it can hand that money over to the debt holders. It means higher unemployment, fewer goods and services, and therefore a restive and unhappy citizenry. Throughout all of history, raising taxes has always been a deeply unpopular move, but even more so if the collected taxes are siphoned away and don't result in any additional benefit to the citizens in the form of an obvious expansion of government services or perhaps a redistribution of wealth within that government's borders.

There are, however, precious few historical examples of governments choosing this option. After the Napoleonic wars, England found itself deeply in debt and chose to put itself through a crushing round of deflation, opting not to default or inflate away its debt. Despite hitting a record of 260 percent debt-to-GDP, England managed to pay its debt down to a quite manageable level of less than 50 percent of GDP by the turn of the twentieth century. However, several conditions were in place that allowed this course of action to be chosen.

First, most of the debt was internally financed, as the ruling class, who were well represented in Parliament, held most of it. As they put the rest of the country through a serious deflationary event, the value of their own bonds surged in relative value. In essence, they voted to give themselves a rather large transfer of wealth, which was a strong motivator. Second, the English economy was just entering the Industrial Revolution, one of the most explosive periods of economic growth and wealth creation in history. Large debts can sometimes be serviced through the miracle of rapid economic growth, and that proved true in this case. Third, most of the debt was accumulated in the form of war expenditures, which were easily and rapidly curtailed once the hostilities were over. In other words, the debt wasn't due to structural deficits, as is the case for many developed nations today that face daunting pension and entitlement expenditures in which the ongoing demands are quite different from those of a war that ends.

The second option, default, is a horrible political option for two reasons. First, defaulting on the external portion of a country's debt is a sure way to render that country an international pariah. Nobody will trade with it, except on a cash-only basis, which is very difficult to do if your currency is collapsing (a typical consequence of a debt default). The economy of the country will suffer through the loss of needed goods, and the citizens will be deeply unhappy.

For example, imagine what would happen to the United States, which imports two-thirds of its daily petroleum needs, if it defaulted on its external debt. If even a few of its exporters decided they would no longer accept U.S. dollars in exchange for their oil, the dollar would quite rapidly lose its international value, oil priced in U.S. dollars would spike enormously, and the U.S. economy would be immediately and quite possibly permanently damaged. This means that "external default" wouldn't generally be a viable strategy even if the political will for this option did happen to exist.

To the extent that debt can be defaulted upon internally, it's also typically an unworkable option because the holders of that debt, as we saw in the England example above, are almost invariably wealthy and well-connected individuals with excellent opportunities to influence the decisions of government. Very rarely do people vote to impose massive losses on themselves, so internal defaults are also extremely rare.

This leaves the third option, money printing (or its electronic equivalent), as the most viable of the three options and explains why it's almost always the preferred choice. The irony here is that it's also the most dangerous path to take, but because its destructive effects are lodged in the future somewhere, it pushes the day of reckoning to a later time (when it could very well be somebody else's problem anyway) and even offers a sliver of hope, however false. *Hey, it just might work this time! This time might be different!*

Alan Greenspan made a number of crucial errors during his tenure as chairman of the Federal Reserve, but before he held that position, he wrote this remarkably lucid and correct assessment of gold and its role in helping to shield people from the effects of governmental money printing (written in 1966, when he was managing the consulting firm Townsend-Greenspan & Co. in New York).

> In the absence of the gold standard, there is no way to protect savings from confiscation through inflation. There is no safe store of value. If there were, the government would have to make its holding illegal, as was done in the case of gold. If everyone decided, for example, to convert all his bank deposits to silver or copper or any other good, and thereafter declined to accept checks as payment for goods, bank deposits would lose their purchasing power and government-created bank credit would be worthless as a claim on goods. The financial policy of the welfare state requires that there be no way for the owners of wealth to protect themselves. This is the shabby secret of the welfare statists' tirades against gold. Deficit spending is simply a scheme for the confiscation of wealth. Gold stands in the way of this insidious process. It stands as a protector of property rights. If one grasps this, one has no difficulty in understanding the statists' antagonism toward the gold standard.[1]

Inflation has the effect of reducing the real value of public debts; it makes them smaller by making the money in which they're denominated worth less. Inflating debt away represents a stealthy form of default, but one which avoids a declaration of a formal breach of contract. Of course, to inflate away debt, the government must have control of the printing press, something impossible in the individual Eurozone countries that are united under the single currency of the euro.

Historically, defaulting nations have typically either been the financially weaker developing countries or nations that have proven to be credit risks in the past. Between 1800 and 2008, there have been 250 cases of external bond defaults and only 68 cases of internal default.[2] So defaults have happened in the past, but in today's globalized economy, food and energy security often lie outside a nation's borders, greatly complicating the situation.

Today there are a number of countries that could not possibly support their populations without a steady supply of imports, which changes the dynamic considerably. For these reasons and a number of others, the safest bet is on printing, with defaults and "paying it back" taking (very) distant second and third positions, respectively.

To draw once again from Rogoff and Reinhart's remarkable 800-year romp through history, we can observe periodic episodes of sovereign defaults against an almost constant backdrop of inflation. What is stunning is that every country in both Asia and Europe experienced an extended period of history with inflation over 20 percent between the years 1500 and 1800, and most experienced a significant number of years with inflation over 40 percent. However, deflations tended to follow each inflationary episode, so after all the ups and downs, prices tended to center around the same levels over the centuries.

In the period from 1800 to 2006, Rogoff and Reinhart note that inflation was ever more frequent and attained higher levels, thanks to the ease offered by modern printing presses. Prior to 1900, their data shows that the world cycled between inflation and deflation on very short cycles of around 10 years, again keeping price levels roughly in check around a median value. But since the last deflationary episode in the 1930s, the world spent the next 80 years in one long, sustained inflationary episode, with no downdrafts to moderate prices.

It is also true that since the 1930s, oil has yielded nearly all of its energy bonanza to humanity, and only in 1971 did fiat money lose its final tether to the firmament of earth when President Nixon cut the dollar's tie to gold.[*] These aren't unrelated events. The particular style of debt-based money on which we operate requires the very sort of continuous expansion that petroleum offers, while spending massively beyond one's means requires that no

---

[*] On August 15, 1971, President Richard Nixon "slammed the gold window," ending the Bretton Woods I agreement, which allowed foreign countries to convert their paper dollar holdings into U.S.-held gold at the fixed price of $35 per ounce. From that moment on, foreign exchange rates lost their anchor to gold and "floated" freely on the international market.

physical, tangible anchor exist to limit the spree. This means that *this time it really is different*, because the story now involves so much more than a relatively simple case of too much debt being held by a single country. This time the entire globe is involved and there are critical resource issues involved. Most of the world is now chained to and operating on a debt-based monetary system that requires perpetual exponential growth to operate. But that's the big-picture conclusion; for now it serves our purposes to simply note that the safest bet is to predict that monetary printing, or its modern equivalent, lies in our collective future.

QUANTITATIVE EASING

The prediction I began making in 2004 was that we'd enter a period of profound money printing by the Fed in order to try and "fix" things. Given the fact that the Federal Reserve and other central banks in Europe and Japan began an aggressive monetary printing program in 2008 that has continued through the time of this writing (2010), this "prediction" is now an observation. The printing has already started in earnest. These money-printing programs go by the fancy name of quantitative easing (QE), which simply refers to creating money out of thin air and then using it to buy various forms of debt, both governmental and nongovernmental. Between 2008 and 2010, the Fed's balance sheet expanded from $800 billion to just over $2,250 billion, all of which represents money created out of thin air for the purpose of monetizing existing debt (Figure 12.1).

How does this practice differ from the historical practice of clipping coins or printing money directly? Essentially, it doesn't, except under the theory that the Federal Reserve can reverse the transactions as rapidly as they entered them, thereby unwinding them and hopefully "sterilizing" the inflationary impacts when they begin to surface. In theory, the kings that clipped their coins could also have recalled them all, melted them down, and reminted larger versions, but that never happened, so history suggests that the expansion of the Fed balance sheet will be permanent.

In reality, putting money *into* the system is far easier than taking it back *out*. When the Fed puts the money into the system, an institution delivers a (possibly flawed) debt instrument to the Fed and receives a large pile of cash in return. Reversing this process requires that an institution have a large and ready pile of cash on hand to give to the Fed in exchange for the (possibly flawed) debt. Cash is rarely left piled up at financial institutions; it is generally put to work quite rapidly when it's received, so raising cash usually requires selling other things elsewhere. For this reason, putting cash out

Figure 12.1
The Federal Reserve Balance Sheet

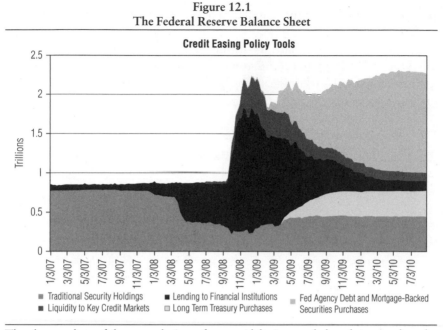

The slow and careful accumulation of assets (debts) turned sharply upward at the start of the credit crisis in 2008.

Source: Cleveland Federal Reserve.

into the marketplace is a lot easier for the Fed than reeling it back in. If they don't (or can't) reverse these monetary injections, then there's an incredibly high chance of destructive inflation emerging at some point in the future.

The point of raising the issue of QE here is simply to illustrate that money printing isn't some future event for which we need to maintain some level of vigilance. It's already happening. As Rogoff and Reinhardt have shown, printing is the first refuge of cornered officials, and those serving today have proven to be no different from those in the past. History may not necessarily repeat, but it does often rhyme.

This means that we can expect large quantities of money to be printed in an effort to forestall the inevitable pain of past decisions—decisions that revolved around not only taking on too much debt, but fashioning the bulk of our economy around its perpetual expansion. It means that if there are other structural reasons for why the economy is not growing as expected or intended, such as resource limitations, we can expect the Fed to deal with that predicament by applying the same 'solution' they've always used in the past: money printing. When all you have is a hammer, everything looks like a nail.

I want you to hold that idea in the back of your mind until we get to Chapter 15 (*Energy and the Economy*), where we'll assess whether there are any additional dark spots on the horizon to further cloud up the story of endless economic growth.

CHAPTER 13

FUZZY NUMBERS

What if it's true, as author Kevin Phillips states, that "[e]ver since the 1960s, Washington has gulled its citizens and creditors by debasing official statistics, the vital instruments with which the vigor and muscle of the American economy are measured."[1] What if it turns out that our individual, corporate, and government decision making was based on deeply misleading, if not provably false, data?

That's what we're going to examine here, uncovering the ways that inflation and Gross Domestic Product, or GDP, are measured, or as we might say, *mis*measured.

Inflation is an active policy goal of the Federal Reserve,[2] and for good reason: Too little inflation, and our current banking system risks failure; too much and the majority of people noticeably lose their savings, which makes them angry and politically restive. So keeping inflation at a "Goldilocks" temperature—not too hot and not too cold—is the name of the game.

Inflation results from a mixture of two components. The first is simple pressure on prices due to too much money floating around. If goods and services remain constant but circulating money rises, inflation will result. The second component lies with people's expectations of future inflation. If people expect prices to rise, they tend to spend their money now, while the getting is still good, and this serves to fuel further inflation in a self-reinforcing manner. The faster people spend, the more they expect inflation to rise, and the more inflation does rise. Zimbabwe was a textbook-perfect example of this dynamic in play during the years 2001 to 2008, when inflation nudged over 100 percent on its way to a peak of more than 230 million percent.[3] On the other hand, if expectations are that inflation will be tame, they're said to be "well-anchored."

Accordingly, official inflation policy has two components. The first is goosing the money supply to just the right level to achieve the desired amount of inflation, and the second is anchoring your expectations to help keep inflation in check. Assuming both components can be controlled, how exactly is "anchoring" accomplished? You might be surprised at the answer. Over time, the management of your inflation expectations has evolved into little more than reporting inflation to be lower than it actually is.

The details of how this is done are somewhat complicated, but they're worthy of your attention because trusting bad data can be hazardous to your wealth. Before we begin, I'd like to be clear on one point: The tricks and subversions that we'll examine did not arise with any particular administration or political party. Rather, they arose incrementally during each administration from the 1960s onward. If I point fingers, I'll be pointing at actions, not ideologies. There are plenty of examples that were implemented by both of the major U.S. political parties, and there's absolutely no partisan slant to this game.

ADMINISTRATIVE BIAS

Under President Kennedy, who disliked high unemployment numbers, a new classification was developed that scrubbed so-called discouraged workers from the statistics, which had the effect of causing headline-data unemployment figures to drop. Discouraged workers, defined as people who desire to work but aren't currently looking due to poor employment prospects, weren't counted; the unemployment numbers that we reported to ourselves went down, and Kennedy was reported to be pleased with the outcome. Of course, the exact same number of people were unemployed both before and after this statistical revision, but the number went down, so things looked better. No president since has seen fit to discontinue this practice, so "discouraged workers" are still dropped from the counted rolls.

President Johnson created the "unified budget" accounting fiction that we currently enjoy, which rolls Social Security surpluses into the general budget, where they are spent just like ordinary revenue. Even though the surplus Social Security funds have been spent and thus represent a debt of the U.S. government, budget deficits are reported after taking into account the positive impact of the "donated" Social Security money (which reduces the cash deficit) but not the future negative impact of this borrowing. In this sense, the federal budget deficits that you read about are fiction.

President Nixon bequeathed us the so-called core inflation measure, which strips out food and fuel, to create a measure of inflation "ex food and fuel," which financial commentator Barry Ritholtz says is "like reporting inflation ex-inflation." For the rest of us, it's very strange to think about inflation as consisting of the prices of our essential daily needs minus the eating, driving, and heating parts.

By adopting the Boskin Commission recommendation on inflation, President Clinton bestowed upon us the labyrinthine statistical morass that's now our official method of inflation measurement, which we'll discuss in detail below.

These are just some examples of a pathological instinct to buff the numbers into a rosier hue that has been a feature of every presidential administration since Kennedy. At every presidential turn, a new way of measuring and reporting was derived that invariably made things seem a bit better than they actually were. I know of no examples where a new economic measure was adopted that served to make things seem a bit drearier or worse off. The process of debasing our official statistics has always been strongly biased. Economic activity was always adjusted higher, inflation was statistically tormented downwards, and jobs were made to seem more plentiful than they actually were.

Unfortunately, the cumulative impact of all this data manipulation is that our measurements no longer match reality. In effect, we're telling ourselves lies, and these untruths serve to distort our decisions and jeopardize our economic future. A few economic fibs during the good years seemed harmless enough, and they probably were. However, with the current and emerging economic difficulties, we will find them to be as severe a liability as defective cockpit instruments would be to a pilot navigating a gap through the Rockies.

Next let's discuss in detail the way the most important indicators that we rely on for understanding our economic picture are adjusted, measure-by-measure.

INFLATION

We'll begin with inflation, which is reported to us by the Bureau of Labor Statistics (BLS), in the form of the Consumer Price Index (CPI). If you were to measure inflation, you'd probably track the cost of a basket of goods from one year to the next, subtract the two, and measure the difference. If you did, your method would, in fact, mirror the way inflation was officially measured right on up through the early 1980s. It's a perfectly logical, defensible, and sensible method.

But in 1996, Clinton implemented the Boskin Commission findings, which championed the use of three new statistical tools—substitution, weighting, and hedonics—that are applied to measured prices after they're collected but before they're reported.

The cost of goods and services are no longer simply measured and reported from one year to the next, now that we have adopted the use of the "substitution effect." Thanks to the Boskin commission, our measurements now assume that when the price of something rises, people will switch to something cheaper. So any time the price of something goes up too rapidly, it's removed from the basket of goods and a cheaper item is substituted. For example, if rib-eye steaks go up too much in price, they'll be removed from the basket and replaced ("substituted") with, say, sirloin steak (or whatever form of steak is the cheapest).

To illustrate the impacts of these statistical tricks, let's imagine that our goal is to accurately assess whether a group of 20 of our former high school classmates have gained weight (in other words, inflated) or lost weight since high school. Following current government statistical conventions in our experiment, we'd first weigh all 20 subjects and choose the 10 showing the least weight gain, and then we'd extrapolate those findings to the entire group regardless of the greater weight gain shown by the 10 that we did not include. We'd substitute the lowest weight gainers for the highest weight gainers under the theory that people should try to lose weight and should succeed if they try, never mind that this might not have been their goal, just like shoppers who "should" be frugally substituting their favorite foods for cheaper ones regardless of what they actually end up buying.

Using this methodology, the BLS reported that food costs rose 4.9 percent in 2007.[4] However, according to the Farm Bureau, which doesn't employ these tricks and simply tracks the same shopping basket of the exact same 30 goods from one year to the next, food prices rose 9.2 percent over the past year.[5] That spread of 5.1 percent makes a huge difference. Recall from the "Rule of 70" in Chapter 5 (*Dangerous Exponentials*) that a 5 percent rate of growth will result in a complete doubling in just 14 years. What this means is that even smallish-seeming underreporting of inflation will result in big differences over time. One critique of using substitution as a method is that our measure of inflation is no longer measures the cost of *living*, but rather the cost of *survival*.

The next statistical method, weighting, has the effect of reducing the amount of those goods and services that are rising most rapidly in price, under the assumption that people will use less of those things as prices rise. This is the least defensible of all the statistical tricks, because over time it has deviated widely from reality. For example, the Bureau of Economic Analysis (BEA) reports that health care represents about

17 percent of our total economy, but the BLS only weights it as 6 percent of the CPI. In our high school weight gain example, this would be like only including a fraction of the weight of those who had gained the most, which serves to overcount those who had gained the least or perhaps even lost weight.

Because health care costs have been rising extremely rapidly, reducing health care weighting has had a dramatic reduction in reported inflation. In 2008, if health care had been weighted at a level that matched its true economic proportion, CPI would have been several percentage points higher. CPI weighting leads to undercounting inflation.

Next comes the most outlandish adjustment of them all, one which goes by the name "hedonics," a name whose Greek roots translate to "for the pleasure of." This adjustment is supposed to account for quality improvements, especially those that lead to greater enjoyment or utility of a product, which makes some sense, but which has been badly overused.

Here's an example: Tim LaFleur is a commodity specialist for televisions at the Bureau of Labor Statistics (BLS) where the CPI is calculated. In 2004 he noted that a 27-inch television priced at $329.99 was selling for the same amount as last year but was now equipped with a digital tuner.[6] After taking this subjective improvement into account, he adjusted the price of the TV downwards by $135, concluding that the benefit derived from the tuner improvement was the same as if the price of the TV had fallen by 29 percent. The price reflected in the CPI was not the actual retail store cost of $329.99, which is what it would actually cost you to buy the TV, but $195. Bingo! Based on that adjustment, the BLS concluded that televisions cost a lot less than they used to, and in response, inflation was reported to have gone down. However, at the store you'd discover that these same televisions were still selling for $329.99, not $195.

Another complaint about hedonics is that they're a one-way trip. If I get a new phone this year and it has some new buttons, the BLS will declare that the price has dropped because of all the additional enjoyment I will receive from using the features attached to those buttons. But if my new phone only lasts 8 months before ceasing to work, instead of lasting 30 years like an old rotary phone, no adjustment will be made for that loss of service life (or the hassle of having to drop everything to go and get a new phone). In short, hedonics rests on the improbable assumption that new features are always beneficial and that these features can be thought of as synonymous with falling prices. I'm not entirely against the practice—I really like the many ways my car is not like a Ford Pinto—but the use of hedonics can easily be overdone, and that's my estimation of the present situation.

Over the years, the BLS has expanded the use of hedonic adjustments and now applies these adjustments to everything: DVDs, automobiles, washers, dryers, refrigerators, and even college textbooks. Hedonics now adjusts as much as 46 percent of the total CPI, and if recent plans to apply hedonics to health care are approved, this percentage will jump to well over half.

What would happen if you were to strip out all the fuzzy statistical manipulations and calculate inflation the way we used to do it? Luckily, John Williams of shadowstats.com has done exactly that, painstakingly following these statistical modifications over time and reversing their effects.[7] If inflation were calculated today the exact same way that it was in the early 1980s, Mr. Williams has determined that it would be roughly 8 percentage points higher than currently reported, which is an enormous difference.

The higher inflation readings offered by Mr. Williams comport better with the economic news than do the (much) lower government readings. They fit better with the observation that most people have had to borrow more and were able to save less over time—because their real income was actually a lot lower than reported. It explains why the elderly on fixed incomes have been having a harder and harder time making ends meet. A higher rate of inflation is consistent with weak labor markets and growing levels of debt, two stubborn features of the current economic landscape. This higher rate of inflation matches up well with the observed rates of monetary growth throughout the 1990s and early 2000s. So many things that were difficult to explain under the low-inflation readings offered by the government suddenly make sense when we adopt a higher rate of inflation into our mental framework. We can either conclude that we are misperceiving all of those other things, or conclude that the inflation reading is the skewed statistic.

The social cost to this self-deception is enormous. For starters, if inflation were calculated the way it used to be, Social Security payments, whose cost of living adjustment (COLA) increases are based on the CPI, would be 70 percent higher than they currently are.[8]

Because Medicare increases are also tied to the woefully understated CPI, hospitals are receiving lower Medicare reimbursements than they otherwise would and are increasingly unable to balance their budgets, forcing many communities to choose between closing their hospitals and cutting off service to Medicare recipients. A little harmless fibbing and self-deception is one thing; losing your only community hospital is quite another. These are a few of the grave impacts in our daily lives that result from living with a statistically tortured CPI.

But aside from paying out less in entitlement checks, politicians gain in another very important way by understating inflation.

GROSS DOMESTIC PRODUCT (GDP)

Gross domestic product (GDP) is how we tell ourselves that our economy is either doing well or doing poorly. In theory, the GDP is the sum total of all value-added transactions within our country in any given year. Just like the CPI (inflation measure), the GDP measure has been so twisted and tweaked by government statisticians that it no longer tells a recognizable version of the truth. As before, there was no sudden, secret adjustment where GDP slipped off the rails; it has been stealthily and systematically debased under every presidential administration since the 1960s, like an old house with a thriving termite colony.

Here is an example of just how far from reality GDP has strayed: The reported GDP amount for 2003 was $11 trillion, implying that $11 trillion of money-based, value-added economic transactions occurred. But that did not actually happen. To begin with, that $11 trillion included $1.6 trillion of so-called imputation adjustments, where economic value was assumed ("imputed") to have been created, but where no cash transactions had actually taken place. Despite the fact that there was no trade and nothing changed hands, a value was still assigned to these assumptions and reported as part of the GDP.

The largest imputation represents something called "owner's equivalent rent," which assigns a value to the benefit that homeowners receive by not having to pay themselves rent. If you own your house free and clear, the government calculates "the amount of money owner occupants would have spent had they been renting."[9] It's not a trivial amount; it totaled $1.225 trillion in 2009.[10]

Another is the benefit that you receive from the "free checking" provided by your bank, which is imputed to have a value because if it wasn't free, then, as the logic goes, you'd have to pay for it. So a value is assigned to all the free checking in the land, and that, too, is added to the tally. Together, all of the imputations added up to $2.27 trillion dollars in 2009, out of a total reported national income of $13.94 trillion dollars, or 16 percent of the total.[11]

Next, like the CPI, the GDP also has many elements that are hedonically adjusted. For instance, computers are hedonically adjusted to account for the prospect that faster and more feature-rich computers must be worth more to our economic output than prior models.

So if a computer costing $1,000 was sold, it would be recorded as contributing more than a thousand dollars to the GDP to account for the fact that it's faster and more technologically advanced than the thousand-dollar model that was sold last year. Of course, that extra money is fictitious; it never traded hands and doesn't actually exist. This is similar to a toilet paper manufacturer reporting higher revenues because its product was softer and fluffier this year, even though the same number of units was sold last year at the same price.

Admittedly, there are perfectly valid justifications for trying to adjust for the role of quality when measuring *price* changes. For example, if we were to compare a 1972 Ford Pinto, with its thin-walled gasoline tank and 8-track player, to a 2010 Camry with anti-lock brakes, CD sound system, driver and passenger airbags, and vastly improved drive train, and we were to find that the Camry had a higher market value than the Pinto, it would be unfair to attribute that price difference solely to inflation.[12] I feel it's quite a stretch to then claim that an improvement in quality is the same thing as having sold more of that item, which is what the GDP purports to measure.

Interestingly, for the purposes of inflation measurements, hedonic adjustments are used to *reduce* the apparent price of computers, but for GDP calculations, hedonic adjustments are used to *boost* their apparent cash contribution to the nation's economy. Using the magic of hedonics, government statisticians are able to simultaneously claim that computers cost less but are worth more—depending on whether the measurement is being applied to the CPI or the GDP, respectively.

So what were the total hedonic adjustments in 2003? An additional $2.3 trillion dollars.[13] Taken together, these mean that $3.9 trillion or fully 35 percent of 2003's reported GDP wasn't based on transactions that you could witness, record, or touch. They were guessed at, modeled, and/or imputed, but they did not show up in any bank accounts because no cash ever changed hands and no product was produced. These adjustments have served to vastly inflate the GDP and overstate the true economic health of the United States.

As an aside, when you read about how the United States' "debt-to-GDP ratio is still quite low" or "income taxes as a percentage of GDP are at historically low levels," it's important to recall that because GDP is artificially inflated, any ratio where GDP is the denominator, such as debt-to-GDP and taxes-to-GDP, will be artificially low.

INFLATION AND GDP

Now let's tie inflation into the GDP story. The GDP that you read about is always inflation-adjusted and reported after inflation is subtracted out. This is called "real" GDP, while the preinflation-adjusted number is called "nominal" GDP. Measuring the real output is an important thing to do, because GDP is supposed to measure real output, not inflation.

For example, if an entire economy consisted of producing nothing but lava lamps, with only one lamp being produced in one year and one of them the next year, we'd want to record the GDP growth rate as zero, because the output, or gross domestic product, was exactly the same in one year as the next. There was no growth in output; only one lava lamp was produced in each period.

However, if one lava lamp sold for $100 in the first year and one sold for $110 the next, we would accidentally record a 10 percent rate of growth in GDP if we didn't back out the price increase. Remember, we're trying to measure our gross domestic *product*, not inflated money flows (that would be a different measure). So in this example, in the second year, the *real* lava lamp economy has a value of $100, while the *nominal* lava lamp economy is worth $110. But we only care about the *real* economy, because what we're trying to measure and report on is what was actually *produced*.

Now we're in a position to appreciate a second powerful reason why DC politicians prefer a low-inflation reading. GDP is expressed in *real* terms, derived by subtracting inflation from the measured *nominal* quantities. In 3Q of 2007, reports indicated that the United States enjoyed a surprisingly strong 4.9 percent rate of GDP growth. At the time, there was a fair bit of rejoicing over this unexpectedly robust number. However, what we did not hear very much about was the fact that an astonishingly low inflation reading of only 1 percent was subtracted from the *nominal* GDP of 5.9 percent, giving us the final *real* result of 4.9 percent.

In order to accept the 4.9 percent figure, we have to first accept that the United States experienced only a 1 percent rate of inflation during a period when oil was shooting toward $100/barrel for the first time, medical insurance increases were measured in double digits, college tuition went up by high single digits, and food inflation was wracking the globe. What would have happened if a far more believable 3.5 percent rate of inflation had been used by the BEA? Reported GDP growth would have been a somewhat lackluster, if not entirely disappointing, 2.4 percent.

Lest you think that I've hand-picked an accidental, one-time statistical hiccup in the GDP reporting series, possibly due to significant one-time events that caused an unusually low 1 percent reading to occur, here's a chart of the so-called GDP deflator (which is the specific measure of inflation that is subtracted from the nominal GDP to yield the reported real GDP).

As you can see in Figure 13.1, between 2004 and 2008 the clear trend has been for the Bureau of Economic Analysis to systematically subtract lower

Figure 13.1
GDP Deflator

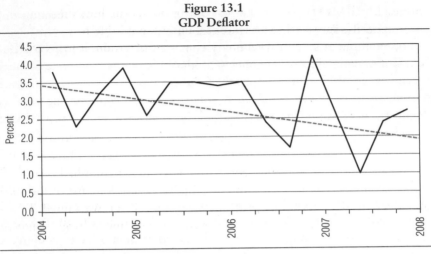

Steadily declining over time.

Source: Bureau of Economic Analysis.

and lower amounts of inflation from nominal GDP, which doesn't comport well at all with real-world inflation data over that period of time. Remember, each percent that inflation is *understated* equals a full percent that GDP is *overstated*.

I invite you to keep this in mind when you next read about how "our robust economy is still expanding," or is "in recovery," or any other pronouncement about the strength of the economy that relies upon the GDP as its yardstick. That measuring tool is no longer giving accurate or useful readings, due to the effects of imputations, hedonics, and deceptively low inflation readings.

In 2007, I began to trust my own assessment that the United States was experiencing higher inflation than reported, while checking my findings against those of John Williams. Because of the need to subtract this higher rate from the GDP, I started investing and interpreting the news as if we were in a period of solid recession, not respectable growth. Suddenly a lot of things that had previously been difficult for me to understand began to make perfect sense. Contracting businesses, rising foreclosures, job losses, rising budget deficits, falling tax revenues, declining auto sales—all of these were consistent with recession, not expansion. All of these warning signs were in plain view in 2007, long before a recession was officially recognized. Those trying to make sense of these economic events by viewing them through the government's rose-tinted statistics were more likely to be confused than helped. Those in a position to appreciate how the game was rigged and then trust themselves to act wisely were able to navigate this period more successfully. When navigating uneven terrain, it helps tremendously if your instruments are reliable.

AND ALL THE REST

Statistical wizardry similar to that which we've explored here for GDP and the CPI is also performed on income, unemployment figures, house prices, budget deficits, and virtually every other government-supplied economic statistic that you can think of. Each is saddled with a long list of lopsided imperfections that inevitably paint a rosier picture than is warranted. Taken all together, I call the economic stories that we're handed by government statisticians "Fuzzy Numbers." To quote Kevin Phillips again: ". . . our nation may truly regret losing sight of history, risk and common sense."[14]

CHAPTER 14

STARTING THE RACE WITH OUR SHOES TIED TOGETHER

In the spring of 2001, while returning from a trip to Europe, I was in the back of a taxi heading home from JFK airport outside of New York City on an important phone call, trying to negotiate a contract with a new client. "What?" I asked, "I couldn't make that out . . ." as my phone connection went fuzzy. Just then, the taxi hit an enormous pothole, its third in as many minutes, and I lost the phone connection. Physics tells me these were unrelated events, but they felt connected. Redialing, embarrassed, and apologizing for the lost connection, I was struck by the thought that I had not had a single dropped call while in Europe, not when traveling through the 26-mile long Chunnel on a train beneath hundreds of feet of rock and water, not even in elevators. While stewing over the lost phone call and the rough ride from the airport, it struck me just how shabby and decrepit much of the U.S. physical infrastructure had become. As I recall, the business deal turned out okay, but instances such as these surrounded some of my first budding doubts about the health of our country.

In a 2005 report, the American Society of Civil Engineers assessed the condition of 12 categories of infrastructure, including bridges, roadways, drinking water systems, and wastewater treatment plants. They gave the United States an overall grade of "D" and calculated that $1.6 trillion would be needed over the next five years to bring the United States back up to First World standards.[1] At the time of this writing in 2010, almost none of these investments have happened. Because inflation has advanced since then and more deterioration has occurred, the bill has certainly grown. "Clean, modern, and efficient" no longer describes the United States in 2010; those days have passed. The United States can get there again, but it will take an enormous fiscal commitment to enjoy First World infrastructure once again.

Choices matter, and the United States has repetitively chosen to defer maintenance and upgrades on essential economic infrastructure until some future date. There's a long story there, but for now, we can simply note that one of the many demands on the United States' limited pool of future funds will be the required investment in, and repair of, its physical infrastructure.

A NATIONAL FAILURE TO SAVE

Even if the United States were about to embark on another 1990s-style economic boom on a par with the Internet revolution, it would still face structural headwinds that will place enormous demands on future funds. Unfortunately, no such savior technology is readily apparent at this time. Given the sheer number of economic currents and other financial demands that lurk in the near future, it would be ideal if the United States were entering the twenty-teens with high levels of rainy-day funds socked away. But this isn't the case.

In 2007, it was reported that the personal savings rate had plunged to historic lows, levels last seen during the Great Depression when people were dipping into savings to buy food and pay the rent. This created the false impression that the modern savings rate was a result of a sudden crisis.[2] In fact, the personal savings rate had been steadily declining since around 1985 (see Figure 14.1), indicating that this failure to save wasn't just a recent notable blip on the economic radar, but rather the culmination of a multidecade process.

Note that the long-term historical average for U.S. citizens between 1960 and 1985 was 9.2 percent. For comparison, in Europe in 2009 that number was just over 15 percent,[3] and between 1978 and 2000 China's national saving rate was a stunning 37 percent of its GNP.[4]

Savings are important to us individually because they form a cash cushion that can get us through economically difficult times. They are also important at the national level, because a nation that doesn't save is a nation that steadily grows poorer. Savings contribute to investments in property, plant, and equipment that lead to the formation of future wealth.

However, Figure 14.1 somewhat obscures the fact that the extremely wealthy raked in most of the income gains during the 1990s and 2000s, which allowed them to save enormous amounts of money, while the lower socioeconomic brackets suffered income declines and posted savings rates that were deeply negative. It all averages out to one low rate of savings, but that's like having one foot on hot coals and the other in a bucket of ice water and saying that, on average, your feet are at a comfortable

Figure 14.1
Personal Savings Rate from 1960 to 2010

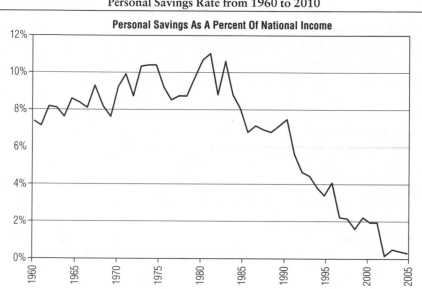

The personal savings rate is the difference between income and expenditures for all U.S. citizens expressed as a percentage.

Source: Bureau of Economic Analysis.

temperature. One group saved a lot because they could, and the rest couldn't save at all. Why is this important? Because, as the Greek philosopher Plutarch once observed, "An imbalance between rich and poor is the oldest and most fatal ailment of all republics."[5]

One possible explanation for the declining savings rate is the rise in the use of credit seen over the same period of time. Where a savings account once provided a buffer to life's vicissitudes, the idea now is that credit cards and home equity lines of credit (HELOCs) can perform that task without the bother of foregoing any of life's pleasures while building up savings. In what qualifies as a case of cultural whiplash, in only 25 short years the United States entirely replaced a "save and spend" mentality with a "buy now, pay later" approach. Lending credence to this overall idea is the observation that the savings rate began its decline right around 1985, coinciding perfectly with our long, steady rise in debt accumulation. Savings and cash cushions were swapped for debt and credit lines.

Another type of saving exists in the form of pension and retirement funds. State and municipal pensions are in horrible shape, and in 2010 were found to be underfunded by $3 trillion and more than $500 billion, respectively.[6] This happened for two reasons. First, various governmental administrations regularly made the decision to defer funding of these promises until some later date. This had the double effect of preserving more money for current spending while also keeping taxes down—two irresistible goals of any town, city, or state administration. Second, the plan administrators were allowed to make absurd projections of future rates of return, sometimes as high as 11 percent per year. These were clearly not achievable, yet the assumptions remained in place. The attractiveness of this practice is that the higher the assumed rate of return, the less money had to be placed into the account.

For example, if a town's pension administrators knew that they'd need $100,000 in 10 years to pay off a pension obligation, their assumption of an 11 percent rate of return would only require them to place approximately $35,000 into the pension fund. If instead they assumed a much more modest and achievable return of 5 percent, which averages out the good years and the bad, they would be required to put roughly $61,000 into the fund, or 95 percent more. This is why plan administrators have often made wildly unrealistic assumptions about plan returns. Once again, the miracle of exponential growth has crept into a story, this time with seemingly minor assumptions about percentages compounding into very substantial predicaments, and once again exponentials are proving to be a substantial foe.

The problem with using such wrong assumptions is that instead of working for you, compounding works against you. Even a slight miss in returns a few years back will mushroom into a very large future shortfall. That's just how compounding works, and that's exactly where hundreds of underfunded pension plans now find themselves.

To illustrate how this will play out, consider the case of Vallejo, California, where mandatory pension payments, long-deferred but finally unavoidable, ate into the current budget too deeply to avoid cutting other current services. Faced with unmovable public employee unions, escalating pension costs, and a rapidly shrinking budget, the city was forced to declare bankruptcy in 2008.[7] By 2010, the city had slashed its police force from 160 to 100, requested that its citizens use the 911 system as little as possible, and cut funding to youth groups, a senior center, and arts organizations. In other words, past promises have caught up with current spending. For the leaders of Vallejo, the future they hoped would never come has arrived. This critical tension between pension promises that were far too generous to ever be supported (even under a regime of healthy economic growth) and the need to direct municipal and state revenues to current services is sure to dominate the financial landscape of the twenty-teens.

What does it mean when we say that the state and municipal pensions are underfunded by a trillion dollars? How is that calculated? The trillion-dollar shortfall is what is called a Net Present Value (NPV) amount. An NPV calculation adds up all the cash inflows and offsets (or "nets") those inflows against all the future cash outflows. Since a dollar today is worth more than a dollar in the future, the future cash flows have to be discounted and brought back to the present. We net all the cash inflows and costs, and discount them back to the present to determine if the thing we're measuring has a positive or negative value.

This is the methodology used to calculate the status of state and munici-pal pension funds. Growth in the value of the pension fund assets plus future taxes are offset against cash outlays to pensioners, brought back to the present to indicate that in order for the pension funds to have zero value (in other words, to avoid having negative value or being "in the hole"), $1 trillion would have to be placed in those funds *today*.* In 2008, corpora-tions, coming off one of the highest levels of profitability in history, had similarly underfunded pension obligations amounting to over $400 billion (again, in NPV dollars).[8]

But it's only when we get to the U.S. federal government entitlement programs that the truly scary numbers emerge. Lawrence Kotlikoff (a Boston University economics professor) has studied the issue as closely as anyone and calculated in 2010 that the U.S. federal obligations are underfunded by $202 trillion, or more than 8 times current GDP.[9] He glumly concluded that the U.S. government has been effectively running a Ponzi scheme and that highly unfavorable math will severely crimp future prosperity:

> And [the Ponzi scheme] will stop in a very nasty manner. The first possibility is massive benefit cuts visited on the baby boomers in retirement. The second is astronomical tax increases that leave the young with little incentive to work

---

*An important realization about NPV calculations is that by definition, all future cash flows have already been taken into account. This means that all expected streams of revenue have been offset against future expenses. Therefore, if a pension has a $1 trillion shortfall, we would need to place $1 trillion in the funds *today* toward future needs, and if we don't do this next year, the shortfall will almost cer-tainly grow. The only way it could be smaller is if benefits are reduced or the fund's assets outperformed the assumed rate of growth that fed the original NPV calcula-tion. That is, reality would have to be different than the initial assumptions. This happens all the time, but for a variety of reasons, initial assumptions have almost invariably turned out to have been overly optimistic, not pessimistic.

and save. And the third is the government simply printing vast quantities of money to cover its bills.

Most likely we will see a combination of all three responses with dramatic increases in poverty, tax, interest rates and consumer prices. This is an awful, downhill road to follow, but it's the one we are on.[10]

Two things are perfectly clear: There will be less money to go around in the future, and standards of living will fall as a result.

In case you're harboring the notion that there's some money socked away in a special U.S. government account, like in some kind of lockbox, I regret to inform you that there's no "trust fund." All of the excess Social Security receipts collected over the years have already been spent. The "trust fund," such as it is, consists of several three-ring binders, locked in a filing cabinet in an otherwise-unremarkable government building in Virginia, which are filled with slips of paper representing IOUs from the government to itself.

Some people are confused by the fact that these IOUs are known as "special Treasury bonds" that promise to pay the funds back when needed in the future, with interest. That certainly sounds official and trustworthy. But the problem is, it's not possible for the government to owe itself money, especially money upon which it has promised to pay interest. It's not possible for *any* entity to owe itself money; by definition there cannot be any value in a promissory note issued by an entity from itself to itself. It would be an accounting fiction to suggest otherwise, and in private industry this practice is considered fraud (e.g., Enron).

All government revenue either comes from taxpayers or from borrowing, so when the time comes to pay off those "special" bonds, those funds must *either* come from taxpayers *or* from additional borrowing. The funds won't come "from the government"; they'll come from taxes or additional indebtedness. Therefore the "special" bonds have no value beyond how much future taxpayers will have to pay due to their presence. They're not an asset of the government; they're a liability of its people. There is a big difference between the representation of the Social Security holdings as a "trust fund" versus a multitrillion-dollar future liability of taxpayers. It's as vast as the difference between night and day.

Depending on whose numbers you use, the federal shortfall in (mainly) entitlement funding is anywhere from $53 trillion (U.S. Treasury, 2009) to $99 trillion (Federal Reserve, 2009) to $202 trillion (Kottlikoff, 2010). Even the lowest estimate is nearly four times the total GDP of the nation. There are no painless ways to close even that gap.

SUMMING IT UP

Putting it all together, we find that a personal failure to save is coincident with a failure to save at the state and local levels, which is mirrored by a corporate failure to save. And all are dwarfed by a colossal failure to save at the federal government level. Adding to this predicament is a profound failure to invest in and maintain existing infrastructure. All of these deficits will exert demands upon our national wealth in the relatively near future, and this leads me to conclude that the next 20 years are going to be completely unlike the last 20 years.

Here are the deficits:

1. A savings rate near zero
2. State and municipal pension deficits of up to $3 trillion
3. Corporate pension deficits of $400 billion
4. Federal shortfalls of somewhere between $60 and $200 trillion
5. Needed infrastructure investments of $2 trillion (or more)

How did we get here? How did this happen? As a former consultant to Fortune 500 companies, I observed that if the leadership of a company was financially reckless or had a moral disregard for its workers, this same behavior could be found reflected throughout all the remaining layers of the company. The U.S. government became fiscally reckless beginning in the mid-1980s, failed to live within its means, borrowed more and more, and not only failed to properly fund the entitlement programs, but raided the funds and then excluded themselves from having to properly report this fact:

From the U.S. Code:
EXCLUSION OF SOCIAL SECURITY FROM ALL BUDGETS Pub. L. 101-508, title XIII, Sec. 13301(a), Nov. 5, 1990, 104 Stat. 1388-623, provided that: Notwithstanding any other provision of law, the receipts and disbursements of the Federal Old-Age and Survivors Insurance Trust Fund and the Federal Disability Insurance Trust Fund shall not be counted as new budget authority, outlays, receipts, or deficit or surplus for purposes of—(1) the budget of the United States Government as submitted by the President, (2) the congressional budget, or (3) the Balanced Budget and Emergency Deficit Control Act of 1985.

Coincident with this loss of fiscal prudence, corporations, municipalities, states, and individuals all took similar approaches toward saving and financial responsibility. Between 1985 and 2010, the United States experienced a profound cultural shift with respect to financial prudence that began at the top, filtered throughout the remaining layers of society, and now permeates our entire economic landscape.

This is our legacy—the economic and physical world that we are choosing to leave to those who follow us. Most of these bills will come due, in a big way, in the twenty-teens. Given the massive amounts of debt, low savings, demographic headwinds, and other economic challenges, we are entering the next 20 years with our economic shoes firmly laced together.

PART IV

ENERGY

CHAPTER 15

ENERGY AND THE ECONOMY

Now that we have seen how our economy is based on perpetual exponential growth and reviewed the ever-accumulating series of debts and deficits with which we've saddled ourselves, we are ready to get to the heart of the matter: linking energy to the economy. This chapter is essential to appreciating why enormous economic changes are coming our way.

One of the many ways that classical economists go astray is by assuming that the economy exists in a vacuum, a complete little private universe that can be understood on its own, without considering "externalities" in the form of the resources that cycle in and the waste that must cycle out. The problem with this view is that the economy is absolutely not a complete little universe all its own. Quite the opposite; it's like an organism, as dependent on its surroundings as a baby in a womb. Where economists assume that needed resources will magically arise because the marketplace demands them, a more holistic model would begin with the observation that the economy only exists because resources are available. The natural world isn't a subset of the economy, it is the other way around—the economy is a subset of the natural world.

Recall from Chapter 9 (*What Is Wealth?*) that primary wealth leads to secondary wealth, which leads to tertiary wealth. Without primary wealth, nothing else exists. The only world in which conventional economics makes any sense is in a world without limits, one where no resource constraints exist. In the physical sciences, the difference between the two views would be described as the difference between an open system and a closed system.

A closed system is any defined set of space, matter, energy, or information that we care to draw a box around and study. The universe itself is a system, and within that largest of all systems, one can define any numbers of smaller systems. For example, our planet is a system, as is your body, your house, or a bathtub full of water. A closed system is a system having no interaction or communication with any other system—no energy, matter, or information flowing into or out of it. The universe itself is a closed system. There is no "outside" the universe, no other system beyond its boundaries that it can interact with.

The second type of system is an open system, with energy and matter flowing into and out of it. Such a system can use the energy and matter flowing through it to temporarily fight entropy and create order, structure, and patterns for a time. Our planet, for example, is an open system; it sits in the middle of a river of energy streaming out from the sun. This flow of energy enables the creation of large, complex molecules which in turn have enabled life, thus creating a biosphere that is teeming with order and complexity.

Closed systems always have a predictable end state. Although they might do unpredictable things along the way, they always, eventually, head toward maximum entropy equilibrium. Open systems are much more complicated. Sometimes they can be in a stable, equilibriumlike state, or they can exhibit very complex and unpredictable behavior patterns that are far from equilibrium—patterns such as exponential growth, radical collapse, or oscillations. As long as an open system has free energy, it may be impossible to predict its ultimate end state or whether it will ever reach an end state.[1]

The most important concept here is that order and complexity arise in any open system (such as our economy) if and only if energy is consumed. Let me restate this critical point: Order and complexity arise as a consequence of taking concentrated energy and reducing it to a less concentrated form, extracting useful work and generating heat along the way.

Our economy has been exponentially growing in complexity by leaps and bounds, as Beinhocker captures in this observation:

Retailers have a measure, known as stock keeping units (SKUs) that is used to count the number of types of products sold by their stores. For example, five types of blue jeans would be five SKUs. If one inventories all the types of products and services in the Yanomamö [stone age tribe] economy, that is, the different models of stone axes, the number and types of food, and so on, one would find that the total number of SKUs in the Yanomamö economy can probably be measured in the several hundreds, and at the most thousands. The number of SKUs in the New Yorker's economy is not precisely known, but using a variety of data sources, I very roughly estimate that it is on the order of 10 to the 10th (in other words, tens of billions).

To summarize, 2.5 million years of economic history in brief: for a very, very, very long time not much happened; then all of a sudden, all hell broke loose. It took 99.4 percent of economic history to reach the wealth levels of the Yanomamö, 0.59 percent to double that level by 1750, and then just 0.01 percent for global wealth to leap to the levels of the modern world.[2]

The amount of economic complexity required to build, track, ship, and utilize tens of billions of items is enormous. We can only describe our economy as a complex system that, like any other, owes its complexity to the continuous throughput of energy.

The purpose of this section of the book is to explore the connection between the economy and energy, and then ask what will happen to our economy when (not if, but *when*) ever-increasing energy (oil) flows through the economy, then suddenly stalls, then goes in reverse. Because open systems can only increase their complexity and maintain their order through the use of energy, the simple prediction is that our economy's growth in complexity will also stall at first and then go into reverse. The hard part is predicting what will happen and when, because one consistent feature of complex systems is that they are inherently unpredictable.

EVEN SAND IS TOO COMPLICATED

Even something as seemingly simple as predicting the behavior of a growing sand pile currently eludes our predictive abilities. Imagine dropping grain after grain of sand into a pile. It grows and grows, but at some point it will slump on one side or perhaps entirely collapse. Knowing when and how much seems as though it should be a straightforward task, but it's not.

In *Ubiquity: Why Catastrophes Happen* by Mark Buchanan,[3] a tale is recounted of three physicists, Per Bak, Chao Tang, and Kurt Weisenfeld, who set about trying to discover if they could predict when, where, and to what degree sand piles would avalanche. Using a computer model to speed things along, they ran an enormous number of simulations and discovered that nothing could be predicted at all. Not the size of the avalanche, which could range from a single grain tumbling down the face to the complete collapse of the whole pile, not the timing between events, and not whether the next grain would trigger either a cataclysm or nothing at all.

They discovered some important properties of systems that are poised on the knife edge of instability, but left the ability to predict the timing and size of catastrophic events to future scientists. For us, the important lesson learned from the sand pile experiments is that when it comes to the timing and the size of changes, complex systems are inherently unpredictable.

But this doesn't mean they're *completely* unpredictable. Knowing something of the "system of sand," we can put some boundaries around what might and might not happen, and can therefore "predict" the future in the largest sense, even though its timing and precise details might elude us. We know that a growing sand pile will eventually collapse; we know that it cannot grow to be ten times taller than it is wide; we know that the higher and more complex the pile becomes, the more likely an avalanche becomes; we know that a sand pile is a complex system and will therefore behave in unpredictable ways. While we cannot predict exactly what will happen and when, we can understand the boundaries of the system and therefore know what is both possible and probable.

We know this from our everyday lives. We don't know when, where, or how large the next earthquake in California will be, but we know that one will eventually happen. Because an earthquake in California is both possible and probable, local building codes seek to mitigate the risks by utilizing specific architectural designs and structural reinforcements. When we sit at the beach on any given day, we cannot possibly predict the form of every crashing wave and the shape of every turbulent eddy in the water's retreat, but we can easily "predict" a range for the size of the waves that will wash in over the next hour. "Between 1 and 4 feet, but most likely 2," we might guess based on the waves we've seen, and then we might let our children play in the surf, confident that an 18 foot wave won't suddenly arrive and ruin the day.

Although events within complex systems are unpredictable in their timing and details, we can still (1) understand that they'll happen, (2) know that when stresses are building the events become more likely (and larger), and (3) recognize the rough boundaries of the system.

THE MASTER RESOURCE

When oil first began to be used for industrial purposes at the turn of the last century, world population stood at 1.1 billion and sailing ships still plied the waters alongside coal steamers. Since then, world population has expanded more than 4 times, the world's economy by more than 40 times, and energy use by more than 10 times.[4]

We're all familiar with the massive benefits bestowed by this explosive liberation of human potential in the forms of technological and intellectual advances. In order to appreciate the delicacy of the continuation of this abundance, we need to understand the actual role of energy in forming our society. If we recall back to Chapter 6 (*An Inconvenient Lie*), I made the point that both growth and prosperity are dependent on surplus. In the case of economic growth and prosperity, nothing is more important than surplus energy.

Imagine two separate societies: One has barely enough food energy to survive, and the other is blessed with a vast surplus of food energy. Assuming that they possessed the same cultural proclivities toward inventiveness, we would find the society with the subsistence food supply to be very rudimentary and not terribly complex when compared to the better-bestowed society. It would be clear that the surplus energy in the food supply had been "funding" economic growth for the more well-endowed society.

So we might say that among all energy sources, food is the one that most commands our attention when it's in short supply. By way of example, we could compare the state of complexity of societies before and after the agricultural revolution some 10,000 years ago. Before the agricultural revolution, humans lived in small nomadic tribes that subsisted by hunting and gathering. There were few job roles, and only small, hand-held artifacts from this period have been found and studied today. After the revolution, complex societies with multiple producing and nonproducing job specializations arose, building enduring works of architecture, art, music, law, and all the other trappings of societal complexity that are familiar to us today. These bold works and levels of complexity only became possible once there was a surplus of food to "fund" specialized roles and activities.

Before agriculture, human society was limited in its complexity by the amount of food that could be gathered and crudely stored, which represented a very limited energy budget. After this agricultural revolution, enormous leaps in complexity were powered by the ability of farmers to create an excess of food calories that effectively freed up other people for other pursuits. But what unleashed the "third epoch"—the exponential explosion in complexity—that began some 150 ago and continues today? It was energy, of course, but it wasn't food energy. It was ancient sunlight.[5]

Instead of waiting for the rather diffuse and comparatively parsimonious energy from the sun to fall upon the earth and slowly grow their planted crops, humans discovered hundreds of millions of years of ancient sunlight condensed into the unbelievably dense and usable forms of coal and oil.[6] Nature will occasionally build up a massive store of potential energy and then wait for something to unleash it in a furious burst. Thunderheads build up enormous electrical potential energy and then discharge it all at once with a bolt of lightning. A steep slope will accumulate an enormous weight of snow before its potential energy is suddenly unleashed to the valley below. Ancient sunlight was stored as immense concentrations of potential energy, waiting in store for some spark to release it. That spark was us humans, and we've consequently liberated close to half of all those tens and hundreds of millions of years of stored energy in a span of a little over 150 years—faster than lightning, in geological terms.

Just as food energy is vital to the effective functioning of our bodies, which are very complex machines, energy that can perform work is absolutely vital to the creation and maintenance of complex economies. The key word here is "work." Without energy, no work could ever be accomplished, but not all forms of energy are useful for doing work. The tiny amount of potential energy stored up in the spring of a wristwatch can perform the useful work of moving the watch's hands and mechanisms, but the enormous heat energy contained in one of the Great Lakes can do almost no work, because it isn't concentrated enough to be of any practical use.

The more energy density something contains, the more useful it is. This is why the fossil fuels—oil, natural gas, and coal—are so desired and desirable. They represent concentrated forms of energy that are capable of doing a lot of work. Without them, our economy would be a pale shadow of its current bright self. Given the importance of energy to the continued smooth functioning of our economy, we owe it to ourselves to understand the ideas and the data that underlie the sources and amounts of energy that course through our economic arteries.

ENERGY BUDGETING

To help us on this journey, let's take a quick tour through the concept of energy budgeting. If you have a household budget or have ever run the numbers for a business, this will be an easy topic.

Imagine that at any given time there is a defined amount of energy available for us to use as we wish. This will be our budget to spend as we see fit, but instead of dollars, this budget will consist of units of energy. Let's put every source of currently existing energy into this budget: solar, wind, hydro, nuclear, coal, petroleum, natural gas, biomass, and so on.

This list represents our total energy to use any way we please; it's our "energy budget." Our first mandatory expenditure from this budget will be the energy that we need to use in order to ensure that we'll have more energy next year. Consider it an unavoidable energy tax. A certain amount of energy must be used to maintain our existing energy infrastructure—all the dams, pipes, and power plants—and an additional amount must be expended to find more energy to replace that which we use up. Along with this, we must also invest some energy in building and maintaining the capital structure that allows us to collect and distribute energy and maintain a complex society. Things like roads, bridges, electrical grids, and even our

Figure 15.1
Energy Budgeting

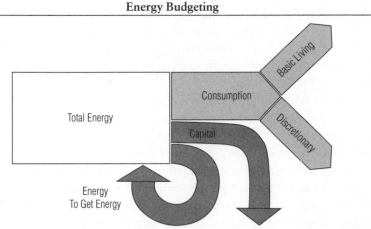

In this energy budget, a certain amount must be reinvested (darkest arrows), leaving the rest to be consumed by basic living and fully discretionary uses.

Image: Jeanine Dargis

buildings go into this category. Together, all of this can be considered our mandatory energy expenditures, meaning that they are unavoidable.

Once we've subtracted all of the mandatory energy expenditures from our budget, the remaining energy can be used for consumption. Part of this must go toward procuring our basic living needs, such as water, food, and shelter, leaving the rest for truly discretionary things like vacation trips to the Galapagos, selling hula hoops to Eskimos, and attending concerts. All of this has been diagrammed in Figure 15.1.

To further simplify this story, we can divide energy up into two big buckets: (1) energy that must be reinvested to maintain existing energy flows, buildings, and basic living needs ("mandatory"), and (2) energy that we can more or less choose what to do with ("discretionary"). Using our prior terminology, the discretionary bucket becomes the surplus energy that we can either apply toward growth *or* prosperity, but not both (unless there is surplus). But our surplus energy is shrinking, for two reasons: Every year there are more people placing more "mandatory" demands on the energy we have, and every year we're getting less and less energy back from our energy investments.

NET ENERGY

This is the most important concept of this chapter and one of the most important concepts of the book. I want you to ignore how much energy costs in money terms, because the cost is actually irrelevant (especially when your money is printed out of thin air). Instead, I want you to focus on *how much energy it takes to get energy*, because, as I'm going to show you, this is even more important to our current and future well-being than the raw amount of energy that we can produce each year. The concept is straightforward, and it's called "net energy."

Because it takes energy to both find and produce energy, we're going to look at the returns delivered from energy exploration and production activities in terms of the ratio between what is invested and what is returned. Imagine that the total energy it took to find and drill an oil well were one barrel of oil, and that one hundred barrels came to market as a result. We'd say that our net energy return was "one hundred barrels to one," or 100:1. In this example, our mandatory expenditure was 1 out of 100, or 1 percent. Another phrase for this that you're likely to encounter in the literature is Energy Returned on Energy Invested, which goes by the acronym EROEI.

I find this easier to visualize in graphical form:

Figure 15.2
The Energy Cliff

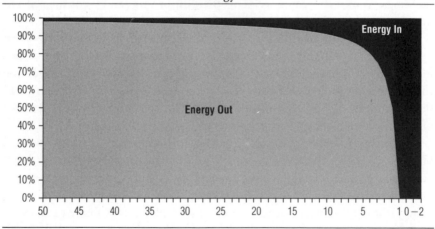

This figure expresses the relationship between energy invested and energy returned. Note that together the invested and returned energy always sum to 100 percent and the lines hit zero percent at a reading of "1" where it takes one unit to find one unit for a zero percent return.

In Figure 15.2, we're comparing the relationship between energy out and energy in. The black part (above) is the amount of energy we put in ("invested"), and the gray part (below) is how much energy we got out ("returned"), representing the net energy that's available for us to use for whatever purposes we desire. All the way to the left of the chart, the energy out divided by energy in yields a value of 50, meaning that 1 unit of energy was used to find and produce 50 units of energy. In other words, 2 percent was used to find and produce energy, leaving us a net 98 percent in the gray part to use however we see fit. This represents the surplus energy available to society; it's the stuff that we use to create the order and complexity that we see all around us. As we scan across the chart, we can observe that the surplus energy available to society remains quite high all the way down to a net energy ratio of about 10, where it suddenly falls off a cliff. We might also note that this is yet another nonlinear chart in our lives.

Now I want to draw your attention to what happens on part of the chart between the readings of 10 and 5. The net energy available to society begins to drop off quite steeply and nonlinearly. Below a reading of 5, the chart really heads down in earnest, hitting zero when it gets to a reading of 1, which is where it takes one unit of energy to get a unit of energy. At that boundary, there's zero surplus energy available and there's really no point in going through the trouble of getting it.

Given that energy is the master resource, and no economic activity is possible without energy, we all care very deeply how much energy is available. What Figure 15.2 allows us to begin to appreciate is that it's not "energy" we really care about, but net energy, the light gray part below, because that's the area that literally makes possible almost everything that you care about. It allows the lights to come on, food to appear on your plate, warmth to fill your home, and the big brown truck of mail-order happiness to pull into your driveway.

To further explore why this is an enormously important chart, let's take a look at our experience with net energy with respect to oil (Figure 15.3).

In 1930, for every barrel of oil used to find oil, it's estimated that 100 were produced, giving us a reading of 100:1, which would be way off to the left in Figure 15.3. By 1970, fields were a lot smaller and the oil was often deeper or otherwise trickier to extract, so, unsurprisingly, the net energy gain fell to a value of around 25:1—still a very good return with lots of light gray beneath it. By the 1990s, this trend continued, with oil finds returning somewhere between 18:1 and 10:1.[7]

It's estimated that new oil resources found after the year 2010 will return a much lower net energy, perhaps as low as 3:1, although nobody really knows for sure because careful analyses have not yet been performed. Still, we might observe that gigantic rigs drilling through thousands and thousands of feet of water and rock as they chase after smaller and smaller fields

Figure 15.3
The Energy Cliff (2) and Oil

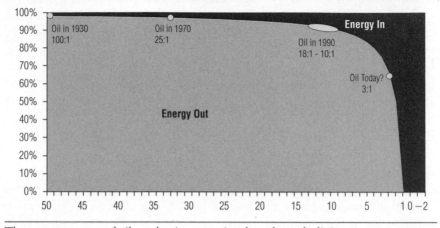

The energy returns of oil production over time have been declining.

Source: C.J. Cleveland, "Net Energy from Oil and Gas Extraction in the United States."

will intuitively have less favorable energy returns than prior efforts located in shallower zones on dry land.

Why is the net yield dropping? In the past, a relatively tiny amount of embodied energy was contained within the smallish rigs that were used to exploit finds that were massive, plentiful, and relatively shallow. Two of the larger finds in the world's history, Spindletop in Texas and the Ghawar field in Saudi Arabia, are both only a little over 1000 feet below the surface. The Macondo field in the Gulf of Mexico, which was the site of the Deepwater Horizon incident in 2010, was beneath 5,000 feet of water and a further 13,000 feet of rock and sediment, and held perhaps 1/1000th of the oil in Ghawar. All that drilling, miles of piping, and a massive oil rig were required to find a relatively minor amount of oil, illustrating why the net energy of oil discoveries of today are so much lower than the past. And the Macondo field was neither particularly deep nor disappointingly small by current standards.

Today much more energy is required to find energy. Exploration ships and rigs are massive, requiring significantly more steel to create than the humble drilling rigs of the 1930s. And today more wells are being drilled to greater depths in order to find and produce smaller and smaller fields, all of which weigh upon our final net energy return.

And what about the massive amounts of oil allegedly contained within the tar sands and oil shales? These are often wrongly described as equivalent to "several Saudi Arabias."[8] The net energy values for these are especially poor and are in no way comparable to the 100:1 (or higher) returns actually found in Saudi Arabia. Tar sands have a net energy return of around 5:1,[9] and tar shales are thought to be even worse, in the vicinity of 2:1 or less.[10] So while there may be the same *volume* of oil locked in those formations as there is in Saudi Arabia's magnificent treasures, there isn't the same amount of useful, desirable, delicious net energy in them. Nowhere near as much.

If we were to try and subsist entirely on the energy offered by a new source that was sporting a 3:1 net energy return, this is the world in which we'd live:

Figure 15.4
The Energy Cliff (3)

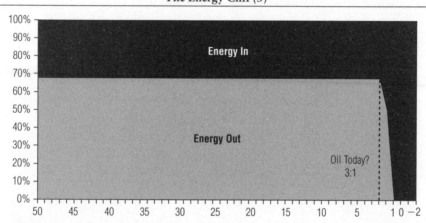

Trying to live on 3:1 net energy.

Look at how much less gray area and how much less surplus energy there is in this chart after we've begun to slide down the energy cliff, compared to the ones where there were 10:1 or 20:1 returns. The gray area represents how we "fund" our growth and our prosperity. The gray area is the net energy that feeds and supports our economic complexity. If we can appreciate how two societies, one abundantly supplied with food and the other nearly starving, can differ on the basis of their available net food energy, then we can also appreciate how a high-net-energy economy will be fundamentally more robust, complex, and interesting than a lower-net-energy economy.

And what about renewable energy sources (Figure 15.5)? Methanol, which can be made from biomass, sports a net energy of about 2.6:1,[11] while biodiesel offers a net energy return of somewhere between 1:1 and 4:1, depending on whether we count just the biodiesel itself or include the energy left in the crushed meal, which can be burned.[12] Corn-based ethanol, if we're generous, might produce a net energy return of just slightly over 1:1,[13] but could also be negative, according to some sources.[14] Ethanol produced from sugar cane in Brazil has an EROEI of closer to 8:1[15] (largely because the sugarcane itself can be burned to fire the process), making it a viable proposition there, and some exciting work is being done on cellulosic and other forms of ethanol that might have much higher EROEIs than any other biofuels, but those are not yet out of the demonstration phase. We should work with all due haste on these prospects, but not count on them to arrive at the appropriate time and at the appropriate scale to save the day.*

Figure 15.5
The Energy Cliff (4): Net Energy from Renewables

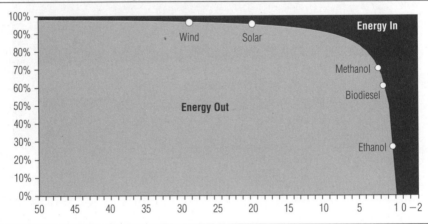

Not all energy forms are fully comparable on the basis of net energy returned. Solar and wind do not produce liquid fuels.

---

*While there are a number of potentially exciting new technologies and energy sources in the labs and even in pilot demonstrations—including cellulosic ethanol, methanol, and algal biofuels—I set a high bar; in order to be included in this book, they actually had to be in commercial production at a level that cracked the 1 percent-of-total-fuel barrier.

Why? Simply because if Peak Oil is only 5 or even 10 years from the writing of this book, any technology that has less than a 1 percent market share already, no matter how promising, is exceedingly unlikely to allow our economy to continue along uninterrupted.

If we add in all the other new usable liquid fuel sources that we've just talked about, we see that they're all somewhere "on the face of the energy cliff." Solar and wind[16] are both capable of producing pretty high net returns, but it's important to note that these produce electricity, not liquid fuels, which means that they are not at all comparable. Peak Oil represents "peak liquid fuels," and that's the primary issue here for petroleum. Once we get to Peak Coal (and we someday will), or begin to operate our transportation infrastructure on electricity, then electricity from the sun is more directly applicable to meeting our needs and solving our challenges. If we were to try and make a go of it on corn-based ethanol alone, this is the world in which we'd (be trying to) live:

Figure 15.6
The Energy Cliff (5): Trying to Live on Alcohol Alone

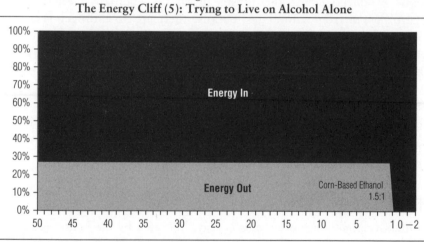

There's no gray zone to speak of left in that chart, and practically no surplus at all to fund even the basics of life, let alone a rich, complex economy full of prosperity and opportunities.

And that's the main point of this book: To illustrate why the next 20 years are going to be completely unlike the last 20 years.

Yes, I will be quite excited by and will closely follow the developments of new energy technologies. But no, I will not be staking a significant portion of my future strategy on the mere hope that these will arrive in time. Hope alone is a terrible strategy.

This book is meant to inject a dose of numerical reality back into the discussion, and that's what I am driving at here. In order to be considered as a potential solution, the technologies and/or processes in question have to have a solid chance of affecting the outcome.

Unless we very rapidly find ways of boosting the net energy of the remaining energy options, we'll simply find that we have far less surplus energy to dedicate to our basic needs and discretionary wants than we came to expect and enjoy from fossil fuels. We'll be using far too much energy in the essential, mandatory practice of finding and producing more energy, and we'll find ourselves with far too little left over to use as we wish. Our energy investment costs will skyrocket even as the returns dwindle. That's just the basic reality of the situation; it's not possible to fool nature with fraudulent accounting.

Oh, and where's the so-called "hydrogen economy" in Figure 15.6? It's below the x-axis in negative territory, meaning that it's not a viable candidate around which to fashion a society. It's negative because it has to be produced from other forms of energy—perhaps electricity (via hydrolysis) or from natural gas. Because there are no hydrogen reservoirs anywhere on earth, every single bit of it has to be created from some other source of energy—and, here's the kicker, *always at an energy loss*. In other words, hydrogen is an energy *sink*, not a *source*; its tiny bubble would have to be placed below the zero percent mark on the above chart. In creating hydrogen, we *lose* energy. That's not pessimism; that's the law—the second law of thermodynamics, to be exact. We'll talk more about the laws of thermodynamics in Chapter 18 (*Why Technology Can't Fix This*).

THE ECONOMY AND ENERGY

A massive abundance of surplus energy, liberated by the lightning bolt of humanity, has enabled historically unparalleled levels of prosperity to be enjoyed by billions of people. But respect for the role of energy in providing this abundance has largely gone missing from the economics profession, which will prove to be a rather tragic mistake. It's somewhat odd that it has been thus ignored, because the evidence for the connection between growth in energy utilization and economic growth (and prosperity) is extremely well documented and also intuitively obvious (Figure 15.7).

Even less well appreciated is the degree to which economic complexity owes its existence not just to the total amount of energy being utilized, but to the net free energy that flows through society. Out of all the sources of energy, petroleum stands out as the most important of them all, due largely to its presence in nearly every consumer product that is made, transported, and sold. Oil is richly woven into our economic tapestry, and there are no substitutes waiting in the wings. Where we once transitioned from wood to

Figure 15.7
Energy Consumption and GDP in the United States

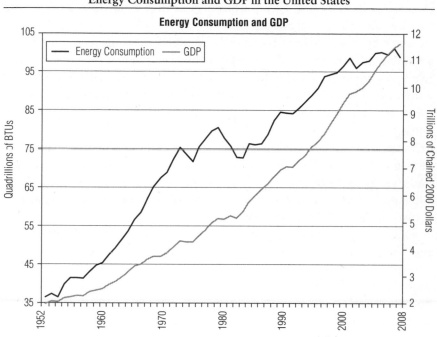

Source: Energy Information Administration & Bureau of Economic Analysis.

coal, and later from coal to oil, there is currently no established candidate waiting to replace oil.

WE LIVE LIKE GODS

In order to understand why oil, in particular, is so important to our economy and our daily lives, we have to understand something about what it does for us. We value any source of energy because we can harness it to do work for us. For example, every time you turn on a 100-watt light bulb, it's the same as if you had a fit human being in the basement pedaling as hard as they can to keep that bulb lit. That's how much energy a single light bulb uses. While you run water, take hot showers, and vacuum the floor, it's as if your house is employing the services of 50 such extremely fit bike-riding slaves in the basement, ready to pedal their fastest, 24 hours a day, at the flick of a switch. When you jump in a car, depending on your engine, it's the same as a king harnessing up a carriage to 300 horses. This "slave count," if you will, exceeds that of kings in times past. Given the fact that even kings of times past could not whip out a credit card on a whim and find themselves halfway around the world in less than a day, it should be said that we enjoy the power of gods.

And how much "work" is embodied in a gallon of gasoline, our favorite substance of them all? Well, if you put a single gallon in a car, drove it away from your home until the gas ran out, and then got out and pushed the car home, you'd find out exactly how much work a gallon of gasoline can do. It turns out that a gallon of gas has the equivalent energy of somewhere between 350 and 500 hours of human labor.[17] Given that a gallon of gas can perform that much human work, how much value would you assign it? How much would 350 to 500 hours of your hard physical labor be worth to you? $4? $10? Assuming you decided not to push your car home and paid someone $15 an hour to do this for you, you'd find that a gallon of gasoline is "worth" $5,250 to $7,500 in human labor.

Here's another example: It has been calculated that the amount of food that an average North American citizen consumes in a year requires the equivalent of 400 gallons of petroleum to produce and ship.[18] At $3/gallon, that works out to $1200 of your yearly food bill spent on fuel, which doesn't sound too extreme. However, when we consider that those 400 gallons represent the energy equivalent of close to 100 humans working year-round at 40 hours a week, then it takes on an entirely different meaning. This puts your diet well out of the reach of most kings of times past. Just to put this in context, as it's currently configured, food production and distribution uses fully two-thirds of the U.S. domestic oil production. This is one reason why a cessation of oil exports to the United States would be highly disruptive; most of our domestic production would have to go toward feeding ourselves.

Aside from the way that oil works tirelessly in the background to make our lives easy beyond historical measure, oil is a miracle in other ways. In the industrial processes, oil is the primary input feedstock to innumerable necessities of life, such as fertilizer, plastics, paint, synthetic fibers, countless chemical processes, and airplane rides. When we consider other potential fuel sources, we find that they are mostly incapable of fulfilling these needs.

It could be said that we all live like kings, but truthfully, even the wealthiest king of times past couldn't click on a link, order an item made halfway around the world, and have it in his hands the next day. That ability is something the ancient Greeks would have recognized as the power of a god, and so it is.

CHAPTER 16

PEAK OIL

If you glance up from this book and scan your surroundings, you'll be challenged to spy a single object that did not somehow, in some way, get there because of oil. In our economic model, petroleum fuels are involved in every step of the economy. Most things that are manufactured involve oil somewhere along the way, and quite a few are made directly from oil. Remember, you yourself are powered by food that is produced and delivered by oil! So even if you're looking at an object created by nature that you personally collected and placed on a shelf in your home, we can still claim that it got there because of oil. Even intangible services are fueled by petroleum, as the people offering them are fed, clothed, transported, and kept comfortable by oil.

If you haven't yet heard of Peak Oil, this chapter is going to be a real eye-opener. My purpose here is not to recreate a complete treatise on Peak Oil—that would take an entire set of books, and they've already been written by others[1]—but to establish just enough logical facts that we can tie the three Es together and arrive at the conclusion that prudent adults should seriously consider the implications and take specific steps in order to mitigate risks.

As we discussed in Chapter 15 (*Energy and the Economy*), energy is the lifeblood of any economy (or any complex system, for that matter). Without energy constantly flowing through that system, order and complexity will shrink as the system inexorably winds down and becomes disordered. ("Entropy" is the name given to this process by scientists). When an economic system has been built around exponentially driven debt-based money, the energy that fuels the exponential expansion of both debt and the economy deserves your very highest attention. Why? Because there's a very high risk that a system that expands exponentially will also contract exponentially. As the old saying goes, what goes up must come down. The worry is that once its energy supports are knocked out, the economy will collapse at the same speed it expanded—*fast*.

Nothing is more important to the continuation of our current way of life than our ability to extract and deploy ever-larger amounts of energy. Our entire economic system is predicated upon the implicit assumption that the future will not only be larger than the past, but *exponentially* larger. This is a feature of our debt-based monetary system, where principal balances on nonproductive loans grow each year, leaving interest payments to provide the "exponential kicker." Tomorrow's economic growth is the collateral for today's debts. If that growth does not occur, what then happens to the value of today's debt?

PETRO-REALITIES

In order to understand what "Peak Oil" means, we need to share a basic understanding about how oil fields work and how oil is extracted. A common misperception is that an oil rig is plunked down over an oil field, a hole is drilled, a pipe is inserted, and then oil gushes from a big underground lake or pool that eventually loses pressure and gets sucked dry. Let's call this the "straw in a firmly gripped juice-box" model.

The reality is that what you find deep underground is pretty much the same thing you find when you dig a hole near the surface of the ground: solid material. No caverns, lakes, or pools; just solid earth.

So how do we find water and oil under the surface? Extractable liquids are only found in porous rocks, like sandstone, or fractured rocks that permit the oil or water to flow through extremely tiny crevices, fissures, and

Figure 16.1
Juice-Box vs. Frozen Margarita Model

One of these more accurately represents an oil field. (Hint: It's the one on the right.)
Sources: Margarita image copyright Wacpan; juice-box image copyright Neiromobile.
Image: Molly McLeod

pores in between and around the granular structure of the rock. If you were to hold in your hand a chunk of rock from an oil-bearing formation, you'd perceive it to be a greasy but quite solid piece of rock. Therefore, it's more accurate to think of an oil field like a frozen drink, not an underground juice box, where the oil is the tasty stuff and the rock is the crushed ice. We'll call this the "frozen margarita" model (see Figure 16.1).

When an oil field is tapped, we find that the amount of oil that comes out of it over time follows a tightly prescribed pattern that typically ends up resembling a bell curve. At first, when the frozen margarita is discovered upon the insertion of just one straw (the exploratory straw, as it were), the rate at which the beverage can be extracted is limited by having only one thin tube through which the drink can flow. As more and more straws are stuck into the delicious slush, more and more drink flows out of the reservoir at a higher and higher rate. But eventually the dreaded slurping sound begins, and then, no matter how many new straws are inserted and no matter how hard those straws are sucked, the amount of margarita coming out of the glass declines until it's all gone and we're left with only ice. That's pretty much exactly how an oil field works.

So far, every single mature oil field has more or less exhibited the same basic extraction profile as the one caricatured in Figure 16.2. The amount of oil extracted over time grows higher and higher until it hits a peak, and then it progressively shrinks. Just like with a frozen margarita, once the oil is gone,

Figure 16.2
Basic Extraction Profile

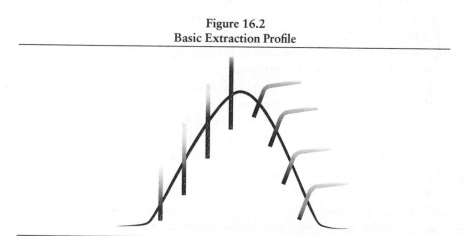

With each new straw, up to the first four, the rate of liquid extraction increases. After a time, the flow rate begins to decline and the insertion of straws #5 through #8 does not increase the flow rate.

Image: Molly McLeod

it's gone, and no amount of late-night wishing or desperate attempts at slurping will cause that circumstance to change. And what is true for one oil field is equally true when we measure across many oil fields and sum the result. Because individual fields peak, so do collections of fields.

Peak Oil, then, isn't a theory, as some have tried to portray it; it's an extremely well-characterized physical phenomenon. We have many decades of data and experience to draw upon when making that claim. This isn't some idle theory that we're waiting to confirm through additional observation. We know that literally thousands of individual oil finds have dwindled, because we've recorded every barrel coming from them over time; entire oil fields comprised of many smaller finds have depleted in front of our watchful eyes, and entire nations have undergone this process of peaking. We *can* theorize about how much oil remains to be discovered and produced, but the *process* by which oil fields become depleted is not up for debate. Peak Oil is not a theory; it's an observed fact.

IT'S NOT "RUNNING OUT"

Far too often, Peak Oil is inaccurately described as "running out of oil," as if we'll produce more and more, and then, suddenly, we'll just run out. This is incorrect. As described above Peak Oil involves producing slightly more and more until the peak, and then producing slightly less and less. In fact, given the difficulty in extracting the second half (which has to be carefully pumped out) in contrast to the first half, there's usually a longer span of time to be found *after* the peak than *before* the peak. One way to think of the process is that at the moment of the peak, roughly half of the oil that was ever there remains to be extracted.

But something interesting happens at the halfway mark. Where oil gushed out under pressure at first, the oil represented by the back half of the curve (the down slope) usually has to be laboriously pumped or squeezed out of the ground at a higher cost, in terms of both energy and money, than before, when it gushed from the ground under pressure. Where every barrel of oil was cheaper to extract on the way up, the reverse is true on the way down; each barrel becomes more costly to extract in terms of time, money, and energy. Eventually it costs more to extract a barrel of oil than it's worth, and that's when an oil field is economically abandoned.

Figure 16.3 shows crude oil production in United States from 1900 to 2007. Starting with the first well drilled in 1859 in Titusville, Pennsylvania, more and more oil was progressively pumped from the ground until 1970 ("the peak"), and after that point, less and less came out of the ground. The

Figure 16.3
U.S. Crude Oil Production, 1900 to 2007

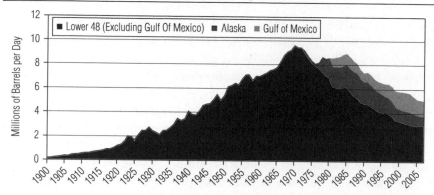

Broken out by major region.

Source: Energy Information Administration.

massive finds in Alaska and the Gulf of Mexico could not overcome the rate of depletion in the lower 48 to achieve a new high water mark of oil production. The United States' peak of oil production in 1970 was just under 10 million barrels a day, and 40 years later it produces just a little over 5 million barrels a day. So "Peak Oil" in the United States isn't a theory, but a 40-year-old fact.

In Figure 16.3, you will notice that the data for the lower 48 is a very close match to the idealized depletion curve in Figure 16.2, but adding the new fields from the other areas serves to create a sort of "bumpy plateau" between 1970 and 1985.

So what we see for the United States is a nearly textbook-perfect example of Peak Oil: a steady rise in oil production to a peak, followed by a steady decline in oil production. Out of 54 oil-producing countries in the world, 40 are now past peak and in decline, leaving only 14 to try to both cover the declines occurring in other areas and add more oil to fuel to the story of growth.[2] Again, these aren't theories, but facts.

The United States consumes far more oil than it produces and by necessity imports two-thirds of its daily needs. Japan, lacking any domestic oil source, imports nearly 100 percent of the petroleum that it needs. The United Kingdom, having gone past peak in the incredibly productive North Sea fields in 1998 (which now produce less than half as much as their peak amount) became a net importer of both natural gas and petroleum in 2004 and 2005, respectively.[3] Australia's oil hit peak in 2000, and by 2009 Australia was importing close to 40 percent of its petroleum needs.[4]

FIND FIRST, PUMP SECOND

It's impossible to pump oil out of the ground that you haven't yet found, so another unavoidable fact about oil is that in order to extract it, you have to find it first. Even after a major oil field is discovered, a fairly significant gap exists between the time of its initial discovery and its date of maximum production. There are two main reasons for this: The first is that it takes time to sink the wells and develop the necessary infrastructure to get that oil away from the fields and to market (pipelines, storage facilities, and separating units all have to be sited and built). The second is that a careful approach to production is often required to avoid accidentally damaging the field and possibly stranding some oil in place by pumping too quickly.

To understand this second point, imagine that you have been given an inflatable mattress glued to the floor and filled with creamy peanut butter, and you have the task of getting as much of the peanut butter out of the fill nozzle as possible. You'd probably begin by massaging the mattress from the edges. If at any time any peanut butter gets left behind, say in a small pocket behind the front formed by your hands, it will be lost, stranded forever by geological circumstance and/or economics. This would be no small challenge, and you'd probably be quite cautious as you worked around the edges, carefully avoiding leaving any behind. Likewise, it's no small challenge for oil producers to maximize the production from oil fields, which are often enormously complicated in their underground topography (imagine that you had to work around random baffles and blind cavities in the inflatable mattress), and they must work carefully and diligently to get as much out of the ground as they can. Given these realities, it can take anywhere from a few years to several decades for any given field to finally achieve maximum production.

In the United States, oil discoveries peaked in 1930 and production peaked in 1970, which yields a gap between a peak in discovery and a peak in production of almost exactly 40 years. Perhaps that 40-year gap was unique to the United State's particular geology and the oil demand of the times, but the United States is a very large country, and we might reasonably consider this experience to be a plausible proxy for the entire world.

This is where the story gets interesting. Figure 16.4 shows that worldwide oil discoveries increased in every decade up to the 1960s, but have decreased in every decade since then, with future projections (2010 through 2030) looking even grimmer.

If you've got to find it before you can pump it, and it takes time to develop fields to achieve maximum production, and the global peak in

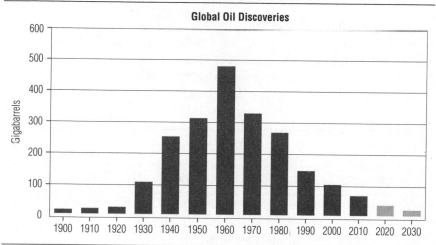

Figure 16.4
Global Oil Discoveries Peaked in 1964

Because discoveries necessarily precede production, a time lag exists between discovery and maximum production.

Source: Association for the Discovery of Peak Oil and Gas (ASPO).

discoveries was in 1964, then we know there's a peak in production coming at some point. The United States' experience of a 40-year gap between its discovery and production peaks suggest that perhaps 40 years is as good a starting point as any to begin looking for a world production peak. (1964 plus 40 equals 2004.)

A Global Peak

Now let's turn our attention to global oil production. In the prior section we made the case that a peak in discovery would lead to a peak in production. That's simple logic. In July of 2008, oil hit an all-time high of $147 per barrel, and there are a couple of tantalizing clues to be found in the run-up to that event.

Figure 16.5 shows *only* global conventional crude oil production over the period from 1990 to 2009—it leaves out biofuels and other liquids that collectively amount to roughly 10 million barrels a day.

What we see in Figure 16.5 is that oil has been bumping along a plateau that began in 2004, exactly 40 years after the world peak in oil discoveries. Sound familiar? One fascinating clue here is that even as conventional crude production was flat between the years 2004 and 2008, prices spiked from

Figure 16.5
Yearly World Crude Oil Production

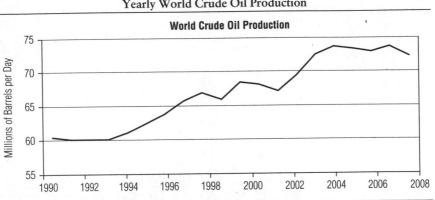

Crude oil production was essentially flat between 2004 and 2008, with 2005 being the technical peak.

Source: Energy Information Administration.

$50 a barrel to $147 a barrel. If there ever was a strong incentive to get oil out of the ground and off to market, a near tripling of the price of oil would be it. Yet oil production did not rise in response to these market signals. Why not? Could it be that oil production was already at its limits? A second fascinating clue, besides the eye-popping coincidence of the 40-year lag between discoveries and an apparent production peak, is the shape of the bumpy plateau, which mirrors the production peaks seen for such large producing areas as the United States and the United Kingdom. The bumpy plateau is made up of old fields going into decline, new enhanced oil-recovery techniques being applied and new fields coming on line. Add them all together and you get a bumpy plateau.

If we're already at peak, as this data suggests, then we've placed ourselves in quite a predicament. The best possible set of responses to Peak Oil will have been started two decades in advance of the actual peak, a much weaker set of responses one decade in advance, and the worst and weakest set only after Peak Oil has already arrived. Let us fervently hope that the data is misleading us, but at the same time, let us deliberately respond as if the peak has indeed already passed.

OIL AND GDP

Let's take another look at the relationship between global GDP growth and oil consumption. Since oil that's produced is rapidly consumed

Figure 16.6
Global GDP Growth and Oil Production

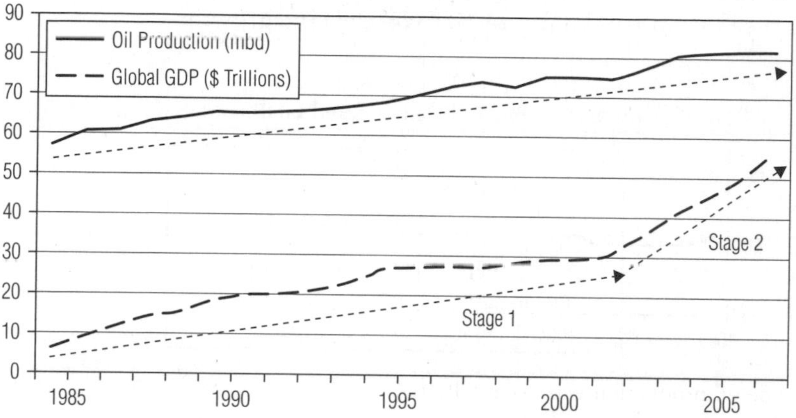

Sources: Global GDP: Central Intelligence Agency World Factbook[5] & Global Oil Production: Energy Information Administration.[6]

(approximately 50 days worth of global consumption is above ground at any one time), we can use oil production as our measure of oil demand. Fortunately, we have access to very good data for oil production, which we can compare against global GDP growth, as in Figure 16.6.

Between 1985 and 2003, growth in both oil consumption and GDP enjoyed a stable relationship, marked as "Stage 1." However, something extraordinary happened to the global economy between 2003 and 2007, where GDP growth accelerated sharply. I've marked this as "Stage 2." This period is characterized by a startling divergence between the rates of growth in oil consumption and GDP.

One explanation for this departure rests with the explosive growth in debt (a.k.a. "credit"), which created a false appearance of growth in world GDP. I call it false because credit-fueled expansions aren't sustainable, and they inevitably must be retraced, as our island nation example illustrated in Chapter 10 (*Debt*). Building off this debt, much of the GDP growth recorded during the 2003 to 2007 period included an enormous amount of purely paper-based growth that wasn't a function of what we might consider to be real production. For example, Lehman Brothers grew strongly during that period, but its paper shell-games collapsed, revealing its additions to "growth" to be largely illusory. Ditto for AIG and quite a number of other financial firms; their "growth" was a mirage.

Figure 16.7 compares the yearly growth in oil demand to growth in GDP, displaying both the yearly growth rates for each for various time periods and then the ratio of GDP growth to oil-demand growth:

Figure 16.7

Yearly Rate of Growth in Global Oil Demand and GDP, and as a Ratio of GDP/Oil

	Growth In . . .		
	Oil	GDP	Ratio
1985 to 2007	1.6%	6.8%	0.24
1985 to 2003	1.5%	5.3%	0.27
2003 to 2007	1.4%	10.2%	0.14

Using the 1985 to 2003 period as our reference case (because it factors out the late stage of the credit bubble), we can see that every 5.3 percent expansion in global GDP was associated with a 1.5 percent expansion in oil consumption. This works out to a ratio of 0.27, meaning that for every 1 percent expansion in GDP, we should assume a 0.27 percent expansion in oil production (or consumption, if you prefer to look at it that way).

We might also note that the period from 2003 to 2007 was marked by an astonishing rate of global growth at slightly more than 10 percent. This is an astounding rate that would lead to a full doubling of total global GDP in less than seven years if it were to continue. Recalling what we learned about doubling in Chapter 5 (*Dangerous Exponentials*), this implies that the global GDP would produce and consume more goods and services in that same seven-year stretch as in *all of history combined*. Given what we have already learned about Peak Oil, and knowing the strong link between oil use and economic growth, you might want to ask yourself how likely this seems.

Because a 10-plus percent rate of growth is clearly unsustainable, we might instead suspect that our monetary and fiscal authorities would settle for a more modest rate of growth, let's say 5 percent, in order to keep the Great Credit Bubble expanding and to match the rate of growth between 1985 and 2003. Unfortunately for their plans, it seems that the oil required to support that growth won't be there.

OIL DEMAND

As further confirmation of the importance of oil to our lives, we might look to the impact of the worst global economic slump in 70-plus years upon global oil demand. Where global trade plummeted by 20 percent to

40 percent in 2009 for most exporters, and where many individual countries have recorded high single-digit drops in GDP, we find that oil demand has not dropped by nearly as much.

In March of 2009, the International Energy Agency (IEA) estimated world oil demand for that year at "84.4 million barrels a day—1.5 percent lower than a year earlier."[7] While a 1.5 percent drop is among the largest ever recorded, it's a fraction of the decline recorded in other areas of economic consumption. Oil consumption is "sticky." In the United States, petroleum consumption fell by only 4.1 percent from its peak in 2008 to 2010. Certainly this is a very large drop by historical standards for the United States, but it's not all that drastic and leaves petroleum demand above where it was in 2003, indicating that oil consumption is perhaps a more essential feature of the economic landscape than many realize.

Or perhaps we could go further and say that oil is a nonnegotiable element of our lives. Where most of us can fairly easily and rapidly cut back on dining out or buying a new house or importing clothing, we cannot simply or quickly do the same thing with gasoline. It is quite difficult to pare back the number of miles driven to and from work or to school, for example, and such changes, if made at all, tend to happen quite slowly. This gives oil consumption its stickiness.

If oil demand is relatively robust and somewhat insensitive to economic difficulties, then what about oil production?

OIL PRODUCTION

In November of 2008, the IEA released its World Energy Outlook (WEO) for 2008,[8] and in it produced the single most startling piece of information that I had yet seen on the subject of Peak Oil. In every prior year, the IEA provided an estimate of future oil availability that was generated after first consulting with economists about likely levels of global growth in GDP in future years. In other words, they modeled oil supply on the basis of what they thought the economy might require, not what could realistically be produced. In 2008, a new methodology was used. It incorporated all the world's major oil fields, over 800 of them, into a single database, and then asked a very different question: *"How much oil can be produced?"*

The answer, as it turned out, was a lot lower than any of the prior estimates. Where IEA estimates of oil production once topped out at 130 million barrels per day by 2030, the 2008 WEO report pegged that number at just 106 million barrels per day—a whopping 19 percent decline. Nearly 1 in 5 barrels of oil that were once thought would be available in 2030 suddenly vanished. Even more important, the report broke down oil supply by its various subcomponents, such as "conventional" and "deep water," and revealed that oil from currently producing fields has been in decline since 2005.

Why is this statement a ground-shaking one? Because "oil from currently producing fields" is a euphemism for "cheap and easy oil" or "high net-energy oil"—the stuff that gives us the large gray territory on the bottom of the energy cliff graphs. With this stark admission that cheap and easy oil has already peaked, the IEA admitted that we're already on the down slope of the same exact type of oil that has fueled the past several decades of economic growth. This earth-shattering news should have been on the front page of every major newspaper, but it wasn't—we might ask ourselves why not—although it did circulate widely in the blogosphere.

Another revelation from report was that the bulk of all new oil-supply growth from here on out is going to come from fields "yet to be developed or discovered," with some relatively minor contributions from "nonconventional oil," which primarily refers to the tar sands of Canada and similar deposits. Neither of these sources can reasonably be expected to offer anything close to the same net energy returns of prior finds.

For example, extracting oil from the so-called "oil sands" of Canada has proven far more costly, capital-intensive, and environmentally destructive than first imagined. These were among the very first projects that were deferred, delayed, or dropped as a consequence of falling oil prices and diminished lending in the aftermath of the 2008 crisis. I strongly suspect that the hoped-for contribution to supply from these sources will be adjusted downward in coming reports, possibly by a lot, due to a combination of poor financing and environmental concerns.

The final bombshell from the WEO 2008 report was the IEA's estimation that the collective decline rate for all existing fields is now -6.7 percent annually. Here again, we're faced with a mind-boggling admission. Using our handy rule of 70, but in reverse, a -6.7 percent rate of decline implies that existing fields will lose *half* of their output over a roughly 10-year timeframe. It should be noted here that the -6.7 percent decline rate averages together all of the fields, including the far healthier OPEC fields along with the stunning double-digit declines being recorded in some non-OPEC countries such as Mexico and Norway.

What this data tells us is that existing fields are collapsing far faster than was thought to be the case as recently as 2007. World expectations in this regard have been consistently lagging behind reality, and rather badly, too.

THE OIL PRODUCTION OUTPUT GAP

To add to this picture, not only are existing fields declining in output, they seem to be doing so at an ever-increasing rate, meaning that we have to run faster simply to stay in place. Some suggest the reason for this is that newer drilling methods and recovery techniques greatly increase the rate of extraction but not the amount that can finally be retrieved. It's like squeezing the toothpaste tube a little harder—yes, it comes out faster, but you don't create *more*. This is another example of where exponential declines can work against us.

Recalling our oil-to-GDP ratio above, which yields a 0.27 percent increase in oil consumption for every 1 percent advance in global GDP, we can estimate required oil production levels under a number of scenarios. In the table below, we address this question: *Given various rates of global growth, how many millions of barrels of oil would we need to pump out of the ground each day to meet the desired rate of economic expansion?*

Figure 16.8 indicates that even a historically modest 4 percent rate of global growth would require an advance from the 84.4 mbd (million barrels per day) in 2009 to 89.1 mbd by 2014, nearly 5 mbd in new, incremental capacity, or about 1 mbd each year. This is equivalent to roughly one-half of the entire output of Saudi Arabia.

Attempting the ludicrous, a 10 percent growth rate seen in the column to the far right (mirroring that seen between 2003 and 2007) would require that global oil production be expanded by 12 million barrels a day, or nearly one-and-a-half times Saudi Arabia's 2009 output, over those five years.

Figure 16.8
Global Oil Supply/Demand Scenarios

	Levels of Economic Growth			
	3%	4%	5%	10%
2010	85.1	85.3	85.6	86.7
2011	85.8	86.2	86.7	89.1
2012	86.5	87.2	87.9	91.5
2013	87.2	88.1	89.1	93.9
2014	87.9	89.1	90.3	96.5

Oil Consumption in 2009: 84.4

Based on various levels of GDP growth.

Any of the above scenarios represent a significant gap between what we can currently produce and what we might seem to require. But the actual gap is even larger than that.

EXISTING OIL FIELDS IN DECLINE

Of course, the above data underestimates the challenge. Based on the IEA estimates of the rate of decline in existing oil fields, we can expect some 18 mbd to vanish over the next five years. This means that if we're producing 84 mbd in 2009 and don't bring any new fields on line, we can expect global daily production from existing fields to decline to 66 mbd in 2014.

Fortunately, there are new projects coming on line all the time, but there's a wrinkle in that story as well. Cambridge Energy Research Associates (CERA), a U.S.-based company, studied all of the individual projects that oil companies planned to bring on line by 2014 and tallied up some 7.6 million barrels per day of new production, which is nothing to sneeze at. However, when we put this all into one spot, we find that quite a large gap exists between what the world will theoretically require (or demand) and what will be available. Figure 16.9 presents a summary of all of this information. Given the native decline in existing field output and the new projects still slated to come on line, we need to fill a gap of slightly more than 10 mbd by 2014 just to stand still.

Forget about new global growth; the world may need to find another 10 mbd of production between the years 2009 and 2014 in order to avoid slipping backward. But as we've seen, our exponential money/debt system isn't content with sitting still; it needs to expand. By the time we seek to grow by

Figure 16.9
The Output Gap

Current Rate Of Decline, Existing Oil Fields	18,000,000
New Production Coming On-Line	7,600,000
Gap to simply "stand still"	*−10,400,000*
Gap to enjoy 3% growth	−13,208,632
Gap to enjoy 4% growth	−14,169,842
Gap to enjoy 5% growth	−15,144,224
Gap to enjoy 10% growth	−20,212,876

How much oil is missing from the equation?

even 3 percent, the gap is already at 13 mbd. Once you understand the lead times, geological limitations, and engineering hurdles involved in trying to close a 13 mbd output gap, this becomes an improbable task.

In 2009 and 2010, various governmental and industry groups began to observe the same potential supply shortfalls and sounded varying levels of concern over the matter, including: (1) the Industry Taskforce on Peak Oil (UK), (2) Lloyds of London, (3) the UK Parliament, (4) the U.S. Department of Defense, (5) the German military, and even (6) the King of Saudi Arabia, who suggested that perhaps they should leave some oil in the ground for future generations.

In no case did any of these reports connect the dots between energy and the economy as we've done in these pages, but it's only a matter of time before they do.

PEAK EXPORTS

However, the most urgent issue before us doesn't lie with identifying the precise moment of Peak Oil. That is of academic interest, but it's also something of a distraction, because the economically important event around oil will occur when a persistent gap emerges between supply and demand.

Dallas geologist Jeffrey Brown developed a very simple and clever way to think about the supply and demand problem, which he calls the Export Land Model.[9] Suppose we have a hypothetical country that produces three million barrels of crude oil per day, consumes one million barrels a day, and exports the balance of two million barrels a day. All things being equal, it can export those two million barrels year after year. But now let's suppose that its oil field output is declining due to depletion issues at a modest 5 percent a year. After 10 years, instead of 2 million barrels a day, this country can now only export 0.89 million barrels a day, or less than half the prior amount. The missing balance has depleted away, and it cannot export what it doesn't have. Now comes the kicker: Let's further suppose, quite realistically, that this country increases their internal demand for oil at a rate of 2.5 percent a year. What happens to exports in this case, where internal demand is rising and production is falling? Under this scenario, exports will plunge to zero in less than seven years.

This illustrates the miracle of compounding in reverse, where exports are eaten into from both ends by declining production and rising internal demand. It turns out that this isn't just a scenario, but a reality for many exporting countries. For example, in the case of Mexico, the number three supplier of oil exports to the United States in 2009, production declines and demand growth will entirely eliminate their exports somewhere between the years 2011 and 2015 (depending on a variety of economic and petro-investment variables). When this happens, the United States will have to turn to the global market in search of a new number three exporter to replace those lost imports, but global competition for oil supplies is likely to be quite stiff by that time.

When world production will peak is a matter of some dispute, with estimates ranging from 2005 to some 30 years hence. But as I said before, the precise moment of the peak is really just of academic concern. What we need to be most concerned with is the day that world demand outstrips available supply. It's at that moment when the oil markets will change forever and probably quite suddenly. First we'll see massive price hikes—that's a given. But do you remember the food "shortages" that erupted seemingly overnight back in February of 2008? Those were triggered by the perception of demand exceeding supply, which led to an immediate export ban on food shipments by many countries. This same dynamic of national hoarding will certainly be a feature of the global oil market once the perception of shortage takes hold. When that happens, our concerns about price will be trumped by our fears of shortages.

THE UGLY POWER OF COMPOUNDING

Remember all those exponential graphs from Chapter 5 (*Dangerous Exponentials*) and how time ran out in a hurry toward the end of the stadium example? In theory, there's nothing problematic with living in a world full of exponential growth and depletion curves—*as long as the world doesn't have any boundaries.* However, exponential functions take on enormous importance when they approach a physical boundary, as was the case in the last five minutes of our stadium example and which will soon be the case for oil. We know that oil is finite and have always known that the day would come when we'd bump up against the roof of that particular stadium. All of the data that I've been collecting and observing over the past five years strongly suggests that we've already reached oil's exponential boundary.

And here are the question that this possibility raises: *What if our exponentially based economic and monetary systems, rather than being the sophisticated culmination of human evolution, are really just an artifact of oil? What if all of our rich societal complexity and all of our trillions of dollars of wealth and debt are simply the human expression of surplus energy pumped from the ground? If so, what happens to our wealth, economic complexity, and social order when they cannot be fed by steadily rising energy inputs? What happens then?*

Figure 16.10
Global Oil Production on a 4,000-Year Timeline

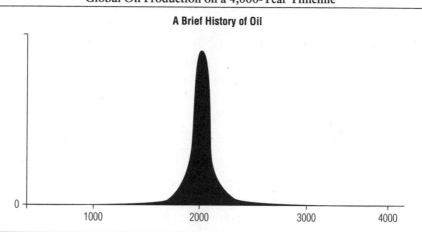

More immediately, you and I would be perfectly within our rights to wonder what will happen when (not if, but *when*) oil begins to decline in both quantity and quality. *What will happen to our exponential, debt-based money system during this period? Is it even possible for it to function in a world without constant growth?* These are important questions for which we currently have no answers, only ideas and speculation.

To put our oil bonanza in some sort of appropriate context, Figure 16.10 shows oil extraction placed on a four-thousand-year time line.

It's now up to us to wonder what we should expect in the future from a money system in which the most basic assumption might be in error. *What if the assumption "the future will be not just larger, but exponentially larger than the present" is not correct?*

CHAPTER 17

Necessary but Insufficient

Coal, Nuclear, and Alternatives

The primary point of this book is that the economy to which we have become accustomed, along with our entire view of wealth in the forms of stocks and bonds, rests upon vast flows of energy (and other resources), the levels of which must not only be maintained but also increased each year. Without this constant growth in energy use, everything else becomes much more difficult, if not impossible, to maintain.

The purpose of this chapter, then, isn't to completely cover the immense technical discussions that can (and should) surround energy, which economist Julian Simon rightfully called "the master resource."[1] Nor will we exhaustively cover all the various technologies and sources that could be alternatives. Instead, for our purposes, we will look at our energy predicament from a level that will permit us to address the question, *How likely is it that other major sources of energy can seamlessly replace oil?*

A prevalent and hopeful line of thinking found all across the political spectrum suggests that we will simply transition away from oil onto some combination of nuclear energy, increased coal consumption, and/or alternative energy sources, such as solar, wind, or maybe even algae biofuels. While each of these energy sources will play an important role in mitigating the down slope of oil, none of them individually or in combination can ever completely plug the gap left by oil's slow departure. Remember, the challenge here is not only to replace what will "go missing" as oil fields deplete, but also to increase the total energy supply of the world by a few percent each year as our exponential economy demands. Simple math, combined with the realities of time, scale, and cost, illustrates why this is improbable.

SIMPLE MATH

Energy itself comes in many forms. We don't value one source of energy over another for the form of the source itself, but rather to the extent that each can do useful work for us. By putting different types of energy on equal footing through a singular measure, we can compare them more easily. For our examples, we'll use a measure of power called watts.[2]

In 2009, the world produced and consumed 84.4[3] million barrels of oil per day (mbd), or 30.8 billion barrels for the year. Converting all of those billions of barrels into their energy content using watt hours, we discover that the world consumed around 52.4 quadrillion watt hours of energy in the form of oil. Assuming we wanted to get the same amount of power from other sources, this would be the same as:

- More than 6,800 nuclear reactors running at the same efficiency as the United States' current 104 reactors (or roughly 6,400 more nuclear reactors than were operating worldwide in 2009)
- Nearly 6 million new 1 megawatt wind towers running at their idealized output (assuming the perfect amount of wind blows every day of the year and no maintenance is ever required), or 17 million running under more realistic conditions
- Nearly 13 million acres, or slightly over 20,000 square miles of land, to be covered by solar PV panels (assuming ideal locations in the southwest United States or elsewhere)
- More than 16 billion acres of farmland converted entirely to soybean biofuel production, representing 135 percent of the total amount of world agricultural land[4]

Those are some big numbers. But that only gives us 2009 levels. Now suppose that we want to increase our total world consumption of energy from petroleum at 1.0 percent per year from here to 2030, as the EIA assumes.[5] Each of the above numbers needs to increase by 26 percent by 2030, according to the assumed rate of growth in oil consumption. Of course, there's demand growth for electricity to consider as well (which we haven't), but the point here is to merely put our petroleum use into context.

Clearly we aren't going to instantly need to replace all of the energy that we currently get from oil, because it will not "run out," but will instead wind down over many decades. So the numbers above are simply a useful way to illustrate how much energy we currently derive from petroleum and how many nuclear reactors and/or alternative sources we'd have to build or pursue to make up for the energy we currently enjoy from oil.

More realistically, instead of scaling these numbers against all oil produced, let's suppose that the world's oil output peaks in 2014 and that our goal is to merely replace the amount that goes missing each year. For this scenario we will assume a very modest 5 percent rate of depletion for existing fields (less than the 6.7 percent recorded by the IEA), and we'll (very) generously assume that OPEC has 5 mbd of spare capacity, Iraq will deliver 9.5 mbd by 2019 (a nearly 500 percent increase from current levels), and another 15 mbd of assorted other new projects will come on line over the next 10 years, which adds up to 30 mbd of new or incremental production. *But,* we'll also need another 1.3 percent of oil growth each year to reflect the amount of petroleum growth that we've enjoyed over the 20 years from 1989 to 2009.

Remember, the point of all this is to see if we can realistically recreate the conditions that will allow the next 20 years to resemble the past 20 years, which means that we will need to keep growing our energy use year after year at the same rate that it grew in the past. A gentle-glide path for our exponentially based economy will require a relatively seamless transition from one source of energy (oil) to some combination of other sources. Can we do it? What's the math?

Under the above scenario, the difference between oil supplied and oil demanded builds in each and every year after 2014, being driven by the 5 percent depletion of oil on the one hand and the "requirement" for 1.3 percent energy growth on the other.

Just by the numbers, once the scenario "settles down" in five years' time (to account for the 30 mbd of projects described above to come on line), our 2019 scenario would require:

- More than 200 nuclear plants would need to come on line each year and every year for the next 40 years, *or:*
- Roughly 200,000 new wind towers would need to be sited and installed each and every year (delivering 1,700 TWh (terawatt hours), or more than 5 times the entire global installed wind base of 2009, (which generated 340 TWh),[6] *or:*
- More than 400,000 acres of land would need to be covered by solar PV panels, *or:*
- More than 500 million acres of farmland would need to be converted to the production of liquid fuels.

Obviously we could utilize some combination of all four possible solutions, but seeing them individually helps to illustrate the scale of the problem. Ignoring other vital considerations for the moment, such as the fact that virtually none of our almost entirely oil-based transportation network can run on the electricity produced by nuclear, wind, and solar PV technologies, that's the basic math. Just by the numbers, none of those alternatives looks very likely, but anything's possible, right?

Now let's look at the reality.

THE REALITY—TIME, SCALE, COST

People who are hoping for a technological solution to our energy predicament sometimes overlook the realities involved in moving to a new energy technology. There are significant issues of time, scale, and cost involved. Above, we've used some simple math to illustrate the scale of the predicament.

From time to time I am accused of significantly underappreciating just how clever and resourceful humans are. Perhaps I do underestimate our species, but the scientist in me knows that cleverness cannot defeat the physical laws of the universe. And the former corporate executive in me knows just how difficult it can be to move from lab, to pilot plant, and then to full-scale operational delivery.

Historically, transitions from one energy source to another have been long, expensive, protracted affairs. Global energy use in the nineteenth century was dominated by wood, not coal, and it wasn't until 1964 that petroleum overtook coal as the main source of transportation energy. Even a 20 to 30 percent share of a national energy market by a new entrant takes several decades, possibly a century or more. At least historically this has been true.[7]

Part of the reason is that the old form of energy has an enormous installed capital base that must be phased out. For example, as our shipping fleets moved from wind power to coal, sailboats were slowly phased out over a period of decades as new coal steamers were individually brought on line. Nobody wanted to dispose of their old capital simply because new technology was available; it wouldn't have made sense economically. The same was true for the switch from horse-drawn carriages to automobiles. So if we want to move from gasoline-powered autos to electric cars, a good guess would be that several decades of transition will be involved. The current crop of petroleum-powered vehicles will have one or two decades of useful life that their owners will want to wring out of them; service stations will have to be phased out, with their pumps and tanks removed; electric charging stations will need to be installed everywhere; and electric grids will have to be significantly upgraded to handle the new loads.

The rest of the reason that energy transitions take so long is simply the scale involved. Even if the world collectively decided that 1,000 brand new nuclear plants were exactly what it needed (and right away), it would still take decades to complete them all. Why? Because there aren't enough manufacturing facilities to build the reactor cores. So those manufacturing facilities would have to be built first. Then, there aren't enough engineers trained in reactor assembly and operation, and training takes time. Further, all of the world's current uranium mines together wouldn't be able to supply the required fuel, so new mines would have to be identified and opened. That, too, would take a very long time.

In every historical case, energy transitions required decades to complete, and there's no reason to suspect that this time will be different. The only way to conceivably avoid this delay would be to override the markets and force the transition by government decree. Perhaps we need the equivalent of a Manhattan Project times an Apollo Project times ten: a massive, sudden, and global decision to put enormous resources into bringing a new energy technology or sources onto the scene without relying on market forces to get the job done. So far there are no signs of that happening anywhere, except possibly China. One example: A 2008 study by the National Research Council found that "plug-in hybrid electric vehicles will have little impact on U.S. oil consumption before 2030" and more substantial savings might be in the cards by 2050, reinforcing the notion that several decades separate the first launch of a new technology from its meaningful contribution to the energy landscape.[8]

THE NUCLEAR OPTION

Even with significant current concerns about carbon in the atmosphere and recent technological advances in the field of nuclear reactor design, nuclear power still cannot step into the lead role and save us all from the effects of depleting oil. It will play a role, just not the lead role. Here's why.

In 2004, nuclear power represented 8 percent of all energy consumed by the United States,[9] while fossil energy represented 86 percent. Worldwide, there were 440 nuclear power plants operating in 2010, 104 of which were in the United States. In 2010, China had plans for or was already building 33 more nuclear plants to be ready by 2030, and a worldwide total of 61 were under construction in 16 countries.[10]

The very first question that must be asked before building a new power plant is, *Where is the fuel for this plant going to be coming from?* Power plants cannot run dry of fuel and need to be constantly fed, so sourcing the fuel is an extremely important task.

When it comes to fueling nuclear plants, there is a bit of an issue. The Chinese are already buying and stockpiling uranium for future use in their plants[11] because they have apparently peered into the future and concluded that fuel security is an issue, so they are buying it now, just to be safe. The United States and France, the two countries with the most operating nuclear reactors, both hit a peak in uranium production back in the 1980s. Both countries only have very modest reserves of relatively low-grade uranium remaining within their borders.

The largest known uranium reserves in the world are located in Kazakhstan, Canada, and Australia.[12] By now, you'll find the story of uranium to be familiar, because it so closely parallels the story of petroleum. The highest grades and most convenient ores of uranium were exploited first and are nearly all gone, and the remaining ores are more dilute and/or more difficult to exploit. It's the same story as that of oil.

High-grade uranium ore deposits, such as those still found in Canada, can be close to 20 percent in purity.[13] But most of the world's known deposits are in the range of 1 percent to 0.1 percent, with a few deposits even listed as "proven reserves," implying that they are worth going after even despite having an ore purity grade of less than 0.01 percent, which is two thousand times more dilute than the higher-grade ores in Canada.

In 2006, the 104 operating U.S. nuclear power plants purchased 66 million pounds of uranium, of which 11 million pounds came from domestic sources and the balance from foreign sources.[14] Over the past decade, the world's nuclear power plants have been running, in part, on the uranium from decommissioned U.S. and (former) Soviet warheads, with some 13 percent[15] of the world's total reactor fuel coming from the "Megatons to Megawatts" program.[16]

If the United States cannot currently meet its own needs for uranium domestically with only 104 operating reactors, how much hope should we place on the idea of building and operating hundreds more over the coming years? Even if the United States somehow managed to double its total number of operating reactors, it would still only be obtaining 16 percent of its total energy needs from nuclear power. And even this assumes that power demand does not grow at all between now and then.

For the world to move significantly to nuclear power above and beyond current levels, it will first need to figure out where the uranium to fuel the reactors will come from. The short answer is that it won't come from conventional mining, because that industry is having a hard time keeping up with the plants that are already in operation. It couldn't possibly service a doubling or tripling from these levels, let alone meet the 18-fold increase implied by the gap being left behind by Peak Oil.

Some hopeful nuclear power proponents then turn to the idea of fast breeder reactors, possibly those running on thorium (which is much more abundant than uranium), which could theoretically provide energy for the next thousand years. At least that's the story brought about in a couple of thought papers put out in the popular media. It bears noting that only a handful of experimental fast breeder reactors have been constructed for demonstration purposes. As of 2010, no commercial breeder reactors have yet been deployed. Not one.[17] Several of the early experiments have already been shut down and/or decommissioned, but a small handful of experimental, demonstration, and pilot breeder reactors remain: one in India, one in Japan, and two in Russia.[18] The basic story here is that fast breeder reactors look very good on paper, but they have proved to be something of an operational nightmare, which is to say nothing of the intense national security risks that they pose by virtue of their production of plutonium if running on uranium, and uranium 233 (a fissile material useful for making nuclear bombs) if running on thorium.

Whether or not breeder reactors are a good idea is relatively insignificant when you consider that no commercial reactors are yet on the drawing boards, let alone currently built, operating, and adding to our available energy. If we are going to entertain hopes that these complicated machines will contribute to our energy story, we must first admit that they can't possibly do this if they aren't built. This seems a trite concept, but you'd be surprised how many people earnestly inform me that we are going to solve our energy predicament with breeder reactors. If Peak Oil arrives in 2014 (as I write this near the end of 2010), it seems incredibly unlikely that the world will somehow manage to build hundreds of breeder and nuclear reactors in the span of a decade, which is what would be required to offset the energy decline.

Here's how the possibility of nuclear energy breaks down:

- **Time:** Decades. It will be at least 10 years (and probably more like 20) before the number of operating nuclear reactors in the world, currently standing at 440 (in 2010), could possibly be doubled.
- **Scale:** Enormous. The world's capacity to build nuclear plants depends upon a limited number of engineers with the requisite training and skills, and there are a limited number of factories that can manufacture the specialty items needed to build a plant. More worryingly, it's not

clear that the necessary fuel will be available from conventional mining sources. Dealing with the waste issue even at the current scales of operation has not yet been solved.

- **Cost.** Trillions and trillions of dollars. The price tag to build a modern 1 gigawatt nuclear plant is $5 billion (in 2010). Maintenance and fuels costs add another $6 million per year per plant. Merely doubling the world's nuclear plants would cost $2.2 trillion. Assuming we could get past the issues outlined in time and scale, and could build the roughly 200 nuclear reactors *per year* required to offset falling oil production, the price tag over just a single decade would be in the vicinity of $10 trillion.

THE COAL STORY

When he was president, George W. Bush gaffed on national television when he declared that the United States still has "250 million years of coal left."[19] Even if he were to have said what he meant, which was" 250 *years* of coal left," he would still have been wrong. In truth, the only possible way to get to 250 years of coal is to start with the most optimistic possible estimate about U.S. coal reserves and then divide it by current consumption, which is unrealistic because our consumption of coal is constantly growing. Realistically, if coal consumption continues to increase as it has done in every decade since at least 1800,[20] it's not possible to have anything close to 250 years of coal remaining.

As Albert Bartlett makes clear, one cannot reasonably leave out growth in consumption when discussing how long something will last. That would be like claiming that you had spent nothing in the past five minutes and that therefore the money in your wallet would last forever. Bartlett has been dissecting the innumeracy of our growth and energy policies for decades, and has pointed out some massive logical errors in our thinking, such as this statement taken from a U.S. Senate report: "At current levels of output and recovery, these American coal reserves can be expected to last more than 500 years." Of this, Bartlett said:

> There is one of the most dangerous statements in the literature. It's dangerous because it's true. It isn't the truth that makes it dangerous, the danger lies in the fact that people take the sentence apart: they just say coal will last 500 years. They forget the caveat with which the sentence started. Now, what were those opening words? "At current levels." What does that mean? That means if—and only if—we maintain zero growth of coal production[21]

He goes on to note that even the Department of Energy admits that perhaps half the coal reserves aren't recoverable, immediately dropping the estimate to 250 years. If we do that and assume that coal production increases at the same rate that it has for the past 20 years, then the known reserves will last for between 72 and 94 years; within the life expectancy of children born today. In terms of outlook, what's the difference between 250 years of coal left and 72 years? In a word, everything.

So what can we say about coal consumption? First, coal is by far the dominant energy source for the production of electrical power (see Figure 17.1).

The use of coal has been growing worldwide at very fast rates, largely driven by China but also by the base growth of power needs in other countries. Even in the United States, where 250 years of coal supposedly remain,

Figure 17.1
Electricity Generation by Power Source

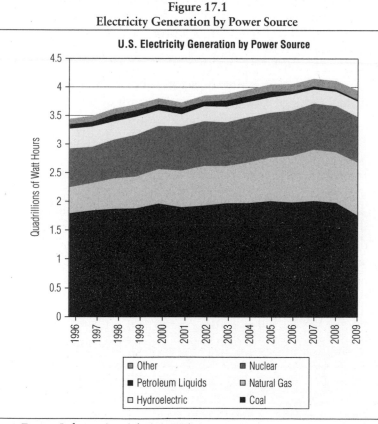

Source: Energy Information Administration.

the United States is likely to become a net importer of coal by 2015 or so[22] because it won't be able to meet its own demand for certain types of coal, principally low-sulfur coal. Not by much, mind you, but a net importer all the same.

Coal production in the United States, as measured by tons mined, has been steadily growing at roughly 2 percent per year since the 1940s. This sort of stable, continuous, but ultimately exponential growth is exactly what our economy and society demand (see Figure 17.2).

Of course, there's a wrinkle in this story. Coal comes in several different grades. The most desirable grade is shiny, hard, black anthracite coal. It yields the most heat when burned, has low moisture content, and is highly valued in the steel-making industry. After anthracite comes bituminous coal, offering slightly less energy per pound of weight, and then subbituminous, and then finally something called lignite (a.k.a. "brown coal"), which is low-energy, high-moisture stuff that really has no use besides burning.

Next let's look at the United States' history with mining coal, separated out by the different grades (see Figure 17.3).

Look at the line labeled "anthracite" in Figure 17.3 and see what sort of trend you can discern. What you see is a steadily declining line, which indicates that less and less of the most desirable form of coal is being mined.

Figure 17.2
Total U.S. Coal Production

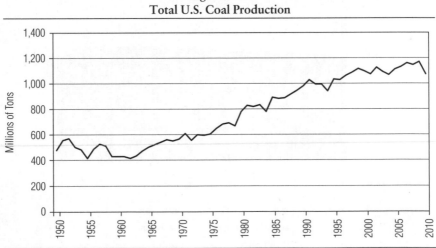

Source: Energy Information Administration.

The reason we aren't mining more anthracite is because we *can't*. It doesn't exist; it's pretty much all gone. Our entire "bank account" of anthracite, formed over hundreds of millions of years, has been largely exhausted in a span of about 100 years. Hundreds of millions of years to form; roughly a hundred years to consume. The point bears repeating: *When it's gone, it's gone*. You can't burn the same lump of coal twice. As with oil, more and more was extracted, and then, due to geological realities, less and less could be extracted. We hit a peak and are far down the backside of that peak here in 2010.

Quite naturally, after anthracite went into decline, efforts then centered on to mining the next-best stuff—bituminous coal—and in Figure 17.3 we observe that a peak in the production of bituminous coal was hit in 1990. Was this because coal companies lost interest in the next-best grade of coal? Hardly. It simply means that we started to run out of that grade, too. Naturally, we then moved on to the next-best grade after that, subbituminous coal, which we see making up the difference to allow U.S. domestic production of coal to continue steadily growing. Most recently, lignite has

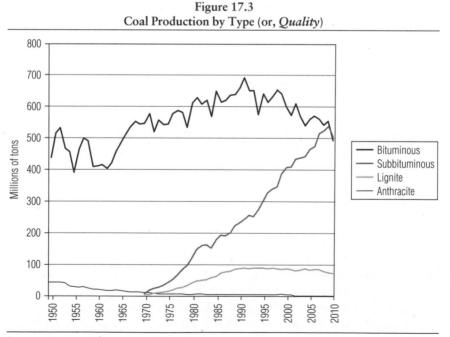

Figure 17.3
Coal Production by Type (or, *Quality*)

Source: Energy Information Administration.

Figure 17.4
Plot of Coal Tonnage versus Coal Energy

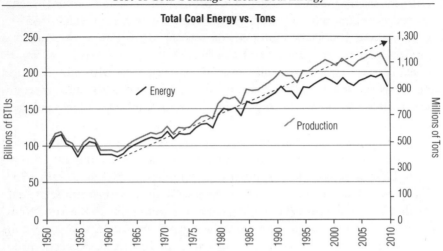

Total Coal Energy vs. Tons

Source: Energy Information Administration.

been getting into the game, although we shouldn't expect to see lignite production really take off before the production of subbituminous coal peaks, which it someday will.

Now here's the really interesting part. Remember when I said that the heat content, or available free energy, of coal got progressively worse with each grade? If we plot the total energy content of the coal mined, instead of the tonnage, we get a very different picture (see Figure 17.4).

Where the tonnage has been moving up at a nice, steady rate of 2 percent per year, we find that the total energy content of mined coal leveled off around 1990 and has gone up by exactly zero percent since then. This implies that the United States is using more energy and spending more money to produce *more tons* of coal, but is essentially getting *less energy* back per ton for its troubles.

This finding mirrors the results of a 2010 study performed by Patzek, et al., which determined that the net free energy from coal mined at all existing mining operations is nearing a permanent peak, possibly as early as 2011.[23] It's important to note that study did not claim that the tons of coal mined will peak in 2011, but rather that the total net energy from those mined tons will hit a peak. This study wasn't about the *quantity* of coal that will be mined (or amount), but its *quality* (or net free energy). After the peak, there will be slightly less and less available net free energy from coal. Of course, this shouldn't surprise anyone, because it's a perfectly logical finding that comports well with common sense. The highest grades of the most-accessible coal were exploited first, leaving the less-energy-dense, less-useful, and less-accessible reserves for later.

Welcome to "later." The Energy Information Administration (EIA) projects that the United States will increase its coal consumption by 25 percent by 2030, reflecting the growth in demand for base electricity production. The International Energy Agency (IEA) projected in its 2010 World Energy Outlook that world coal demand for all uses will advance by an astounding 47 percent between 2008 and 2030.[24] Given the fact that coal grades are declining in their energy content, it's safe to say that mining operations will have to increase enormously just meet the projected growth in demand for coal to be used for the production of electricity. Whether operations can be expanded that much (or that rapidly) is an open question. The bottom line here is that coal isn't a nearly endless resource with hundreds of years of increasing production left in front of it, but a quite limited resource whose energy peak may not even be a decade away.

On top of this story, some people like to introduce the idea of converting coal to liquids to use in our fuel tanks. The coal-to-liquids (CTL) idea has a certain appeal. If the United States and other areas of the world have a lot of coal, then why not convert some of that coal into liquid fuels that we can put into our vehicles?

Unfortunately, you don't have to scratch very hard at that idea to discover its flaws. First, there are no CTL plants running in the United States, and there are precious few anywhere in the world, raising the question of whether we could even build them fast enough to make a difference. Second, it's a horribly inefficient way to use coal, wasting a lot of the energy content in coal at a time when we really shouldn't be wasting much of anything. Third, there may not be enough coal coming from existing and planned mines to handle our base electricity needs, let alone supply an entire new industrial use.

On this last point, we will note that in 2010 China is building the equivalent of one new 1 gigawatt coal-fired plant every week[25] and consumed a full 50 percent of all the coal used in the world that year.[26] Given that China doubled its energy consumption between 2000 and 2008, and given its current plans to continue building out its coal-fired electricity infrastructure at a very rapid clip, it's a pretty safe bet that there will be some stiff competition for available coal supplies in the future.

Putting it all together for the United States, if coal becomes a net import product by 2015, the energy quality of existing coal declines, and demand ramps up worldwide by significant margins, the idea that coal will play any sort of a redeeming role for the loss of petroleum production might qualify as wishful thinking.

While some still, even today, mistakenly claim that the United States has 250 years of coal left, once we factor in declining coal grades plus the need for increased consumption to support increased energy growth, it's entirely possible that U.S. coal won't last even 50 years. Will coal play an important role in our energy future? Undoubtedly. Will coal be the energy savior that will enable us to make a seamless transition away from oil to something else and last for hundreds of years? No.

Here's how coal breaks down as a possible candidate to fill the liquid fuels gap being left by Peak Oil:

- **Time:** Decades. There are no operating coal-to-liquids (CTL) plants in the United States, nor are there very many anywhere in the world. It would take several decades to open up new mines to feed additional coal to this industry and to build sufficient CTL plants.
- **Scale:** Assuming the world wants to get to the equivalent of 105 million barrels of oil a day by 2030, but that oil has instead peaked and slipped slightly to 65 million barrels per day, this implies the need to construct and feed 800 CTL plants, each with an average daily output of 50 thousand barrels.
- **Cost:** Assuming that each plant costs $5 billion to build and produces 50,000 barrels a day, the world will have to invest $4 trillion just in the construction of the plants.[27]

THE ALTERNATIVES

When people think of alternative energy, they are primarily talking about means of getting electricity from the sun, wind, and waves. While we still don't have a means of running our transportation network on electricity, perhaps we could someday, and that's the hope (dream?) of some. The reality is that alternative energy sources are generating such a low percentage of current electricity, even if they grew at astonishing compounding rates it would be a very long time before they made a majority contribution to the global energy outlook. In 2006, Simmons & Company International, an investment banking firm focused on energy, estimated that if solar power capacity grew at the incredibly high rate of 25 percent per year over the next 14 years (from 2006 to 2020), it would provide roughly 1 percent of global electricity demand.[28]

The story with wind power is much the same as solar. Yes, these technologies can play a role, but the idea that they could somehow replace oil—even ignoring the fact that they are sources of electricity, not liquid fuels—is simply not rooted in the reality of the scales involved. Further, wind power only works when the wind is blowing, solar electricity only works when the sun is shining, and wave power only works when the waves are a certain height. The problem with electricity is that it needs to be constantly supplied to be useful, especially to noninterruptible processes such as those found in hospitals and manufacturing. If we could ever find a convenient large-scale way to store electricity, it would certainly help, but so far success has eluded us in this matter.

One area that deserves an enormous input of resources is the advance of batteries. The biggest game-changer out there isn't to be found in developing a new energy source, but in figuring out how to store electrical energy more effectively. If we could store electricity better, a host of issues could be resolved. Right now, it's sad to say, most batteries in use are little changed in design from the one invented by Allesandro Volta in 1800. If ever there were an area that deserved a massive government investment, electrical storage would be it.

The other point to make here is that 95 percent of all energy used to transport things within and across the global economy is supplied by petroleum-derived liquid fuels. Even if we obtained massive amounts of electricity from alternative sources and figured out how to store it effectively, we'd still have to retrofit our entire transportation fleet to run on electricity. Again, we need to raise the prospect of the time, scale, and cost of such an elaborate undertaking.

Biofuels, such as ethanol and biodiesel, were both initially presented as viable energy sources and ecologically protective products. This introduction turned out to be overly optimistic. The net energy returns from corn-based ethanol is a paltry 1.3, give or take a little, and requires the constant and unsustainable application of fertilizers and other industrial interventions to achieve the desired yields. If the United States were to try to completely replace its oil imports with corn ethanol, it would require nearly 550 million acres of farmland to be put to use,[29] representing 125 percent of all the cropland in the United States (which totals ~440 million acres). Anything that requires more than 100 percent of your arable land cannot supply your demand for liquid fuel (or anything else).

In Europe, where a lot of biofuels are used, concerns have mounted about the destructive practices associated with such enterprises as Indonesian palm oil plantations, resulting in significant and legitimate controversy on ecological grounds. It turns out that the way the Indonesians produce the palm oil is to grow it on peat bogs, which has the unfortunate result of both destroying sensitive ecologies and liberating more CO_2 than if oil alone had been burned.[30] Where people initially thought biofuels represented a "green" alternative with the lowest impacts (if any), now they are more aware of the quite significant environmental costs of biofuels that sometimes even exceed those of fossil fuels. We may someday discover a free lunch, but so far biofuels are not it, at least not at the scale required to run a global industrial society.

There are promising signs from algal biodiesel,[31] which I am interested in because it offers the prospect of nutrient recycling and supplies liquid fuels. But as pleasing as the early signs are from this promising technology, here in 2010 we might note that virtually zero algal biodiesel is yet on the market, meaning that an enormous build-out and scale-up of this technology will be required for it to have any meaningful impact. Again, there's a world of difference, and usually several decades, between the birth of an idea and full-scale implementation and adoption.

Here's how the alternatives break down:

- **Time**: Decades. Achieving even modest percentage footholds in our macro energy-use profiles will require a colossal investment. But it needs doing and should be done with all possible haste.
- **Scale**: Absolutely massive. Alternative energy technologies relying on wind, waves, or sun have extremely low (read: unfavorable) "energy densities," meaning that instead of installing a single power plant, thousands of individual units have to be installed over a much larger area. To simply construct the factories needed to build wind, solar, and other equipment will be a significant undertaking. Serious questions remain as to whether sufficient rare resources exist to build all the panels and wind mills using current technologies. For example, neodymium magnets may run short due to a lack of the neodymium itself, as it is one of the rare-earth elements that China crimped off from the export markets in 2010.
- **Cost**: At this point, electricity from solar and wind sources isn't cost-competitive with fossil fuel sources.[32] While estimating the trillions of dollars necessary to make alternatives a viable replacement for petroleum is a difficult prospect, we can easily state that alternatives would be the highest cost of any of the options. But still, these investments should be made.

NATURAL GAS

Of all of the potential alternative fuels, natural gas is best suited to become a "bridge fuel" that we can use to transition into a new future of less energy. Recent advances in shale bed drilling seem to have opened up vast new supplies of natural gas, although environmental concerns (around the chemicals used to "frac" the tight shale open so the gas will flow, and their effects on water tables) and the issue of rapid depletion of the wells remain to be clarified before these new supplies can be relied upon.

But if the reserve numbers are to be believed, then there is ample supply of natural gas to "fund" a transition period. Of course, we'd have to tap that account wisely and preferentially use whatever there is to build a more resilient and efficient energy infrastructure, not waste it trying to increase retail sales and other forms of consumption. The EROEI is very high for gas wells, believed to be somewhere over 30.[33]

However, if we're seriously and credibly going to use natural gas, then we have to immediately begin the enormous task of retrofitting our energy and transportation infrastructure to use it. Cars will have to be modified, new natural gas fuel tanks must be installed, service stations will need new refueling equipment and storage tanks, pipelines will have to be built, and so on. However, converting a vehicle to run on natural gas is a snap compared to conversion to electricity, and there's no compelling reason why such conversions should not be done as quickly and as urgently as possible.

As before, there are issues of time, scale, and cost to be considered if we want to credibly exploit natural gas as a meaningful replacement for oil. It's certainly possible that we can make the switch, but here in 2010, there is no sign that any such plans are even being considered, let alone approaching a scale of implementation that matches the urgency of the situation.

Yes, we could move toward natural gas as a prime energy source. But to do so, we would have to make the shift within a single decade, and no major energy transition has ever been accomplished in that short of a period of time. Is this possible? Sure, anything is possible. Is it probable? Not if we leave it up to "the markets," which seem to remain blissfully unaware of Peak Oil even as we have already passed the peak of conventional oil and appear ready to pass a peak of all types of oil in just a few years. I won't get excited by the prospect of a transition to natural gas until I hear the U.S. president get on television and announce the equivalent of a World War II–era effort to immediately begin building out the necessary infrastructure to make it happen.

If there was one area where we might want to pressure our elected officials to support one energy transition over another, it would be for natural gas over corn-based ethanol. Hands down, natural gas is the winner due to its massively higher EROEI. Unless we get serious about making this transition, and soon, there's not much hope that natural gas will ever do more than play "catch up" with a receding oil horizon.

CONCLUSION

Together, nuclear, coal, and the alternatives will definitely play a role in our energy future. But none will be the energy savior that some are hoping for (or even counting on). Perhaps if we had started transitioning to these alternatives 10 or even 20 years ago, they could have slipped more comfortably into a lead role, but just like oil, none of them could have provided exponentially more energy forever. That is just the basic reality of living on a finite planet with finite resources.

Unfortunately we did not even begin *mentally* transitioning away from oil in the decades before its imminent peak, let alone structurally or economically. In order to have facilitated any kind of soft landing, several decades of preparation would have been required, given the realities of time, scale, and cost involved.

A set of structural, wrenching, and possibly disruptive changes are on the way. At this point, I'm confident that we will rely more heavily on nuclear, coal, and alternative energy sources in the future because we will have to, but I'm also just as confident that these resources will never be able to fully plug the gap left by depleting oil. We may *hope* that they might, but we shouldn't count on them. The numbers are too large; the math doesn't work.

The most probable outcome, given the level of funding priority and other actions by various world leaders, is for these alternative sources to play limited, albeit important, roles in our energy future. Nuclear, coal, and the alternatives can help to mitigate the impacts, but they cannot prevent them.

The implications of this are profound. The economy that you and I have come to know and love—the one predicated on a constant flow of ever-increasing quantities of energy—will have to operate on less energy. Even though having a few percent less energy instead of a few percent more sounds relatively minor, for an intertwined set of economic, financial, and monetary systems that are all based on perpetual exponential growth, the potential impacts are enormous.

CHAPTER 18

WHY TECHNOLOGY CAN'T FIX THIS

By now, some of you are probably thinking I've seriously underestimated the role that technology and innovation will play in our future. Perhaps I have, but my background as a scientist keeps intruding into my optimism about the ability of technology to solve the predicaments we face. In truth, I love technology and what it has brought us over the past centuries and will bring us in the future. I will stand up and applaud new discoveries and new advances louder than anyone in the crowd—when they are rolled out. But we need to face a few facts and assure ourselves that we haven't placed too much optimism where it doesn't belong.

FACT 1—TECHNOLOGY DOES NOT CREATE ENERGY

Because technology seems to produce so many miracles, it's sometimes easy to forget what it can and cannot do. Technology can help us do things more efficiently and effectively than in the past, and it can help us do far more with less. It can entertain and connect us in ways that we couldn't have conceived of only a decade ago. It can boost productivity. It can help us transform and use energy through innovative applications. It allows us to connect instantly with each other in new and exciting ways. But it cannot *create* energy.

Energy can neither be created nor destroyed. So says the First Law of Thermodynamics. Energy can only be transformed from one form to another, such as when coal is turned into electricity, which becomes the cold air blown into a dentist's office in summer. Not once, not ever, not in any laboratory in the world, not even for a millisecond, has technology created more energy than it has used. Energy has certainly been transformed in

177

quite brilliant ways, but the final accounting is always the same: Just as much energy exists as before the transformation; it's just that some of it is now in the form of diffuse heat that is useless for performing any work.

This is where the Second Law of Thermodynamics comes in. It governs what happens to energy when it's transformed: Every transformation always loses at least a little energy (and sometimes quite a lot) in the form of diffuse heat. Diffuse heat is the tax that the universe places on all energy transactions. There's nothing wrong with diffuse heat—those of us in the northern United States happen to love it in our offices in February—it's just that diffuse heat cannot perform any work, and it's the work that energy performs that we're mainly after. It bears repeating: *Every single time we convert energy from one form to another, we lose some of that initial energy content to the universe in the form of heat.*

For example, we might burn coal to turn into electricity, which we then use to split water so that we can capture and use hydrogen. Following this same set of transformations using the Second Law of Thermodynamics as our guide, we get the following: (1) When that coal is burned, about 40 percent of the energy it initially contained goes toward turning the electrical turbines, but 60 percent of its energy is lost to the universe as waste heat. (2) The electricity travels to the site where the water will be split, losing 7 percent of its energy along the way in the form of nicely warmed transmission lines that gently radiate their heat into the universe. (3) The electrolysis is performed, splitting water into oxygen and hydrogen, with 80 percent of the energy in the electricity captured in the form of pure hydrogen and a final 20 percent lost as heat. At every step, the universe demanded and received its tax in the form of diffuse heat. In this example, the final efficiency of converting coal $\rightarrow$ electricity $\rightarrow$ hydrogen is $0.40 \times 0.93 \times 0.80 = 30$ percent. In other words, the act of converting coal to hydrogen loses 70 percent of the energy in coal to the universe.

The universe always tends toward randomness as it ceaselessly strives toward its goal of someday reaching one very average and uniform temperature. This is the law of entropy. Entropy represents the amount of energy in a system that is no longer available for doing mechanical work. At each stage of our conversion of coal into hydrogen, entropy (randomness) increases. Perhaps confusingly, *lower* entropy means there's a *higher level of order* in a system. As entropy increases, so does disorder and randomness. Entropy then, is the name of the tax that the universe places on all energy transformations.

Entropy is the reason that your coffee cup starts hot and gets cold, but never starts warm and gets hotter all on its own. Cold molecules are slower-moving, closer together, and more orderly than heated molecules. They have less entropy than warmer molecules. It is the rule of the universe that high entropy always runs toward low entropy and never the opposite, just as running water always heads toward the sea. All molecules with higher disorder (heat energy) seek to share their wild exuberance with molecules that have less disorder, never the other way around. So your coffee cup starts hot but grows cooler, until it has shared as much of its entropy as it can and reaches room temperature. If entropy ever ran in reverse, you'd be as surprised as if you saw a river flowing uphill or a jumbled pile of books fly up onto a shelf in perfect alphabetical order.

Energy comes in many forms, ranging from highly concentrated to diffuse, from extremely useful to utterly useless for the task of performing work. The least-concentrated form of energy is diffuse heat at the background temperature (whatever that happens to be), and that form lives over on the "completely useless" end of the work spectrum. No machine in the world can perform net work from a single temperature reservoir, no matter how much heat energy it contains; work can only be extracted from heat if there's a temperature difference between two separated reservoirs. For example, there is an enormous amount of heat energy contained within Lake Superior, but we cannot hook a machine up to it and use that energy to perform any work.

The second law states that as we transform energy, we always start with a concentrated form, like diesel fuel or a stick of wood, and after we've transformed it into something else, we're left with whatever work that energy performed plus heat—random, diffuse heat. Our unavoidable entropy tax.

Think of the Second Law of Thermodynamics as a frictionless slide (meaning you can't wriggle back up the slope to a higher spot), where at the top of the slide is beautiful, wonderful, concentrated energy, and at the bottom is diffuse heat. At the top of the slide we might put heating oil and 50 degree air molecules, and at the bottom we might put 70 degree air molecules. Once that heating oil descends and is converted into heat along the way, the trip down the slide is over and done. Once that heating oil has taken its trip down the slide, no more work can be performed from the energy that the heating oil once contained.

Suppose we put some natural gas, a marvelously concentrated form of energy, at the top of the slide and then use it to turn an electrical generator. The natural gas, when burned, performs some work by turning the generator, while the rest is turned into heated exhaust molecules. In asking the natural gas to perform this work, we nudge it down the slide, and it races to the bottom, while performing some useful work and paying the entropy tax along the way. Work and heat.

When energy takes a trip down that frictionless slide, it's a one-way trip. Water never flows uphill and burned hydrocarbons never magically reform themselves out of exhaust fumes. Every form of energy gets only one turn on the slide.

Given this, I like to think of the concentrated energy that we have been given as a one-time free gift of energy perched at the top of a frictionless slide. Our choice is whether we're going to do something truly useful with that energy when we push it down the slide, or simply turn as much of it as we can into useless heat as fast as possible. Either way, we only get to do it once.

In all of history, we've never, not once, violated this law of entropy. If we did, it would be the most spectacular news in scientific (and human) history, and many people, especially me, would scour the findings with great excitement to be sure they were true. But we quite regularly read about people who have claimed to violate this law. Nearly every year, claims surface that a perpetual motion machine that produces more energy than it consumes has been invented. The inventors of these magical devices demonstrate a remarkable ability to secure gullible media interest, and sometimes even deep-pocketed investors, but not one of them in all of history has ever produced a surplus-energy-perpetual-motion machine that actually works as claimed. To do so would mean that a perpetual motion machine would be able to nudge some energy down the frictionless slide *and* harvest enough work along the way that the same amount of energy could be pushed back up the slide as was used. You might as well try and lift yourself into the air. Needless to say, the law has yet to be broken, and a perpetual motion machine has yet to be invented.

If you find the Second Law of Thermodynamics a bit esoteric and want to observe a more direct and observable law of nature that has also never been violated, consider the law of gravity. Not once has anything that has been dropped on Earth ever floated upward instead of accelerating downward. Despite our technological prowess, not once have we ever found a way to defeat gravity here on the surface of the earth with our technology. We can temporarily defeat gravity using the powerful forces found in rockets and magnets, but we've never permanently diminished it. Just as the Second Law of Thermodynamics has proven to be an immutable law of nature that is immune from our technological reach, so, too, has gravity. The latest high-tech gizmos may intrigue and impress us, but they are as firmly straitjacketed by the laws of energy and entropy as you are glued to the earth by gravity.

Our first step toward understanding the limits of technology is to fully appreciate that technology can find, produce, and transform energy, but it cannot create it. Once we really understand the fact that technology does not (has not, will not, *cannot*) create energy, we're in a better position to appreciate its offerings and shortcomings.

Fact 2—Transforming Energy Is Expensive

Once energy has taken the trip all the way to the bottom of the frictionless slide, it's lost to us as a form of energy that can do useful work. Technology will permit us to take less concentrated forms of energy and make them more concentrated, perhaps even push them back up the slide, but only at an energy cost. By now you know this cost is "diffuse heat." Any time we decide to concentrate a form of energy, we lose some energy to heat. Put another way, if we want to create one unit of concentrated energy, we will have to start with *more than one unit* of less-concentrated (but still useful) energy, with the extra balance representing the portion that will be "donated" to the universe as heat. Pushing things back up the slide is possible, but only if we're willing to pay.

This is why the much-advertised "hydrogen economy" is an energy bust waiting to happen. There are no existing deposits of hydrogen to mine or tap. Hydrogen is energy-expensive to make, and there's simply no way to make it without losing energy along the way. We might make it from natural gas, or from electricity, but we lose heat with every step of the conversion process. The more hydrogen we make, the less energy we have. Hydrogen might make sense economically and/or politically, but it's an energetic flop. I'm picking on hydrogen a bit here, but the principle applies to any and every energy transformation.

And there's nothing that technology can do to circumvent this reality. Transforming energy is expensive; it costs energy. Heat is lost, the entropy tax is unavoidable. This isn't techno-pessimism—it's the law: the Second Law of Thermodynamics, to be exact. The universe always applies its tax; entropy constantly increases.

Fact 3—Energy Transitions Take Time

If Peak Oil arrives before 2020, as seems likely at the time of this writing, then very little time remains to effect a transition to alternative sources of energy, whatever they may be. Energy transitions take time. A lot of time.

Figure 18.1
Energy Use by Source, 1800–2010

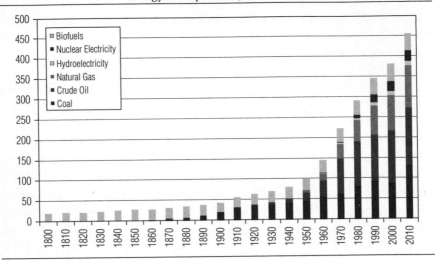

And that is not so much a function of technology, but of human behavior and the economics of already-deployed capital.

For example, note in Figure 18.1 how long it took for coal to equal the energy contribution of wood ("biofuels" in the chart), and for oil to then equal the energy from coal, and that natural gas has still not equaled either of those (although it could). Nuclear and hydro remain distant competitors in the energy game.

These transitions took decades, typically four or more, to happen. This is one more reason why we might not expect or hope for technology to fix the energy predicament we face: markets, economics, and behaviors operate on their own time scale, independent of technology itself. History suggests that a good time to begin the energy transition away from petroleum would have been a good 30–40 years prior to the peak. An excellent study by Robert Hirsch (then of SAIC) made a compelling case that 20 years prior is the cut-off for undertaking mitigation strategies to avoid damaging consequences.[1]

WHY TECHNOLOGY CAN'T FIX THIS

Technology can help us exploit what energy we do have more cleanly, cheaply, and more efficiently, but it cannot create energy. And when we transform energy, we lose energy to the universe along the way in the form of diffuse heat. Therefore, it's appropriate to view the fossil fuel store of the earth as if it were a gigantic pile of food that can only be eaten once. When we eat this bounty of the earth—our inheritance—it's gone, never to be seen again. And technology holds little sway over economic and sociological impediments to rapid energy transitions.

Because economic order, complexity, and growth all require energy, and because our original allotment of energy cannot be increased by technology, technology alone cannot "fix" the predicament of needing more energy than we have. Technology has an enormous role to play in helping us to use our energy more wisely and with greater efficiency and utility, but these efforts will only slow the eventual day when our giant pile of free food is gone. At that point in time, we revert to eating what we can grow ourselves—an apt metaphor because we'll be living within the energy budget supplied, once again, by the sun.

Between here and there, it's up to us to decide what to do with this once-in-a-species energy bonanza. *Shall we increase our prosperity by creating enduring works of architecture and lavishly funding our best and brightest minds to stretch the limits of what's possible? Or shall we use energy's one trip down the frictionless slide merely to promote the most rapid economic growth and consumption that we can?* Both are choices that we could make, and in either case, nature doesn't care; energy will be converted from concentrated forms into diffuse heat, remorselessly and relentlessly, whether we wish that to be the outcome or not. Nature will carry on whether we use up our energy stores wisely or shamefully, quickly or slowly, without any concern for how much or how little useful work we extract along the way.

Technology can provide a lot of things, but it cannot violate the laws of the universe. They are immutable and working just as they always have. And that is why technology can't fix this—nothing is broken.

PART V
ENVIRONMENT

CHAPTER 19

MINERALS

Gone with the Wind

These next few chapters won't be a recitation of the various environmental stresses and issues that currently plague the world. There are many incredibly detailed sources chronicling the depletion and mismanagement of the earth's resources, perhaps none better than Lester Brown's *Plan B* series (currently in version 4.0) from the World Watch Institute, from which these next few chapters will draw heavily.

Instead, we're going to tell a story around our dependence on and use of those resources, coupled with the energy story, to make the case that seismic shifts are in store for the economy. This isn't to diminish the importance of environmental issues, or to intentionally or unintentionally subjugate them to money and the economy. Rather, the main point to which I adhere is this: *The most immediate "environment" impact we will feel in our own lives will be transmitted to us via the economy.* It responds more quickly and provides immediate feedback. More important, if the economy suffers and stumbles, or even collapses, then the environment will only suffer more. In that case, we will lack the resources to protect and preserve it, as we will be worrying about survival, which inevitably trumps all other considerations.

QUANTITY AND QUALITY (AGAIN)

The story of energy basically boils down to two "Qs," quantity and quality. We noted that for oil, global discoveries peaked in 1964, which means that someday, inevitably, the *quantity* (amount) of oil coming out of the ground will someday peak as well. We noted that the issue isn't just how much energy is coming out of the ground; it's also the *quality* of that energy, with quality being an expression for the net free energy returned from those exploration and development activities.

This same story of quantity and quality applies to all other mineral resources, as well as any other primary sources of wealth that come from the earth. Our economy as we know it is an industrial economy that really began when we started harnessing the energy of coal to do work. The industrial economy began about 150 years ago, during which time the world has transformed considerably. Where abundant mineral resources were once lying around for the taking, now every last major deposit has been mapped and lesser and lesser grades of ores are being pursued at higher and higher costs, both energetic and monetary.

One hundred and fifty years, it should be noted, is a relative blink of an eye. Consider that Cleopatra was born and ruled closer in time to the launching of the space shuttle than to the building of the Great Pyramid of Cheops,[1] and somehow 150 years doesn't seem like all that much time. It's not, really, and that's the point.

One of my favorite images from the past shows two dapper gentlemen reclining on what appears, in the grainy black-and-white 1800s-era photo, to be a large rock in a streambed. In fact, that "rock" happens to be a copper nugget, an enormously concentrated form of mineral wealth that was just lying around waiting to be found and used. Before long, all of the large copper nuggets were swept up and used, so smaller and smaller nuggets were pursued, until finally all of those were commercially depleted, too. Then we moved onto the highest-grade copper ores, which were soon exhausted, and today we find ourselves consigned to and chasing after lesser and lesser ore grades.

In the United States, one of the largest copper mines is the Bingham Canyon Mine in Utah. It's 2.5 miles across, three-quarters of a mile deep, and used to be a rather sizeable hill that has since been hauled away, crushed, smelted, and transformed into a very large hole. The ore grade at Bingham Canyon is quite low, only 0.2 percent when all the waste rock is factored in. Now think of a hole in the ground that's nearly 4,000 feet deep, and imagine trying to get the ore and waste rock up and out of that hole without using gigantic diesel trucks. Think of the energy involved in hoisting rocks and earth thousands of feet into the air just so that we can get at the remaining dregs of copper in the earth's crust.

Where our financial markets might tell us that this is a reasonable thing to do, perhaps because copper is at \$3.00/lb., while diesel fuel is only at \$2.85/gal., it doesn't make a lot of sense on an energetic basis. Once we convert that highly concentrated diesel fuel into waste heat, humans will never be able to use that energy again to do anything else. Perhaps bringing rocks up from 4,000 feet down so that we can extract a relatively tiny proportion of copper from them really is the best use for that energy, or perhaps there are more pressing priorities. This is one way that financial markets can lead to perfectly rational *economic* decisions that also happen to be perfectly irrational *energetic* decisions.

The other point that I want to be sure to communicate here is the stunning sense of pace in this story. From giant nuggets lying in streambeds to 0.2 percent ore bodies in only 150 years. That's an astonishingly short amount of time. What will we do for an encore over the next 150 years? When put in this context, it's sobering to consider just how fast the mineral wealth of the earth has been exploited and how relatively few years remain until all of the known deposits are completely exhausted.

Actually, that's an overstatement. The deposits will never be completely exhausted, as that would likely require far more energy than we actually have. As we recall from Chapter 15 (*Energy and the Economy*), one gallon of gas is equivalent to between 350 and 500 hours of human labor. How much is 350 to 500 hours of your labor worth to you? My prediction is that once petroleum energy begins to be priced at something closer to its intrinsic worth based on the work it can perform, most marginal mining activities will cease, and we will never get around to removing those last few flecks of mineral wealth.

Instead of thinking of the dollar costs associated with chasing after 0.2 percent copper ore, I want you to think of the energy costs, because those are what are going to shape the future. Remember how difficult it is to instantly appreciate nonlinear curves? Another nonlinear curve relates to the amount of energy required to go after and produce metals and other minerals that must be extracted from depleting ore bodies. Figure 19.1 and Figure 19.2 illustrate the declining quality of mineral ores.

It's clear that the energy requirement of chasing depleting ore bodies is very much a nonlinear story. Assuming that the ore is coming from mines that are a similar depth and distance from the processing mill, every decrease in the ore concentration requires a big increase in the amount of ore that is removed for processing to obtain the same amount of the desired material. This is ore that must be broken away from surrounding material, transported, crushed, and refined. Every step is energy intensive.

One trait that humans share with all animals is that we go after the easiest, highest-quality sources of materials first. That's just natural. Those that are more concentrated and nearer to the surface (or markets) are preferentially exploited first. We tend to farm the best soils first, harvest the

Figure 19.1
Ratios of Mined Ore to Produce One Pound of Mineral or Metal

Ore Grade	Pounds of ore to produce one pound of mineral
20%	5
10%	10
8%	13
6%	17
4%	25
2%	50
1%	100
0.7%	143
0.5%	200
0.3%	333
0.1%	1,000
0.08%	1,250
0.06%	1,667
0.04%	2,500
0.02%	5,000
0.01%	10,000

Figure 19.2
Pounds of Ore to Create One Pound of Refined Mineral

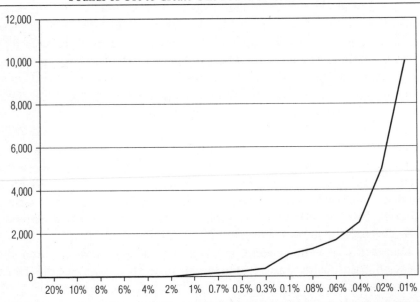

tallest trees, and go after the most concentrated ore bodies. It's a process called "high grading," and it simply means doing the obvious: using up the best and most convenient stuff before the other stuff. Which means that by the time we're chasing the less-attractive ores as a second order of business, there's a very good chance that these ores are inconveniently located, perhaps deeper in the ground or in a more remote location, or both, and/or in more dilute form. Because of this, as we go forward, the energy required to chase the lesser ores will be even more than is implied by a simple chart comparing the ore percentages to processing amounts.

Quite simply, the key point here is this: To get more and more minerals from depleting ore bodies in the future won't require just a little bit more energy, it will require exponentially more energy.

ECONOMIC GROWTH AND MINERALS

The economy, which I've attempted to convince you is due for a shake-up, depends on ever-increasing flows of materials (and energy) running through it. That's what an exponentially increasing economy implies—more stuff in ever-increasing quantities. The predicament is that sooner or later this will no longer be possible, because there's a limit to all resources. Even the most pie-in-the-sky optimists admit that eventually there will be limits, although some cling fast to the belief that those limits are still very far off in the future, maybe even too far off to concern ourselves with at this time.

One of the favorite devices used by such optimists is to state that we have many remaining decades of resources x, y, and z "at current rates of consumption." The problem with that, as I hope you can now immediately appreciate, is that an exponential economy cannot be satisfied with "current rates of consumption" because that amounts to the same thing as saying "zero growth." Our particular brand of economy is based on ever-increasing amounts of everything flowing through it. More money, more debt, more gasoline, more cars, more minerals, more profits, more buildings, more clothes, more, more, more of everything.

So if you ever hear the phrase "at current rates of consumption" in regard to a nonrenewable natural resource, this is a sure sign that the person wielding the statistics has painted an erroneously rosy picture of that resource, either accidentally or on purpose.

To illustrate the importance of mineral wealth to economic growth, consider what goes into our cars and trucks. Automobiles are a perfect starting point because mobility is extremely important to people everywhere on the globe. We can easily appreciate how economic growth translates into more cars on the road, and cars use up lots of different minerals in their construction and operation.

To manufacture a car or truck, the following mineral elements are needed (Figure 19.3):

Figure 19.3
Types of Metal or Element (by Weight) in a Typical Automobile

Metal/Element	Purpose	Pounds in Car
Steel (Iron Ore)	Frame mostly, engine	4,960
Petroleum	Plastics: body and interior, rubber tires, paint, fabrics, gas and lubricating oils	980
Aluminum	Also in the frame, lighter than steel	240
Quartz	Silica to make glass	170
Glass	Windows	85
Copper	Wiring, starter motor	70
Carbon	Used to make iron ore into steel, tires	46
Rubber	Tires	44
Silicon	Ceramic components	41
Lead (Galena)	Battery	24
Zinc	Galvanizing agent	18
Manganese	An alloy with steel that is resistant to wear in axles, pistons, crankshafts	17.6
Nickel	Stainless steel plating	9
Magnesium	Alloy used to strengthen aluminum	4.4
Sulfur	Used in battery	2
Asbestos	Brake pads	1.2
Molybdenum	Strengthens steel and lubricants	1
Vanadium	Used to form alloys that are fatigue-resistant	1
Oxygen	Combustion in engine	Varies
Antimony	Makes car upholstery fire resistant	Trace
Barium	Coat electrical conductors in the ignition system	Trace
Cadmium	Electrolytically deposited as a coating on metals to form a chemically resistant coating	Trace
Clays	Used to make spark plugs in engine	Trace
Cobalt	Makes thermally resistant alloys (superalloys)	Trace
Fluorospar	Used to manufacture aluminum, gasoline, and steel	Trace
Gallium	Mirrors, transistors, and LEDs	Trace
Gold	Electronics	Trace
Mica	Fills the shocks	Trace
Nitrogen	Ceramic materials (spark plugs) and in battery	Trace
Platinum	Catalytic Converter	Trace
Palladium	Catalytic Converter	Trace
Rhodium	Catalytic Converter	Trace
Strontium	Phosphorescent paint on dials	Trace
Tin	Solders	Trace
Titanium	Makes metallic alloys and substitutes for aluminum Paint, lacquers, plastics, rubber	Trace
Tungsten	Fliament of light bulbs, spark plug	Trace
Zirconium	Alloy of steel and glass, light bulb filaments	Trace

Source: McLelland, "What Earth Materials Are in My Subaru?"[2]

Figure 19.4
Total Registered Vehicles in the United States

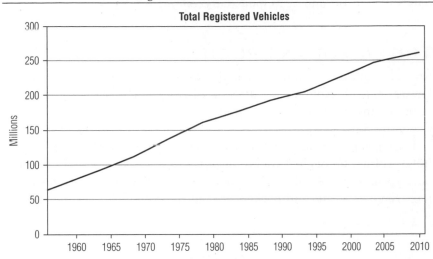

Total Registered Vehicles

Source: Research and Innovation Technology Administration Bureau of Transportation Statistics.[3]

Even if we assume 100 percent recycling of the materials in a car or truck (an impossibility, as some things are lost along the way to rust or just otherwise diluted and dispersed), one thing that we can't get around is that each year, with economic growth, there are more cars and trucks plying the global highways than the previous year (Figure 19.4).

More cars and trucks mean that more of those things in the table above must be extracted from the earth. More copper, steel, aluminum, and everything else in that list must come up out of the ground to be converted into vehicles. The same is true for cell phones, computers, televisions, and everything else that includes some form of mineral wealth.

When we look at the world's undisputed, number one consumer economy, that of the United States, a country enormously well endowed at its inception with mineral wealth, we find that it currently imports 100 percent of its needs for 18 critical, economically important elements or minerals.* The implication of this is clear: The U.S. economy now requires more mineral wealth than can be secured from within its own borders, and in several

---

*Please refer to the Appendix for a list of the minerals that the United States must fully or partially import.

cases it has entirely depleted its natural endowment of mineral wealth after only 150 years of running its industrial economy.

THE END OF AN EPOCH

Several high-quality studies have already peered into the future of our known mineral resources and determined that some of them are now past peak and that several will be entirely exhausted within just a few decades (Figure 19.5).

It's startling to realize that nearly all of these mineral resources were in fully pristine, untouched condition just 150 years ago. Where the earth once spent hundreds of millions of years concentrating these ores into a relatively few seams and pockets around the globe, humans managed to

Figure 19.5
Known Mineral Reserves and Depletion

Mineral	Years left at sustained 2% growth, based on reserves
Strontium	11
Silver	12
Antimony	15
Gold	15
Zinc	15
Arsenic	18
Tin	18
Indium	19
Zirconium	19
Lead	19
Cadmium	20
Barium	20
Mercury	22
Tungsten	23
Copper	23
Thallium	28
Manganese	29
Nickel	30
Molybdenum	32
Rhenium	35
Bismuth	38
Yttrium	40
Niobium	40
Iron	48

Source: Diederen, "Metal Minerals Scarcity and the Elements of Hope."[4]

eat through a significant quantity of those in only 150 years. But that, too, underplays the situation. The amounts of minerals extracted each year have been steadily climbing through time. If we assume a 2 percent rate of increase in yearly extraction, this would mean that world extraction and use of mineral resources will double every 35 years.

And we're continuing to increase the amounts that we extract by a fairly steady 2 percent per year, which means that in just another 35 years, we will be seeking to extract twice as much from the ground as we are today. Thirty-five years after that, we'll want to extract four times a much. And so on, forever and ever. Or at least that's the story as it currently stands.

Your job is simply to ask yourself if that seems either likely or doable. If, like me, your answer is, *No, this is neither likely nor doable*, then it makes sense to begin planning for a future that will be very different from today.

REDUCE, REUSE, RECYCLE

There can be no doubt that an important tactic of the future is going be careful stewardship of our remaining resources. By reducing, reusing, and recycling our nonrenewable natural resources, we will be able to extend and blunt the day of reckoning. Unfortunately, however favorable or well-executed this strategy might be, it won't be sufficient to prevent seismic shifts in the superstructure of our economy.

Our economy is based on a high-throughput, a somewhat disposable approach to natural resources that acts as if there were no limits to either extraction or excretion. The transition to an economy that can function on static or even diminishing supplies of certain essential raw materials is a fundamentally different economy from the one we currently have.

However well-implemented, a strategy of reduce/reuse/recycle won't be able to mitigate any of the following:

- *The impact of the loss of materials for which no substitutes exist.* There are a variety of extremely critical rare elements for which no substitutes are known to exist for certain applications. Their loss will necessitate finding acceptable workarounds that may be less advantageous than the original—an example of technology going backward.
- *Materials that are combined or used in ways that prevent their easy extraction and reuse.* One of the many uses for cobalt is as an alloy material to make stainless steel. Once it is mixed in dilute amounts with steel, it would take an enormous amount of energy to recover

that cobalt to use it in a different way. In fact, economically and energetically speaking, that's really not an option; the cobalt in the steel is far too dilute, so in every practical sense, the cobalt is effectively locked into the steel. When mined potash is spread upon a field in Iowa as fertilizer, and then washes down the Mississippi River and into the Gulf of Mexico, it's far too dilute to be recovered (although it's plenty concentrated to support algal blooms).

- *Materials lost through dispersion. When steel rusts, it's essentially lost forever*, because it's in too dilute a form to be economically recoverable. Over time, our activities have the effect of taking relatively concentrated ores, using a lot of energy to concentrate and purify them to exceptional levels, and then carefully spreading them evenly over the surface of the earth, rendering them forever unrecoverable.

GONE WITH THE WIND

The bottom line is that our activities tend to disperse our mineral wealth in ways that often prevent their reclamation and reuse. In many cases this is a one-way trip that isn't amenable to recycling or reuse.

After (just) 150 years of industrialization, we can already see the end of several key mineral resources *just a few years or decades out*. And even these projections blithely assume that the energy is there to complete the task of depleting the known reserves, an assumption that I'm not willing to make.

With the depletion of certain key minerals, things will change, possibly dramatically. Am I saying that I expect the economy to come to a crashing halt if a key mineral is exhausted? No, absolutely not. But I am saying that it will no longer work the same way that it did before, and that's what this book is about—alerting you to some seemingly quite obvious and predictable changes that are clearly headed our way.

CHAPTER 20

SOIL

Thin, Thinner, Gone

In January of 2009, an architect who'd arranged for me to speak in his community was driving me from San Francisco to an event in his hometown of Sonora, CA. As we passed through some of the most fertile farmland I had ever seen, I remarked on the bounty I could sense just outside the glass as we drove by at 65 miles per hour. Row after row, field after field, dark soil beckoning now and again from freshly turned operations spoke of the immense agricultural treasure of the place as we zoomed our way east.

Then, all of a sudden, the flat fields turned into row after row of neat, tidy houses, all squished together as if the prior 40 miles of flat expanse were irrelevant and space was suddenly hard to come by. "Hey, what's going on here?" I asked. He briefly dipped his head and brought it up to say, "I'm embarrassed for my profession. We should, of all professions, know better than to build on farmland, but there's no awareness yet in my colleagues of the tragedy that what you see represents."

This silent tragedy, converting rich soils into tract housing, is happening all across the United States and elsewhere in the world and is, again, driven by financial—not necessarily thoughtful—decisions. Civilization has always grown up around and depended on the thin layer of soil that covers the earth, and we're as dependent on it today as we've ever been. Without soil, food won't grow. We would do well to remember that without primary wealth, there's no secondary wealth, and without *that*, nothing else really matters, certainly not your stocks and bonds.

THE COMING FOOD CHALLENGE

In 2010, a United Nations (UN) commission reported on the state of the world's food situation and made these statements:

> . . . satisfying the expected food and feed demand will require a substantial increase of global food production of 70 percent by 2050.
>
> Much of the natural resource base already in use worldwide shows worrying signs of degradation. Soil nutrient depletion, erosion, desertification, depletion of freshwater reserves, loss of tropical forest and biodiversity are clear indicators.[1]

One-tenth of the world's land mass is suitable for growing crops, while another four-tenths is only suitable as range land due to the thinness of the soil, steepness, dryness, or some combination of those factors. The remaining half of the world's landmass is unsuitable for food production. The UN report examined the issue of how we will manage to feed 9.5 billion people (a 46 percent increase), given that virtually all the world's available farmland is already under production. Increased demand is expected to require an enormous increase in crop production.

Over the past few decades, improvements in irrigation, use of fertilizers, and better crop varieties have combined to dramatically improve crop yields on a per-acre basis. But can we complacently assume that another 46 percent can be wrung out of the system over the next 40 years? What might happen if petroleum energy in the future costs too much to support the use of ever-increasing quantities of fertilizers, irrigation, and pesticides?

THE IMPORTANT DIFFERENCE BETWEEN SOIL AND DIRT

Our modern, industrial agriculture system feeds more people while employing fewer people than at any time in history. Even more remarkably, crop science has delivered ever-increasing yields on a per-acre basis at ever-lower costs. As impressive as this is, you probably won't be surprised to learn that such gains come with hidden costs. One of the most important costs has been incurred by the soil itself.

There is an important distinction between soil and dirt made here:

> What is the difference between soil and dirt?
>
> Soil is alive. Dirt is dead. A single teaspoon of soil can contain billions of microscopic bacteria, fungi, protozoa and nematodes. A handful of the same

soil will contain numerous earthworms, arthropods, and other visible crawling creatures. Healthy soil is a complex community of life and actually supports the most biodiverse ecosystem on the planet.

Why is it then, that much of the food from the conventional agricultural system is grown in dirt? The plants grown in this lifeless soil are dependent on fertilizer and biocide inputs, chemicals which further destroy water quality, soil health and nutritional content.[2]

In our quest to grow more food, more cheaply, on the same amount of land, year after year, we have been strip-mining the soil of its essential nutrients and qualities and converting it into lifeless dirt. What would happen if modern farming suddenly had to make do without fertilizers, pesticides/herbicides, and other petroleum inputs? Yields would fall, probably by quite a lot. Our increased yields have less to do with better technology and understanding, and more to do with the forceful application of external energy.

Industrial agriculture is marvelously cost-effective, but also remarkably brittle. It depends on a perpetual inflow of chemical fertilizers to replace the nutrients that are stripped, as well as petrochemical inputs in the form of herbicides, fungicides, and pesticides to counteract the deleterious effects of soil sterilization and monocropping.

What is the difference between Wal-Mart and an industrial farming operation? Not very much, as it turns out. Both are extremely cost-effective, and both are desperately fragile. If anything disrupts the just-in-time delivery systems around which their methods of profitability are built, either operation will experience profound difficulties. If there's a gap in the ability to deliver shipping containers from China to Wal-Mart's operational distribution centers, wares rapidly vanish from the shelves. It may be a cost-effective way to do things, but it's not robust; it's fragile.

Similarly, if an industrial farming operation is deprived of the chemical inputs required to enforce growth in their crops, yields will almost immediately suffer and plummet. Various studies of the impact of fertilization have proven that anywhere from 40 percent to 100 percent gains in grain crop yields are dependent on the application of fertilizers.[3] Sufficient supplies of fossil fuel products are essential to the success of both of these ventures.

Exporting Nutrients

The United States exports some 80 million tons of agricultural products each year (primarily grains), which represent a massive amount of water, as we'll see in Chapter 21 (*Parched*), and vital nutrients that are harvested from the soils and shipped overseas. Without the nutrients being completely recycled back into the soils, the farmed soils quite rapidly become depleted of the vital elements that plants use to support their biological functions and growth.

One puzzle that you might have read about recently comes from the observation that plants grown and tested for their nutrient content some decades ago contained far more nutrients than plants harvested today. The quoted evidence below was assembled by Dr. Donald R. Davis and reveals the following patterns of depletion in food nutrition and soil nutrients:

- In wheat and barley, protein concentrations declined by 30 to 50 percent between the years 1938 and 1990.
- Likewise, a study of 45 corn varieties developed from 1920 to 2001, grown side by side, found that the concentrations of protein, oil and three amino acids have all declined in the newer varieties.
- Six minerals have declined by 22 to 39 percent in 14 widely grown wheat varieties developed over the past 100 years.
- Official U.S. Department of Agriculture (USDA) nutrient data shows that the calcium content of broccoli averaged 12.9 milligrams per gram of dry weight in 1950, but only 4.4 mg/g dry weight in 2003.[4]

There is no mystery to these results. If you constantly harvest minerals from the soil and then truck them away without replacing them, eventually the soil will become depleted and there will be less of those minerals available to plants. In this sense, then, many farmers are in fact "mining" the soils upon which their livelihoods depend. Without closing that loop somehow and getting those nutrients back into the soils in measures equal to the rates at which they're harvested and transported away, the practice of farming on those soils is thoroughly unsustainable. Sooner or later, those soils will become utterly sterile, suitable only for the type of farming that uses massive amounts of energy (somewhere along the line) to transport and replace those nutrients by some other means. The bidding wars that broke out in 2010 for various fertilizer companies, such as the hostile pursuit of Potash Corporation by BHP Billiton, reveal the mounting interest in securing ownership of the best remaining sources of essential (and profitable) crop nutrients.[5]

THE HIGH (ENERGY) COST OF LOW-COST FERTILIZERS

The three key nutrients that are mandatory for crop growth are nitrogen (N), phosphorus (P), and potassium (K), which you'll see listed together on the front of a bag of fertilizer as "NPK." Virtually all of the world's nitrogen is made using natural gas to supply the energy (and hydrogen) needed to convert gaseous nitrogen into ammonia, a form of nitrogen that's biologically available to plants. (The gaseous form of nitrogen that makes up more than 70 percent of the atmosphere is inert and useless to plants.) It's an enormously energy-intensive process; a pound of ammonia fertilizer requires the equivalent of a pound of diesel fuel to create it.

Therefore, any study of the extent that plant yields are dependent on nitrogen applications is really the study of the effect of fossil fuels on farming yields. As long as there are ever-increasing amounts of natural gas to dedicate to making nitrogen fertilizers, then the system we currently use should continue to function. But if this isn't the case—if it turns out that natural gas becomes limited in some way (which indeed it someday will)—then we need to seriously think about how we'll manage that situation.

If we lacked the energy to make nitrogen fertilizers, then plant yields would suffer enormously, until and unless we could figure out a practical way to return the harvested nitrogen back to the land in a usable form. Currently, the number one eventual destination for applied farming nitrogen is the ocean, which is where we send most of our sewage. Right now we can "afford" to do that because we have the energy to waste, but in the future it will be a sure bet that we'll have to find ways to close the loop and return these essential nutrients to the land and the soils upon which we depend.

The story of phosphorus is even more urgent, if not alarming, as our only source for this utterly essential element is from mined rocks. Again, we "mine" phosphorus from our farming soils and send it out to the sea to become hopelessly diluted, never to be recovered. Once thought to be virtually inexhaustible, rock phosphate has been mined in ever-larger quantities over the years to support our exponential need for more food, and we can now see that a peak in this important mineral resource is plainly in view.

Our supply of mined phosphorus is running out. Many mines used to meet this growing demand are degrading, as they are increasingly forced to access deeper layers and extract a lower quality of phosphate-bearing rock (phosphate is the chemical form in which nearly all phosphorus is found). Some initial analyses from scientists with the Global Phosphorus Research Initiative estimate that there will not be sufficient phosphorus supplies from mining to meet agricultural demand within 30 to 40 years. Although more research is clearly needed, this is not a comforting time scale.[6]

This is the exact same story that we've seen already for petroleum and other minerals. There is a fixed quantity of this vital mineral. It's being mined in ever-larger amounts, and it's depleting rapidly. That it will someday run out isn't in doubt; such a fate lies in the future of any finite material that's consumed. But "running out" isn't really our most immediate concern; "peaking" is. If farming yields must grow to meet future demand, and those yields depend on phosphorus, then the peaking of phosphorus is going to put enormous pressures on efforts to increase yields.

Modern farming practices represent the effective mining of nutrients—a one-way trip from the soil to the sea—which we combat by mining or creating replacement nutrients elsewhere and then spreading them back on the land, using a lot of energy in the process. Right now our approach to nutrients is like a giant arrow that begins where the fertilizers are mined, passes through a farm, goes to a plate, and then out to sea.

SOIL EROSION AND DESERTIFICATION

Even if all the soil (and its critical minerals) were staying in place, instead of being dispersed out to the ocean, there is another way in which modern farming practices aren't sustainable. Much of the soil itself is being lost, and this, too, is a concern. Fertile soil builds up only very slowly, often requiring 100 years of natural processes to create a single inch, and it is being lost at a rate that far exceeds its rate of accumulation. Some of it is lost slowly through simple erosion over time, and sometimes it is lost rather dramatically, as was the case in the U.S. dust bowl in the 1930s, when a single dust storm on April 14, 1935 was calculated to have contained 300,000 tons of topsoil, twice as much material as was dug from the Panama Canal.[7]

Desertification is another destructive process that is often initiated and accelerated by the actions of humans. The process usually involves overgrazing of already marginal, dry lands, which destroys the meager plant cover that protects what little soil there is. Eventually a fine wind storm comes along and blows that soil away, and then nothing is left to absorb the sparse rains when next they come. Plant roots themselves also play an important role in both capturing and liberating water; they perform vital functions lost to overgrazing and difficult to reestablish once gone.

CONCLUSION

All of this is to say that instead of building up our primary wealth—soils—we're rather steadily, and sometimes dramatically, eroding and depleting them. Sustaining our current farming yields currently requires enormous energy inputs to create the fertilizers and run the irrigation pumps. But these practices are themselves unsustainable. Sooner or later, the energy won't be there to create the fertilizers and irrigate the fields.

Taken together, these facts about the fate of our soils and available farmland lead me to a stark conclusion: The cost of food is going to go up rather dramatically in the years to come. Farming on arid land isn't sustainable. Farming in a way that depletes the soil isn't sustainable, nor are methods that cause soil to be eroded faster than it's created.

The whole story of farming on an industrial scale is one of low costs and even lower sustainability. In order to farm sustainably, soils must be minimally maintained at their current depths and levels of fertility. In a world of surplus energy, these defects can be hidden by "nutrient subsidies" hauled in at great energy costs from far away. But when the energy subsidy is withdrawn, the true state of our croplands will be revealed.

The alternative to this bleak story of lost soil and squandered nutrients begins in your local area. There are farming practices available that build soils and nutrients; these have begun to "close the nutrient loop" and are therefore on the path toward being sustainable. It would be a useful exercise to explore how these options are (or aren't) being applied in your area.

The bottom line with regard to soil is that it is the single most important form of primary wealth. Without soil, we'd be entirely lost. Without food, nothing else is possible. It is past time to reconnect with our soil and treat it with the respect and admiration it deserves.

CHAPTER 21

PARCHED

The Coming Water Wars

When you were young, perhaps your mother admonished you to turn off the tap while brushing your teeth to conserve water. That's good advice, and I don't want to diminish it, but the coming water predicaments will be driven more by the food on your plate than by what swirls down your drains. Water tables all across the globe are falling fast as aquifers are pumped at rates far faster than they are being recharged.

As Lester Brown explains:

> The link between water and food is strong. We each consume, on average, nearly 4 liters of water per day in one form or another, while the water required to produce our daily food totals at least 2,000 liters—500 times as much. This helps explain why 70 percent of all water use is for irrigation. Another 20 percent is used by industry, and 10 percent goes for residential purposes. With the demand for water growing in all three categories, competition among sectors is intensifying, with agriculture almost always losing. While most people recognize that the world is facing a future of water shortages, not everyone has connected the dots to see that this also means a future of food shortages.[1]

While turning off the faucet while brushing your teeth is a good idea, residential water use comprises only 10 percent of the total. Even if we could cut our domestic water use by 100 percent, we'd still have 90 percent of the issue to deal with.

As with Chapter 19 (*Minerals*) and mineral wealth, my purpose in this section isn't to write exhaustively about water issues. For that I refer you to other excellent sources for the details.[2] Instead, I want to simply illustrate

205

that the exact same exponential dynamics of depletion and growth are present with respect to water as they are in petroleum and minerals. It's the same story all over again: *Exponential growth is driving extractive behaviors that are creating water issues, problems, and predicaments all across the globe*. No longer can clever engineering deliver all of the desired water to some places in the world; even now, there simply isn't sufficient water to meet the level of desired consumption.

Therefore, the story with water is more or less the same as the story for oil and minerals: We're placing exponentially increasing demands on what, in many cases, is essentially a fixed supply. The drive for water demand is no more complicated than population growth. The 70 million new people on the surface of the planet each year (equivalent to 8.3 New York Cities annually) need to eat, and food takes a lot of water to grow. For example, a single pound of wheat takes a thousand pounds of water to grow, and this 1:1000 ratio coupled with population growth is the key driver for increasing water demand across the globe.

Running Dry

The water with which we are most familiar is above ground in the form of ponds, lakes, rivers, and reservoirs; that form of water has the wonderful characteristic of recharging and replenishing itself from the rain and snow that falls from the sky. We can easily view the water levels in rivers and reservoirs and see for ourselves whether the levels are rising or falling enough to be cause for alarm. Over just the past 40 years, as the world's population has more than doubled, many of these rivers and reservoirs have gone from being sufficient to being nearly depleted.

The mighty Colorado River no longer roars into the sea, having been reduced to a trickle by the innumerable demands placed along its entire length. The Yellow River in China is in the same condition. All over the globe, once-mighty rivers now limp toward the ocean, often drying up entirely during the dry season before they reach the sea. While there's some latitude to push things a bit further along with conservation efforts and altered-use practices, the surface water of the world clearly cannot stand any more "doublings" in demand. Already practically every major river has been dammed, diverted, sluiced, and sliced up into apportioned allotments, and many minor rivers have disappeared entirely. The conclusion is clear: Sooner or later, fresh water will be a major limiting factor to population growth and economic expansion.

WHAT LIES BENEATH

Because we can see it, we often tend to think of surface water as the main story, but really the relationship between surface water and the totality of the water we use is very similar to an iceberg's dimensions above and below the water. The most important sources of water for most cities and agriculture lie in the aquifers hidden from view deep beneath the ground, which means that precious few people truly appreciate what's going on down there. What we find here are rapid and increasing rates of depletion. Many of these aquifers recharge so slowly, often over the course of tens of thousands of years, that Lester Brown rightly calls them "fossil aquifers" to link them to same depletion dynamics that plague petroleum reservoirs. In the United States, the massive Ogallala aquifer lies under eight western states, supplies 21 million acre-feet of water for irrigation every year, and may dry up in as little as 25 years.[3]

In this sense, extracting water from deep, ultra-slow-recharging aquifers is no different from mining: Once the ore (or water) has been removed, it's as good as gone forever, at least on a human timeline. This is where our intuitive sense of water, which regularly falls from the sky, can lead us astray. Instead of thinking of it as an infinitely renewable resource, we need to be aware that an enormous proportion of the water we use is effectively a nonrenewable resource. Aquifers like the Ogallala are more like a non-interest-bearing bank account gifted to us by a distant relative. Because it won't last forever, a prudent person would have a strict budget and a solid plan for what to do on the day that the account runs dry.

Ancient aquifers all over the globe are being pumped at unsustainable rates and will therefore someday fail to provide sufficient water to local populations. The list of problem areas are nearly endless, and very few of these locations have any sort of credible plans for what to do when the water runs out.

EXPORTING WATER—THE FOOD STORY

Water is an indispensible factor in the story of ever-increasing crop yields over the past several decades. World food harvests have tripled since 1950, and irrigation is responsible for a large portion of those gains. Most people are surprised to learn that every pound of harvested wheat requires one thousand pounds of water to grow. In a sense, this 1000:1 ratio means that when the United States exports wheat, it's really exporting water. A million tons of grain is the same as a billion tons of water, which explains why many water-starved countries prefer to buy their grains rather than try to grow them on their parched soils. It's cheaper than digging wells or building desalination plants.

Without the use of aquifers, much of the dryer agricultural land in the world, such as the wheat fields in Saudi Arabia, would have to be abandoned altogether. And agriculture in the more temperate regions would have to revert to dry land farming practices—which means depending on rainfall alone, rather than irrigation—and this would lower yields. This is an inconvenient reality at a time when future food security is already an open concern of world leaders and population is slated to grow by approximately 40 percent over the next 40 years.

To quote Lester Brown again, "Knowing where grain deficits will be concentrated tomorrow requires looking at where water deficits are developing today."[3] The dryer and more populous nations are already struggling with severe water issues today. So as we ponder the predicament of falling water tables, we might also ask what the impact of these will be on our ability to support even a few more decades of exponential growth, let alone an endless amount of it. Given the enormous litany of water issues that are already upon us, I find it quite improbable that we will be able to support even one more economic doubling without running into serious issues.

THE FOOD BUBBLE

Because water is so indispensible to agriculture, and the more populous and dryer regions are so heavily dependent on ancient aquifers to meet their irrigation needs, some stark conclusions are apparent. Again from Brown's *Plan B*:

> Many countries are in essence creating a "food bubble economy"—one in which food production is artificially inflated by the unsustainable mining of groundwater. At what point does water scarcity translate into food scarcity?[4]

David Seckler and his colleagues at the International Water Management Institute, the world's premier water research group, summarized this issue well:

> Many of the most populous countries of the world—China, India, Pakistan, Mexico, and nearly all the countries of the Middle East and North Africa—have literally been having a free ride over the past two or three decades by

depleting their groundwater resources. The penalty for mismanagement of this valuable resource is now coming due and it's no exaggeration to say that the results could be catastrophic for these countries and, given their importance, for the world as a whole.[5]

As was the case with our money system, which was essentially born in its current form on August 15, 1971 with the slamming of the gold window by Nixon, we don't have thousands of years of experience to help guide us through what happens when the aquifers that allowed the emergence of large populations above them are depleted. It can rightly be said that we are currently experiencing a "food bubble," in the sense that the harvests are now running at a rate higher than the aquifers can sustain.

The story of water is another tale of an unsustainable practice that's playing out right before our very eyes and getting surprisingly scant attention, given the stakes involved. The mystery here is why so many clearly unsustainable practices are running at once without more pointed national and global discussions about exactly how and when we'll terminate the practices on our own terms so that we can enter a future shaped by design, not disaster.

ENERGY AND WATER

Because water is a liquid and flows so easily, down rivers and through pipes, its other primary characteristic often gets overlooked: It's heavy. A cube of water measuring just slightly over three feet on a side weighs a ton. It is wonderful that huge amounts of water will flow so readily down an incline, such as 100-mile long culvert. However, if you want water to go uphill, there's an enormous energy price to pay.

In certain states in India where the irrigation pipes now reach deep into the earth to draw up the precious but retreating water, irrigation now accounts for more than half of the electrical energy used. Unsurprisingly, bringing water up from great depths is enormously energy intensive, and irrigation is one of the major uses of energy in farming, consuming 13 percent of the direct energy used to grow food.[6]

As aquifers deplete and retreat to lower and lower depths, the energy—and cost—required to pull those waters up mounts. In the future, we'll see twin pressures on food-growing costs: The direct increase in petroleum prices and the mounting costs of drawing water up from ever-greater depths. And even then we're assuming that the aquifers will remain viable indefinitely.

The other primary use for water that often goes overlooked is the production of energy itself. Nuclear and coal-fired plants both require enormous amounts of water, used in the cooling cycle, to operate. If we express the amount of water required on the basis of kilowatt hours, we find that it takes two gallons of water to produce a single kilowatt hour of consumed electricity. Surprisingly, hydroelectric plants "consume" the most, as their reservoirs lose a lot of water to evaporation. For all new thermoelectric plants (coal, nuclear, etc.) the average is approximately 0.5 gallons per end-use kilowatt hour. This may not sound like a lot, but it means that more than half of all the water consumed in the United States is consumed by electrical power plants. If we want more electricity, we'll need to use more water.[7]

THE FUTURE OF WATER

Once again, if we take a hard look at the facts as they stand, we come to the conclusion that the correct question isn't *How do we manage our water resources to allow perpetual growth?* but rather *Since our use of water will someday hit a limit, would we rather approach that limit on our own terms or on nature's terms?*

Fresh water isn't evenly or very well-distributed across the globe, and neither are these water-based problems—some places are in much worse shape than others. The future of water is already upon us, as evidenced by the number of farm operations and regions that have been systematically losing their water access by expropriation or selling their water rights to cities. When economics sets the rules, farmers lose, because the monetary value of the crops that can be grown with a given amount of water is a fraction of the value at which water can be sold to residential and industrial customers.

We're already at the point where water is a limiting factor for societies and economies all across the globe. With 6.5 billion souls (and counting) living the way we do, all the fresh water on the face of the earth, and even that beneath the surface, is barely meeting our needs. What happens when the world's population goes to 9.0 billion, as the UN suggests is likely by 2050? At a simple level, this nearly 40 percent increase in population implies that there will be 40 percent less water per capita in the future. More realistically, we might wonder if the number will be a lot larger due to the permanent loss of several or more ancient aquifers.

The future of water is one of scarcity. It's a future where "water refugees" will need to move from regions where the local aquifers can no longer support the populations above them, and where nations will squabble and possibly go to war over water rights and access. It's hard to imagine how this water scarcity won't translate into crop and food scarcity.

Water use provides a perfect illustration of the gap between the "grow now at any cost" mentality and a rational, thoughtful approach. If a city is drawing upon a depleting ancient aquifer, has no other plans for water, and continues to grow, then it's being led by people who are either deeply irrational or who lack an appropriate horizon of concern.

Unfortunately, this description applies to many cities all over the world, including many in so-called developed nations. The evidence is dramatic and overwhelming, and it's time for us to come to terms with it. The alternative is to wait for circumstances to force the issue, risking prosperity and even water wars.

CHAPTER 22

ALL FISHED OUT

I loved fishing with my grandfather when I was a child. I can't recall us ever talking about anything—not one conversation comes to mind—but there was no need for words; we were *fishing*. He took me to the Branford public pier on the Long Island Sound, and we caught many different types of fish there. The waters were teeming with life. I remember an abundance that, sadly, is no longer in evidence there when I take my kids fishing.

Once again, this chapter isn't designed to be a long recitation of the many challenges that our oceans are facing—there are too many to list—but I'll continue to make the simple point that we're already up against hard limits with respect to what the oceans can provide. More growth? Another 10, 20, or 30 years of increasing exploitation of the ocean's riches? It's not going to happen. They're already fished out.

Ninety Percent Gone

A recent study published in the esteemed journal *Nature* concluded that the combined weight of all oceanic large fish species has declined by 90 percent.[1] If something supposedly renewable is being harvested at a rate that causes its mass to shrink alarmingly, then it's a poster child for the concept of "unsustainability."

As Lester Brown put it in Plan B 3.0:

After World War II, accelerating population growth and steadily rising incomes drove the demand for seafood upward at a record pace. At the same time, advances in fishing technologies, including huge refrigerated processing ships that enabled trawlers to exploit distant oceans, enabled fishers to respond to the growing world demand. In response, the oceanic fish catch climbed from 19 million tons in 1950 to its historic high of 93 million tons in

1997. This fivefold growth—more than double that of population during this period—raised the wild seafood supply per person worldwide from 7 kilograms in 1950 to a peak of 17 kilograms in 1988. Since then, it has fallen to 14 kilograms.[2]

As population grows and as modern food-marketing systems give more people access to these products, seafood consumption is growing. Indeed, the human appetite for seafood is outgrowing the sustainable yield of oceanic fisheries. Today, 75 percent of fisheries are being fished at or beyond their sustainable capacity. As a result, many are in decline and some have collapsed.

Cod, bluefin tuna, swordfish, shark, herring, and innumerable other species are in rapid decline and are in danger of collapsing or becoming extinct. This isn't some future issue that we might worry about; it's happening right now.

While overfishing puts serious pressure on oceanic health, probably the worst problem of the lot right now, there are other problems as well, ranging from destruction of estuaries, loss of coral reefs, oceanic "dead zones" caused by pollution runoff, and the build-up of toxic metals and other industrial pollutants in the top species.

> Sperm whales feeding even in the most remote reaches of Earth's oceans have built up stunningly high levels of toxic and heavy metals. [R]esearchers found mercury as high as 16 parts per million in the whales. Fish high in mercury such as shark and swordfish—the types health experts warn children and pregnant women to avoid—typically have levels of about 1 part per million.[3]

What sort of signal should we receive from the fact that whales—mammals just like us—now carry toxic loads of mercury so far beyond what the EPA would allow in humans that they would probably require a person so infused with mercury to be buried in a special leakproof casket to prevent the release of hazardous materials?

THE AIR YOU BREATHE

I was taught in middle school that the oxygen I breathe comes from trees. That's not entirely wrong; it's just not entirely accurate either. The source of half the world's oxygen is not majestic trees in the Amazon rising hundreds of feet into the mist, but microscopically invisible one-celled creatures that live at the ocean surface, tossed hither and yon by majestic waves and currents.[4] Called "phytoplankton," which is a fancy way of saying "photosynthetic organisms that are really small and live in the ocean," these little "trees of the ocean" are responsible for far more than half the oxygen you breathe; they are the very base of the food pyramid in the ocean.

On land, plants form the base of the pyramid, and these plants are eaten (for example) by the rabbits that are eaten by the foxes. In the ocean, phytoplankton are the plants, which are eaten by slightly larger plankton and larvae, which are eaten by . . . well, you get the picture. There's an entire ecosystem and food chain in the ocean which exactly mirrors the one on land in its basic pyramid shape, but it is eons older in terms of its layers, complexity, and structure. Life started in the sea and has a billion or more years of a head start on terrestrial life when it comes to complexity (e.g., interrelationships, dependencies, feedback loops, and the like).

This is all well and good and perfectly ignorable until we read things like this:

> The microscopic plants that support all life in the oceans are dying off at a dramatic rate, according to a study that has documented for the first time a disturbing and unprecedented change at the base of the marine food web.
>
> Scientists have discovered that the phytoplankton of the oceans has declined by about 40 per cent over the past century, with much of the loss occurring since the 1950s.[5]

While we don't know if this finding will hold up, or what might be causing it if it is real, it's a trend that has been tracked by scientists for quite a long time.[6,7] If such findings are true, we should be just as focused on why half of the world's supply of oxygen is disappearing as why our GDP is not growing as rapidly as we might like.

The very air you breathe is dependent on a form of life that you almost certainly have never seen with your own eyes, and something seems to be amiss with it. Whether the cause is global warming, nutrient imbalances, or an upset in the normal predator-prey relationships is utterly unknown at this point. Wouldn't it be good to know what the cause is? Without (hopefully) belaboring the obvious, human pressures on the oceans, in whatever form, are a ripe candidate for speculation and inquiry.

THE BOTTOM LINE

All of the data coming from the oceans says that even at a population of 6.5 billion, humans are exerting unsustainable pressures and demands upon the world's oceans. There is much we don't understand about our saltwater resources, probably because, like aquifers, they are out of our direct sight and therefore our appreciation.

But one thing that we can be sure about is that, by definition, unsustainable practices must someday stop. *As we head toward 9.5 billion people, what are the chances that we'll be able to wrest 40 percent more fish from the oceans?* The answer is somewhere between zero and none.

We're already at limit, and probably beyond, when it comes to the oceans. The story of perpetual economic growth, then, will have to be told without getting more resources from the oceans. They are all tapped out and headed toward collapse, with reductions in certain key areas and species upon which we already depend for much of our protein.

For any who care to look, signs are present that we have either hit or are rapidly approaching hard, physical limits all around us. This isn't a case of pessimism; this is simply what the data is telling us at this time. Whether or not you choose to heed the warning signs and adjust your life to the implications of this information is for you to decide.

In my own lifetime, a mere blink by historical human standards, I've personally witnessed what seems like the complete demise of shore-based fisheries. In many places, there's nothing left to catch. The water is beautiful on the surface, but underneath it's a desert. Our oceans are rapidly growing devoid of all the larger forms of life, and now, as we're finding out, this sad fact extends to even the microscopic ones as well. When I consider just how rapid this depletion of the ocean's resources has been, I think back to our stadium example—as far as the oceans are concerned, the water is already swirling up the staircase to the bleachers.

PART VI
CONVERGENCE

CHAPTER 23

CONVERGENCE

Why the Twenty-Teens Will Be Difficult

The next 20 years are going to be completely unlike the last 20 years. Perhaps this sounds trite, in the sense that change accompanies every decade, but I mean to convey something more profound, and possibly more disruptive, than the usual pace of change that we've seen in the past. A trait that all humans share is that we extrapolate from the past into the future. Whatever just happened becomes our model for what is most likely to happen next. If the surly store clerk has treated us poorly six times, we will expect the clerk to respond similarly on the seventh. If we slip on ice outside our front door twice, we're more careful the third time we step out. But in the case of the past 20 years, in which we've learned that economies grow, technology improves, and the cure to bursting bubbles is cheap money, it's most likely that these lessons will prove to be more misleading than helpful.

If I'm right (or more accurately, if the data in the prior chapters has been correctly assembled and interpreted), then we're on the cusp of major change—the kind where the amount of time and resources we dedicate to mitigating the risks will prove to be the best investment we could ever make. As someone who has done a lot of recreational rock climbing and some over-the-horizon boating, I have a strong appreciation for the difference between "sort-of" prepared and actually prepared. When you're 600 feet up a rock wall, either you have a critical piece of gear or clothing with you, or you don't. Trust me, being stuck that high up without rain gear because it was too nice at the bottom to justify hauling it up can result in a very memorable experience. Once you're out of sight of land, if you get into boating trouble, you either have an emergency locator beacon with you—or you don't. If you do, the rescue crews can find you instantly; if not, they may never even know you're in trouble, let alone where to look once you've been reported missing.

It is my central belief that our future contains exceptionally high risks that could usher in political and social unrest, a collapsing dollar (and other fiat currencies), hyperinflation (or hyperdeflation), and even full economic collapse. But it's important that you understand that these are merely risks, not certainties. My background as a pathologist trained me to view the world as a collection of statistics and probabilities; nothing is ever black and white to people in my (former) profession. People who smoke four packs a day are at higher risk of certain diseases, but are not certain to die of anything in particular. Cancer exists on a continuum of aggressiveness, which we segment into stages, but even then, there are no guarantees as to the outcome of an individual case. Similarly, when I look into the future, I don't have any certainty about what might come next; instead, I see risks to be weighed and mitigated.

It's also important to note that I don't get rattled easily. I undertook no preparations for Y2K, and I don't fret about flying or driving or being near secondhand smoke. I rock climb and shoot and eat meat. To me, everything is a series of risks, some large and some small, with relatively few above my personal threshold of attention and most below.

The risk that I'm most focused on isn't any particular one of the individual predicaments laid out in the previous chapters. Rather, I'm primarily concerned about the general *possibility* that two or more may converge on a very narrow window of the future in a fashion that could overwhelm the ability of our systems and institutions to adapt and respond. Like a rogue wave formed of lesser parts, two relatively small issues could join forces and prove to be far more destructive and disruptive in combination than individually. Let's review the key elements now in order to better appreciate the risks.

THE FOUNDATION

Exponential growth defines the human experience of the past few hundred years. With the advent of effective medicine and abundant energy, exponential population growth became so embedded in our collective reality that we designed both monetary and economic systems around its presence. Without such robust economic growth, as was the case in 2009 when global GDP shrank by a mere 2 percent, our banking system practically collapsed and was said to have been only hours away from meltdown.[1]

All growth requires energy, and if there happens to be abundant surplus, both growth *and* prosperity can result. However, if there is insufficient surplus to "fund" both, then you can only enjoy one or the other. If this comes to pass, it will not be a problem to solve, but a predicament to manage.

The Economy

To review, our understanding of the economy began with the fact that money is loaned into existence, with interest, and that this results in powerful pressures to keep the amount of credit, or money, constantly growing by some percentage each year. This is the very definition of exponential growth, and money and debt have been growing exponentially (very nearly perfectly) for several decades.

Keeping this dynamic in mind, we dove into the data on debt, which is really a claim on the future, and saw that current levels of debt vastly exceed all historical benchmarks. The flip side to this (a significant sociological trend in its own right) is the steady erosion of savings that has been observed over the exact same period of time. Combined, we have the highest levels of debt ever recorded, coincident with some of the lowest levels of savings ever recorded. We also saw that our failure to save extends through all levels of our society and even includes a notable failure to invest in infrastructure.

Next we saw how assets, primarily housing, have been part of a sustained bubble that is now bursting and will take many years to play out. When credit bubbles burst, they result in financial panics that end up destroying a lot of capital. Actually, that's not quite right; this quote says it better:

> *Panics do not destroy capital; they merely reveal the extent to which it has been previously destroyed by its betrayal into hopelessly unproductive works.*
> —John Stuart Mill (1806–1873)

We learned that a bursting bubble isn't something that's easily fixed by authorities, because such attempts to "limit further damage" are misplaced. The damage has already been done; the capital has already been betrayed. It's contained within too many houses, too many strip malls sold for too high prices, and too many goods imported and bought on credit. All of that's *done*. What is left is figuring out who is going to end up eating the losses.

Then we learned that the most profound financial shortfalls of the U.S. government rest with the liabilities associated with the entitlement programs that are underfunded by somewhere between $50 trillion and $200 trillion dollars, neither of which are payable under the most optimistic of assumptions. A number of other governments around the globe are suffering similar shortfalls and constraints.

Throughout the last several decades, the economic numbers that we reported to ourselves were systematically debased until they no longer reflected reality. They were (and continue to be) fuzzy numbers. Bad data leads to bad decisions, and this is another reason why we find ourselves in our current predicament. The longer we continue to fib to ourselves, the worse the eventual outcome is likely to be.

Energy

Next we learned that energy is the source of all economic activity—it's the master resource—and that oil is a critically important source of energy. Our entire economic model rests upon continuous growth and expansion. This means that it's built around the flawed assumption that unlimited growth in energy supplies is possible, which, unfortunately, is an easily refuted proposition. Individual oil fields peak, as do collections of them. Peak Oil isn't a theory; it's simply an observation about how oil fields age.

We explored the tension that is obviously present between a monetary system that *must* grow and an energy system that *can't* grow. All complex systems, of which the economy is a textbook example, owe their order and complexity to the energy that flows through them. Remove the energy, and by definition (and universal law), order and complexity will be reduced. Starving our economy of fuel risks crashing it.

The amount of fossil energy that we have at our disposal is fixed. Like a trust fund that earns no interest, it can only get spent once, and then it's gone. Technology can help us to utilize that energy more efficiently, but it cannot create new energy.

The Environment

Finally, we noted that the environment, meaning the world's resources and natural systems upon which we depend, is exhibiting clear signs that we're approaching its limits. We're finding ourselves in the position of needing to exploit the poorest-quality mineral ores, peaks in critical resources are being noted at a faster and faster pace, and we're scouring the globe for the last few concentrated sources of primary wealth. We're also depleting water in fossil aquifers at unsustainable rates, farmers are mining soils of essential nutrients, and our oceans' rich ecosystems are suffering.

"UNSUSTAINABLE"

Putting it all together, we come up with a story that's very simple and virtually airtight: *Our present course is unsustainable.* Perhaps we can console ourselves with the idea that somehow we won't reach the limits of our resources during *our* individual lifetimes, but we cannot argue that finite energy resources can last forever. If something is unsustainable, it will someday stop.

Many theoretical thinkers—including economists—reject the idea of limits, but individuals armed with the proper facts almost never do. The landmark modeling work done for *Limits to Growth* in the early 1970s was spot-on in virtually every respect, but economists and the media trounced on it because it did not fit their preferred view of a world without limits.[2] To economists at the time (whose ideas unfortunately still hold sway), resources just show up on time and as needed in response to "market demand," and any intrusions on this tidy arrangement are often rejected out of hand.

If we had taken the time to heed the lessons in *Limits to Growth,* we would be in far better shape today, but we didn't. In addition, we failed to take the lessons offered by Oil Shock I seriously, also in the 1970s. And so here we are with a lot more water in our stadium and the shackles still firmly affixed to our wrists.

CONVERGENCE: THE TIMELINE

If all we had to do was face any *one* of the predicaments outlined above, I'm confident that we would collectively do our best, respond intelligently, accommodate the outcome, and carry on. But if we allow for the possibility of facing several of these predicaments at once, the concern mounts considerably. A timeline stretching from 2010 to 2020 reveals a truly massive set of challenges converging on an exceptionally short timeframe (see Figure 23.1).

Placed on a timeline, we see that a bursting housing bubble began in 2008, just one year before the first wave of boomers entered retirement in the United States (January 1, 2009). Somewhere along the way, let's call it 2015, Peak Oil and rising demand will conspire to outpace oil supplies, forcing an enormously expensive adjustment for every economy currently dependent on cheap oil. Soon thereafter, other depleted resources will peak, as their energy costs of extraction and refining will finally outweigh their economic utility. Unpredictable costs associated with a shifting climate are another potential demand on our limited budgets. And further limiting our options, a failure to save and invest, along with historically unprecedented levels of debt, will cast a shadow over the possible solutions or responses we might envision to all of the other predicaments.

The primary question is, *Where will the money come from to dedicate to each of these challenges if our savings are depleted and our debt levels are*

Figure 23.1
The Twenty-Teens

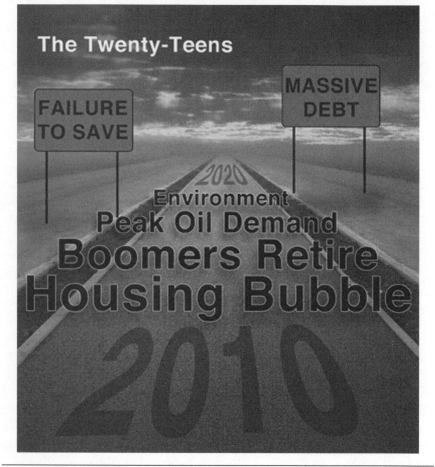

Image: Jeanine Dargis

already in uncharted territory? This one question encompasses a whole host
of others:

- *Where will the tens, if not hundreds, of trillions come from to make up
  the shortfalls in pensions and the entitlement programs?*
- *How many trillions will be required to reshape our transportation
  infrastructure to cope with the reality of Peak Oil?*
- *Where will the money come from to clean up the aftermath of the
  bursting housing and credit bubbles?*

- *How much more expensive will food and minerals be in the future, when many more people are placing higher demands on increasingly marginal resources?*
- *How will we cope with any of these extraordinarily expensive challenges while burdened with the highest debt loads and lowest savings levels ever seen?*

Any one of these events will prove to be a difficult strain on our national economy, but what happens if two of them arrive simultaneously? What about three? It's not hard to appreciate that potentially enormous risks lie along this timeline.

Each of these key trends or threats will take years, if not decades, of careful planning and adjustment to mitigate. And yet we find them all parked smack in front of us, without any serious national discussions or planning, as if they weren't even there. With every passing day, we squander precious time while the problems grow larger and more costly to remedy, if not becoming thoroughly intractable. The mark of a mature adult is someone who can manage complexity and plan ahead. In my opinion, with few exceptions, the current political and corporate leadership of this country is neither managing nor planning well. That needs to change, and soon. It's time to return to the habit of living within our natural and economic means. We need to set priorities, set a budget, and stick to both.

THIS TIME *IS* DIFFERENT

I can hear the critics now: *Doomsayers have been predicting the end of the world since the beginning of time, and the doom has never happened.* Or perhaps, *What's the difference between the story that you have laid out and the one that Thomas Malthus expounded upon back in the late 1700s?** For starters, we have access to a lot more data than Malthus could ever dream of. Where he had access to a limited number of physical books to refer to, we can happily web-surf and spreadsheet our way through more energy data in day than Malthus could manage in a lifetime.

---

*In 1798, Thomas Malthus postulated that the human population's geometric growth would at some point exceed the arithmetic returns of the earth, principally in the arena of food. To paraphrase, he recognized that the exponential growth of human numbers would meet with the constraints imposed by a finite world. Because this has not yet happened, some have claimed perpetual victory over the entire concept of limits. It should be noted that Thomas Malthus had no way of knowing that oil and coal would dominate the energy landscape for the next 200-plus years.

Second, in Malthus's time, the laws of thermodynamics were incomplete and rudimentary, and something we take for granted, the germ theory, had to wait another 90 years to be fully accepted. Hopefully it's not too much of a stretch to suggest that we've progressed in our understandings of things somewhat since Malthus's time, and our circumstances are quite different from those in 1798.

Lastly, I am not predicting doom, only massive change. Whether someone interprets that as a crisis or an opportunity has nothing to do with facts and data, but psychology. Both of the listed objections fall under the same logical fallacy (inductive): "Because "A" hasn't happened before, "A" can't (or won't) happen in the future."

What truly is different this time is that collectively, as a species, we have never before faced declining energy flows. Never. So we're about to enter completely uncharted waters. All we have are snippets and fragments from history to suggest what happens to localized cultures that run low on food or fuel, but these are poor analogues to our own globalized, just-in-time, highly complex, multibillion-person system of economic organization and delivery.

As we squint into the next few decades and ponder the numerous challenges converging on a very narrow strip of time, we would do well to consider the risks and question just what might happen if they converge to form the economic equivalent of a rogue wave.

CHAPTER 24

CLOSING THE BOOK ON GROWTH

Exponential economic growth is in its final throes. The only question is whether we recognize this early, on our own terms, or later, as a consequence of a series of final and regrettable collapses that will result in enormous suffering to humans and ecosystems.

The economic predicament as I've laid it out goes like this:

1. Over time, debt-based money grows exponentially due to interest, and this is an immutable feature of the system.
2. Due to nonproductive loans that can't be serviced with interest flows, the accumulation of debt also "goes exponential" over time.
3. Debt is a powerful motivator, and therefore exponential debt drives exponential economic growth and behaviors.
4. Any growth, but especially exponential economic growth, requires ever-increasing amounts of energy to sustain its order and complexity.
5. Because energy cannot, through any combination of known technologies, grow exponentially into the future forever, economic complexity and order will someday shrink.

The only sure conclusion from this line of thinking is that someday our current model of economic growth will end and something new will take its place. It's only a question of when. Of course, any child could tell you that nothing can keep growing forever, and we've always known somewhere, perhaps deep down, that our current model was unsustainable. The end of the growth paradigm is now making its presence felt as the world economy and financial systems lurch from rock to rock, seemingly immune from the magic money incantations and spending potions that have always worked

227

in the past. The predicament of stagnant economic growth resulting in financial chaos can only be "solved" by increasing the flow rate of energy (and other resources) through our economy. It cannot be solved by pouring more money into a congealing economic cauldron.

What happens when an economy that *must* grow is being fueled by an energy source that *cannot* grow? My prediction has always been that the economy would begin to wobble and collapse, debts would prove to be unserviceable in total and begin to default, and monetary policy would lose traction and cease to be effective, as it is finally revealed that money is merely a tertiary abstraction that gets its meaning from real forms of wealth. My secondary prediction has always been that the monetary and fiscal authorities would attempt to solve this predicament by printing money out of thin air and spending wildly in an attempt to keep things moving along.

This isn't an indictment of capitalism or any particular "–ism" at all. I'm an equal-opportunity critic who places under indictment any particular "–ism" that seeks perpetual growth. Ditto for any political party, religion, economic model, or any other social organizing structure that seeks endless growth in any form. It really does not matter to me in the slightest whether someone calls their perpetual growth paradigm Marxism or Capitalism or Socialism or whether they hail from a country that is located south of the equator or north of it. Perpetual growth of resource consumption is mathematically impossible. Sooner or later the growth must stop; the only unknowns are when and under what terms.

I focus on the economy because this is where the most immediate impacts to our daily lives will surface, but the warning signs have been available for some time to those in the fields of mining, petroleum engineering, oceanology, ecology, farming, climatology, fishing, and every other specialty that taps into or studies the earth—our primary source of wealth. If you care about your future prosperity and access to wealth, then an initial focus on the economy is the right place to start.

More broadly, perhaps it's time to think of ourselves as one of many interconnected strands that together form a robust, but not indestructible, web of life, and not separate in some important way. The sound of snapping strands has been with us for a while, some more frightening than the rest:

- 40 percent decline in oceanic phytoplankton since 1950
- Birds, bees, and bats in serious population decline over the past few years
- Fisheries collapsing all over the globe

- Mercury levels in marine mammals so high that the EPA would treat their carcasses as toxic waste
- Sterilized soils and advancing deserts
- Species extinction rates that rival anything in the geologic records

And so on. The point here isn't to be alarmist over the fate of the planet and its species (there are plenty of more rigorous books in which that can be addressed), but merely to illustrate that signs abound, for anyone who cares to look, that the age of growth is drawing to a close. We're not closing it by ourselves on our own terms; nature is doing it for us, which is somewhat concerning because nature doesn't do bailouts.

When we turn our gaze to minerals and energy, we see the same sorts of warning signs:

- Oil discoveries peaked in 1964.
- New oil discoveries have been outpaced by oil consumption by nearly 4 to 1 each year.
- Known deposits of several critical minerals will be completely exhausted within 20 years, assuming the energy is there to extract them. Others will peak all on their own soon thereafter and even sooner if Peak Oil limits our ability to obtain them.
- New ore deposits are getting harder to find, more remote, deeper down, more dilute, and/or all of the above.

Again, we see more warning signs for food and water:

- World population will climb to 9.5 billion by 2050.
- Nearly all high-quality arable land is already under production.
- Food yields are heavily dependent on fertilizers, which are either energy intensive to make or are being depleted and will someday peak.
- Soils are being mined by the practice of removing essential nutrients without replacing them.

As we scan these lists, my hope is that reasonable and prudent people will arrive at the conclusion that our current economic approach to the world and trends in our use of resources are unsustainable, and that something should be done. Given the scope and enormity of the implied challenges and the speed with which they appear to be arriving, the sooner actions are taken, the better. Again, my purpose here is not to sow fear or breed depression; it's quite the opposite—to nudge you awake and prompt you toward individual and collective actions.

Your first challenge, then, is to accept the implications of the data that I've presented—that hard, physical limits aren't some vague condition of the far-off future; they are concrete and immediate concerns. The story that many take for granted is drawing to a close, and a new one is beginning. There may be some hard times along the way as we adjust. Perhaps not everyone will successfully make the transition. But I know deep down that we can live within our means and create any sort of a future that we desire—except, of course, one that looks exactly like the past 20 years.

It's time to close the book on growth and open a new chapter.

CHAPTER 25

FUTURE SCENARIOS

By now your head may be spinning. You've absorbed a lot of information in the prior pages. Perhaps you can feel the first edges of the three Es touching, but they haven't yet knit together in your thoughts. It has taken me years to deepen and hone my appreciation for this material. It's weighty, but it's also of utmost importance. *How do we take that next step and integrate this material into our thoughts, minds, and hearts so that we can take effective actions to change ourselves willingly, before outside factors force change upon us?*

One technique that I favor is the use of scenarios, which are detailed stories that help weave together the disparate pieces so that we can test the plausibility of the plot for ourselves and assess whether the material rings true. As you read through the following three scenarios, keep these major elements in mind:

- An exponentially based system of money and debt, designed to flourish under conditions of constant growth
- Energy sources—principally petroleum, but also, soon enough, coal— that will fail to deliver more net energy to the economy than in the past
- Critical resources from the environment (our primary sources of wealth) that are depleting, growing ever more dilute, becoming difficult to find and refine, and requiring more energy to obtain
- An already distressingly large global population that is expected to grow by nearly 50 percent between 2000 and 2050
- An agricultural system that already has nearly every useful acre under production, loses topsoil to the winds and the rivers each year faster than it can be made, mines the soils, is heavily dependent on fossil fuels, and sends critical nutrients on a one-way trip to the oceans where they are diluted beyond all recovery

SCENARIO 1: A SLOW TUMBLE

Framing: *In this scenario, nothing ever goes horribly wrong, but neither does anything ever quite work "right" again. What has worked in the past doesn't seem to work anymore, greatly puzzling the economic and financial authorities.*

It is October of 2014, and the U.S. and European economic leaders are meeting for the second time in six months for another summit on how to combat the persistent economic weakness that has stumped and embarrassed central bankers and politicians alike. Unemployment has remained stubbornly high—well over 10 percent in both economic arenas—and successive rounds of stimulus, both monetary and fiscal, have perplexingly failed to have any lasting impact on either employment or final demand.

Factions and rifts are starting to develop within and across the various political and ideological camps. Nerves are fraying. One school of thought, led by the U.S. central bank, believes that debt overhanging the markets is to blame, and wants to remove the debt by purchasing even more debt off the open markets. The theory is that with cash instead of debt, the financial centers will push the funds into the economy, which will then sputter back to life.

On the other side is a group that has grown weary of trying the same thing, but with increasingly bigger and bolder steps, without success. They quietly observe that the definition of insanity is trying the same thing over and over while expecting a different result each time. They also note with growing alarm that debt levels are now well past levels that have historically ever been paid back.

For their part, the markets, especially the bond markets, have become impatient and are showing signs of severe strain, with aggressive sell-offs and rallies beginning to resemble the violent lurching of a fast-moving car that has just lost its grip on a wet road. The whipsaws take out a couple of sizable hedge funds, creating new opportunities for the central banks to ride to the rescue and bail out the broken bets of the well-monied risk players. Public opinion of such bailouts is at an all-time low, so these interventions are now carried out in as much secrecy as possible.

The data the summit participants have before them is truly puzzling. Asia, especially China, is still enjoying economic growth, whereas the developed world is mired and sinking. Some point out that China isn't burdened with the same debt loads as the developed world, assuming, therefore, that this must be the root of the problem. Others note that China produces actual *things*, while the developed world has become overly dependent on financial *services* that produce wealth by virtue of their ability to shuffle paper back and forth, so perhaps the problem is fundamentally one of production. Still others note that a command economy like China's might have some advantages after all.

On day two of the meeting, an energy analyst responsible for one small piece of the data landscape quickly recounts her part to the assembled teams: Global oil production, while down from last year, is still sufficient to supply the markets, because the developed world is using less oil as it sorts through its economic troubles. China continues to import more coal and now accounts for 55 percent of world consumption of this resource, which, again, isn't an issue at present for the developed economies because their own demand is down. Because there are no major issues over energy supplies at present, the participants quickly turn their attention back to the pressing matter of jump-starting the economies of the developed world.

Ideas are bandied about, but finally, inevitably, the decision is made: They must be bolder than before—a true crisis calls for true leadership. It's time to double down on the amount of thin-air money that is printed up and distributed into the economy through a complicated variety of quantitative easing efforts and governmental fiscal stimulus.

The markets go wild—for a while. In nine months, the efforts wear off, the economy resumes shrinking, and yet China continues to consume more and more energy. The developed world remains stuck in an economic rut, puzzled as to why fiscal and monetary policy no longer seem to be working. They decide, boldly, that next time they'll have to pull much more aggressively on the fiscal and monetary levers than ever before, because the problem must certainly be one of insufficient quantity. They soon do this in marvelously coordinated fashion, with every media outlet faithfully repeating the prepared talking points, but once again, the results prove to be disappointing.

All are stumped, all are mystified; the tried-and-true theories have failed again. More money, more liquidity, more spending . . . but it has not worked this time as it has in the past. What could be the problem?

Unemployment continues to climb. Individual U.S. states are nearly fully insolvent, due to a combination of excessive pension promises that are now coming due and falling state revenues. Whole industries, especially in the discretionary sectors, fare especially poorly, even as basic goods and services manage to neither grow nor shrink. It's almost as if the simpler industries are somehow more robust than the complicated ones. Along the way, there are numerous false rallies and signs of economic life, which give hope but soon wither.

Finding the true bottom takes 15 long years. When the bottom finally arrives, the economies of the developed world have been reduced by anywhere from 20 percent to 50 percent, government budgets are finally reduced to bring them in line with the actual pace of economic activity, and the citizens of the developed world look back on this period as the Great Destruction. Stock markets in the developed world, which have been trading as if they were a single market for the past 10 years and sharing the ups and downs without any distinction between them, finally separate and begin trading somewhat independently, reflecting the prospects of each country more accurately. The most heavily indebted countries, those that lived most fully beyond their means for the longest, suffer the greatest corrections in their domestic stock markets.

Maddeningly, not every country participates in the despair, with some, particularly energy-rich Brazil and the commodity-exporting nations of Australia and Canada, performing significantly better in a relative sense, although Canada does have to expend considerable resources in tightening up its long border against economic refugees from the south, which drags down its overall performance.

Throughout the Great Destruction, uncertainty and fear continue to rule. *Will the financial system suffer a systemic collapse? Which governments will mindlessly print, and which will face the music? Where is the risk, and where are the safe harbors (if any)? How will $600 trillion in notional value derivatives be settled? Are capital controls about to be imposed by any country? Will war break out?* The rumors swirl, uncertainty builds, nerves fray, and fear settles like a thick mat of thorns across the land. Gold emerges as the best-performing asset during these times.

Throughout the entire period, oil remains firmly bid and even creeps up, as exploding demand from China and India more than consumes the surplus left by retreating demand in the West. The elevated price somewhat bolsters exploration and development activities, but liquidity and credit problems in the developed world prove to be like sand in the gearbox, preventing these activities from progressing to their full potential. Accordingly, oil supplies remain tighter than they otherwise might, and this proves sufficient to maintain a firm price floor on oil in particular and energy in general.

The basic pattern, so easy for some to see, eludes detection by the monetary authorities in the OECD central banks, whose training does not extend to fields of energy or basic science. Those countries with increasing flows of energy are doing well, while those with decreasing flows are struggling. It takes another decade for this idea to rise up high enough that it can find a seat at the polished mahogany table at the center of the 2024 meeting.

SCENARIO 2—PEAK OIL RECOGNITION AND A HARD LANDING

> **Framing:** *In this scenario, once again, market skeptics thoroughly underestimate the ability of the central banks to engineer yet another business cycle using a flood of liquidity. The new flood of freshly printed money works—for a while—but then runs headlong into the next energy crisis.*

While structural debt problems persist throughout 2010 and 2011, they prove to be less of a threat than initially feared. Quantitative easing by various central banks, along with government stimulus spending, apparently does the trick to stave off fiscal woes, and the developed economies lurch to life and eventually begin to trot.

Markets rebound, global trade picks up momentum, elections continue to reward incumbents, the FIRE sector (Finance, Insurance, Real Estate) returns to its former glory days by dominating corporate earnings with 40 percent of the entire take, and people everywhere breathe a sigh of relief. ("Whew! The emergency is over!") Everyone hurries back to business as usual.

Oil use ticks up by 1.6 million barrels of additional consumption in 2011 over 2010, taking the total to 87.6 million barrels per day, which is easily met by the oil producers. However, in 2012, the trend takes total consumption to 89.2 million barrels per day, requiring that new production records be set. Unfortunately, these new demands can't be met.

Production difficulties, notably in Mexico and Saudi Arabia, combine with rising domestic demand to squeeze exports. Despite official pronouncements that supply issues are only temporary, oil traders and other astute insiders seem troubled by the fact that, for a variety of reasons, less oil seems to be making it to market than in prior years. These glitches, although constantly spun by the U.S. Department of Energy as temporary, are sufficient to drive oil well beyond $147/barrel, the previous record.

A combination of rising internal demand in several key oil-exporting nations and the decision by some countries to export less of their oil (as they prefer to hold it in reserve for future generations) leads to a far more rapid drop-off in the total amount of oil available for purchase on the global markets than most analysts expected. Compounding the predicament, the lighter and sweeter grades of oil are preferentially withheld, forcing a glut of heavier and less desirable grades on the world market. Tuned for the sweeter grades, refineries are unable, and in many cases unwilling, to invest in the expensive retrofits required to process the heavier grades of oil, leading to the widest-ever spreads recorded between the prices for sweet versus sour grades.

Already on edge over the highly volatile and uncertain oil prices, the world is shocked when, in February 2012, the energy minister for Germany announces during an interview on the BBC that Peak Oil is real and that Germany has been quietly preparing for its eventual emergence on the world stage through a combination of efficiency measures, transportation strategies, and industrial realignments. Internal documents detailing German responses to Peak Oil surface from multiple branches of the German government, ranging from the military to the interior ministry. Peak Oil shifts from an eventual worry to a present reality seemingly overnight.

Within a few weeks, a number of countries announce that they are no longer exporting their oil and that they have nationalized the resource to preserve it for future generations. Chaos erupts in the oil markets. Oil prices shoot up to previously unimaginable heights. First $200 per barrel, then $300. People keep thinking, *It can't go any higher; it's not worth it* . . . but it turns out that oil is, indeed, "worth" a lot more than that. And so it goes higher, to $300 and then $400, in fits and starts, sometimes gaining or losing as much as $10 a barrel in a single tick of the trading tape. Volatility reigns.

Fuel rationing quickly occurs in the most dependent of importing countries, including the United States, Japan, and much of Europe. Fuel triage plans already in place[1] call for the military, food suppliers, and emergency services to get first dibs; mass transit is next in line. Hapless automobile commuters find themselves second-from-dead-last on the priority list, just barely edging out recreational users. Unable to get to work on their individual fuel allotment, many turn to carpooling, while others, especially in the United States, discover just how little spare capacity exists in the mass transit system. Embarrassed city and regional planners and administrations promise rapid enhancements to the mass transit system and are shocked when the bus and train car suppliers inform them of already-existing multi-year waiting lists.

The worst impacts result from fuel shortages wreaking havoc on finely tuned just-in-time delivery systems for all sorts of industries and sectors. Spot shortages erupt in numerous supply chains, leading to a variety of unpredictable delays in an enormously wide range of services and products. Grape growers in Chile find themselves with mountains of unsellable product, computer manufacturers can only run their assembly lines for brief periods when key components finally show up, airlines cancel flights headed to airports that cannot guarantee fuel service on a plane-by-plane basis. Systems that were highly cost-effective are suddenly exposed to be lacking the necessary inventory buffers to smooth over initial glitches in product supplies. Faced with shortages, companies in nearly every industry attempt to build their individual inventories to create a buffer for their operations, but discover massive shortages everywhere they turn. The highly cost-effective lean-inventory practices of the 1990s and 2000s turn out to be enormously brittle constructs, unable to meet even minor surges in demand with any sort of grace, let alone the massive surge in inventory demand now being felt.

The world has never before faced such a profound shock to its critical infrastructure. Economic growth is no longer possible, at least not in the old style, and it slowly dawns on the capital markets that growth might never be coming back. The entire future has to be repriced, leading to massive losses in the stock indexes and in long-dated bond funds as growth premiums are stripped out of their valuations. In response to concerns that whole portions of the debt markets might enter default, interest rates shoot up, crushing the economic recovery and leading to an immediate debt spiral that results in a fiscal crisis of unimaginable proportions in the United States, Japan, and other oil-dependent, developed economies that entered this period bearing massive official debt structures.

Perversely, many so-called undeveloped economies fare far better, as they are already less dependent on oil for their day-to-day functioning and have lower debt loads. Having experienced development late in the global game, they benefit from the twin advantages of modern systems built primarily around the latest, most fuel-efficient technologies and a populace with low expectations for energy usage, resulting in a far lower per-capita energy dependency.

To deal with the sudden needs of a collapsing fiscal situation that results from mounting interest-rate costs, along with the need for more and more export dollars to compete for what oil remained on the world spot markets, the United States and Japan resort to even more outright printing of money beginning in 2013. The Fed's balance sheet swells with new acquisitions, while Europe, still fearing the inflationary demons of its past, remains far more restrained in this regard. Europe's per-capita energy-use profile, measuring just half that of the United States at the start of this crisis, proves to be an enormous advantage.

Japan fares even worse. Importing 99 percent of its petroleum needs, saddled with more official debt than any other nation, and strained by severe demographic realities, two decades of profligate yen printing boomerang with a vengeance. The persistent efforts by Japanese authorities to debase their currency suddenly and unexpectedly bear fruit that rots before it can be savored. The yen plummets, as no one has any use for hundreds of trillions of yen from an export-dependent island nation that now lacks the fuel needed to manufacture and export a surplus of products. Japan's internal production and consumption collapse alongside the yen. Many there look wistfully back on "the lost decade," recalling better times.

Throughout 2012 and 2013, gold soars as systemic financial instability strikes fear into the hearts of investors and wealthy individuals. Various sovereign nations attempt to print their way out of their economic difficulties. Faith in all things paper is lost to varying degrees; nobody knows where the risks lie, which claims will be honored, or what to do. The U.S. markets, long thought to be the deepest and most trustworthy in the world, suffer a mortal blow: A number of legitimate trades that were dangerous to the financial health of a major, well-connected bank were unilaterally reversed by the stock exchanges with the blessing of the SEC, to the benefit of the bank but the detriment of all the parties on the other side of the trade. While an expedient move at the time, the long-term damage is 100 times larger; capital begins to flee U.S. borders, necessitating capital controls from which the U.S. financial markets never truly recover.

In 2014, interest rates are finally hiked in efforts to defend the dollar, but it is too little, too late. What follows next in 2015 shocks the world to its financial core: Faith in the U.S. dollar, having dwindled to the point that it is no longer revered as a store of wealth, loses its reserve currency status[2] in March of that year. The U.S. government is suddenly forced to issue new debt denominated in a basket of currencies that doesn't include the dollar, consisting instead of the Chinese renminbi; Brazilian real; euro; and Canadian, New Zealand, and Australian dollars. Forced to denominate its debts in foreign currencies, the United States must reduce its trade deficit to zero almost immediately. U.S. citizens rapidly discover the dramatic difference between living above your means and living within your means. Domestic production must now exceed domestic consumption—an enormous swing in the fortunes of a people long accustomed to the opposite arrangement.

U.S. federal and state government budgets are finally slashed, leading to profound but necessary economic pain. Other world governments follow suit. At the first signs of this shift toward financial prudence, some investors who previously invested in gold begin transitioning away from the yellow metal and back into productive enterprises, which now stand a chance of flourishing under a more solid and sound monetary system. These investors are among the fortunate few who managed to preserve a relatively large portion of their wealth during the turbulent years of Oil Shock III. The keyword is "relatively," as no one is better off than before; everyone has taken a hit, but some just took more of a hit than others.

In the postanalysis, it is revealed that many members of the U.S. government had been tempted to wage a war to try and salvage the situation. Several plans were developed whereby the United States would secure much of the Middle East's and Venezuela's oil production and then protect the transport of that oil to U.S. soil. Some even mention Canada as a preferred target, noting its proximity, rich resources, and weak military.

However, in every war game attempted by the staff at West Point, no way is ever found to both secure the oil resources at their source and protect them during extended shipments across the sea. The resources just don't exist. In every war scenario, it proves nearly impossible to defend the required number of ship convoys from attackers equipped with modern missile technology. No simulations are ever successful for more than a few months, and the ideas are dropped, despite a number of vigorous proponents.

In the end, the reality of Peak Oil takes the world by storm, although the evidence has been in plain sight for decades. There's nothing left to do but rapidly realign expectations, ideas, and hopes around this new reality. Some places, just like some people, manage this transition more gracefully than others. Large fortunes are made and even more massive ones are lost; the past becomes like a fairytale to many who continue wonder how such abundant wealth could ever have existed at all. In the future, stories of roads so packed with cars that they couldn't move are told to wide-eyed children who wonder to what extent their grandparents are exaggerating the truth.

As usual, the solutions adopted in the aftermath of this crisis are those that happened to be most convenient, and much of the world reverts to "backed" money of some form or another. In the case of oil producers, the backing is oil. For others, it's gold. A few smaller, more culturally coherent countries are able to use unbacked fiat currencies effectively, but only because strict and inviolable legal constructs are deployed to remove human weaknesses from the management of these currencies.

The changes are so profound that humanity divides itself into two new eras: BO and AO. *Before Oil* and *After Oil*.

Through all of this, as oil zooms to formerly unimaginable heights, old lessons about energy are relearned. The folly of poorly insulated houses built to face streets, instead of south, is rather painfully revealed, as is the practice of developing exurbs far from food, work, play, and even water.

House prices follow new rules, where proximity and energy efficiency replace "grand entryway" and "granite countertops" as the coveted, desirable, must-have features. Houses with active and passive solar designs command premiums as monthly energy bills are prominently factored into the cash-flow streams of buyers alongside principal, interest, taxes, and insurance. The resulting acronym changes the popular pronunciation for this stream of payments from "pity" (PITI) to "piety" (PIETI).

The Midwest of the United States, long an importer of diesel and a nearly complete exporter of ethanol, rapidly increases its local use of ethanol, creating a regional energy advantage rivaling that enjoyed by the Gulf Coast and Alaska. Not surprisingly, the regions with controllable access to energy fare far better economically than other regions, but those with both food and fuel do the best of all.

Localities everywhere discover the importance of having local control over as many of the key staples of life as possible. Land-use zoning laws are rapidly amended to protect local land suitable for crops. Eminent domain is utilized to support the rapid reintroduction of certain parcels back into local production.

As with any economic shock that creates shortages, this energy shock changes perceptions and behaviors profoundly. When the dust finally settles, it's clear that the old economy has shattered, a consumer culture has been replaced by a culture of thrift, and a new set of values with careful stewardship at their core has emerged.

SCENARIO 3: THE UNDULATING PLATEAU

Framing: *One reasonable prediction of how the economy and oil prices might respond to Peak Oil can be described as an "undulating plateau." Under this scenario, oil prices and economic activity run counter to each other, creating a jagged see-saw pattern over time.*

After wallowing about in the early part of the twenty-teens, the world economy finally responds to money printing and takes off. It moves grudgingly at first, but then faster and faster, as the global economy feeds off low oil prices, which cratered during the prior period of economic weakness. Naturally this economic resurgence causes oil demand to spike, but supplies of oil are somewhat pinched due to several years of underinvestment in field discovery and maintenance. The shortages, while not overly severe, serve to cause relatively large jumps in the price of oil, which

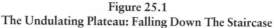

Figure 25.1
The Undulating Plateau: Falling Down The Staircase

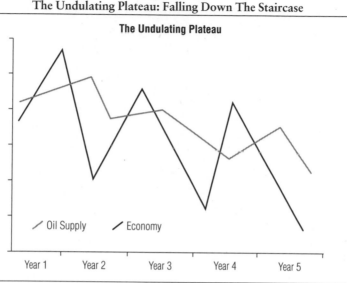

Image: Jeanine Dargis

unfortunately puts a crimp in the economic recovery. The "undulating plateau" goes through its first complete cycle.

Falling economic activity once again leads to a decline in the price of oil, which in turn sparks another economic recovery a bit later on. On this next leg up, the economy, again benefitting from reduced oil prices, dusts itself off and gets going again. However, this time the world has slightly less total oil production capacity than before, due to the combined effects of depletion in existing fields and a lack of investment in new and existing oil fields. Because there's slightly less oil in each succeeding leg of the cycle, the economy can neither attain nor exceed its prior heights, as the energy simply isn't there. This dynamic is represented in Figure 25.1, where we see that the economy rebounds to a lower and lower height on each leg of the cycle as it cycles back and forth across slowly declining oil supplies.

But even as economic activity slowly trips down a stairwell, oil prices are doing the exact opposite, as seen in Figure 25.2. Oil prices make a series of "higher highs" on each leg of the cycle (as well as "higher lows"). The swings in the price of oil also grow larger and more volatile as time progresses, further inhibiting additional investment by oil companies, which cannot trust their ability to model and manage cash flows

Figure 25.2
Oil Prices During the Undulating Plateau: Rising to the Sky

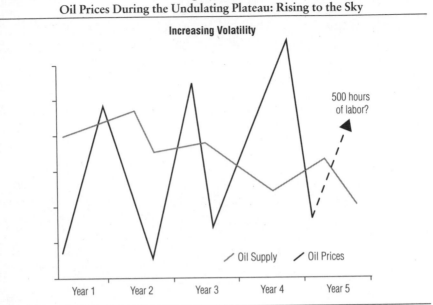

Image: Jeanine Dargis

against investment returns. The safest bet is to hoard cash, hoping for smoother sailing in the future. The ultimate price for oil is far higher than most people can imagine, but its intrinsic value—350 to 500 hours of human labor per gallon—ultimately supports these much higher prices. The most magical of natural resources is no longer taken for granted.

At every turn of the cycle on the undulating plateau, social and economic complexity shrinks. Adjustments are made to the new reality of less energy, which for many brings an unpleasant and unwelcome period of transition. Thousands of job classifications, mainly service-oriented and not directly connected to the production of secondary wealth, are no longer relevant and disappear. Patterns of living re-form around the new reality of less energy and a greatly simplified economy. People find ways to live closer to work and food, adjust to having less mobility than in the past, and retrain or "reskill" themselves in order to find income-producing work.

The good news is that the undulating plateau offers people and nations the luxury of time to mentally, emotionally, physically, and financially adapt to the unavoidable new reality. No major financial disasters or wars break out, allowing critical resources to be marshaled and appropriately directed.

PREPARE TO BE SURPRISED

The biggest surprise to me would be if the future actually resembled any of the scenarios I just described. I'm both prepared and expecting to be surprised. The basic rule about complex systems is that they're inherently unpredictable, at least with respect to the precise details of exactly what, when, and how much will transpire.

However, the larger model, in which a complex system will become simpler if starved for energy, is a known quantity. Imagine that our economy is a snow globe. As long as it continues to be shaken vigorously, the flakes will remain in a suspended state of complexity. Cease the input of energy (the shaking), and the flakes will settle and assume a much less complex state of existence, no longer bumping into hundreds of their neighbors in interesting and unique configurations. We may not be able to predict exactly how, where, and when all the flakes will settle, but we know that they will.

I'm not at all sure how a massive, complex global economy predicated on exponential growth will change when net energy declines. But here are my best guesses:

1. Tertiary wealth in all of its many forms, but especially those whose major value derives from the assumption of future growth, will decline in value and prominence. Said simply, we face decades of sub-par (at best) to catastrophic (at worst) returns in stocks and bonds. Pensions and 401(k)s will fail to deliver the future that many have been counting on. Paper wealth will lose value to the degree that it bore unrealistic assumptions about growth at its core, as well as the degree to which it is overcreated by governments and central banks during the transitionary period.

2. The recent great trends in manufacturing and globalization will reverse; the pendulum will swing the other way. Economies that had previously shifted to become 80 percent service-oriented will need to shift back to being more manufacturing- and production-oriented. Where products were shipped and reshipped in various states of assembly to the lowest-cost production centers regardless of their global location, supply chains will have to be significantly shortened and production relocalized.

3. The proportion of personal income devoted to food and energy, which reached all-time lows in the late 2000s, will steadily increase. This will leave correspondingly less income for other discretionary expenditures.

4. Monetary magic—the application of stimulus and thin-air money—will be tried and tried again, but in the absence of increases in net energy, it will fail to work as intended. The more these responses are attempted, the higher the likelihood of a destructive collapse in the currency or currencies involved. The United States is especially at risk, given that trillions of its dollars are housed offshore, which means that they could be redeemed at any time on the whim of their holders.

5. The U.S. government has a future date with a fiscal crisis and will have to trim its expenditures (possibly by as much as 50 percent) and increase taxes enormously (by perhaps 100 percent) to deal with the fact that it is fundamentally insolvent. The chance of this fiscal crisis morphing into a currency crisis is exceedingly high. Retirement dreams will have to be deferred by tens of millions, if not abandoned.

6. Similar difficulties to the United States will be faced by other overly indebted countries facing their own entitlement difficulties, including Japan, Greece, Ireland, Spain, the United Kingdom, and France.

You'll note that the scenarios I put forth are relatively benign: I propose no wars, no social unrest, no political upheavals, or anything else of that stressful nature. However, historically, the number one cause of wars has been resource conflicts. Given that we're about to enter one of the most significant resource shortages in the history of a world that is more well-armed than ever before, it will take a rare combination of events and diplomacy to avoid heading to war over the remaining resources.

I maintain hope that we can avoid such an outcome, but this hope rests upon enough people, especially those in power, understanding the actual source of our predicament, choosing prosperity over growth, and using our remaining surplus to build rather than destroy.

STAY ALERT

Because we can only glimpse the broad outlines of what is likely to happen, not the details or the timing, it's important to remain alert. I like to think of myself as being an "information scout" for my clients, and I'm constantly sifting through every facet of information that develops in politics, geopolitics, and, of course, any of the three Es. It's all potentially important. I wish I could extract a few thousand words of simple advice that would work for every person and any company, but this is neither possible nor feasible.

The broad outlines are easy enough:

- Invest defensively.
- Build resilience into your physical systems and financial dealings.
- Favor liquidity and safety over the potential for higher returns.
- Mentally prepare yourself for a very different future.
- Practice doing more with less.

But the details are endless and specific.

The information in this book has hopefully prompted you to consider that there's some value in becoming better prepared, whatever "prepared" means in your individual context. At my web site (www.ChrisMartenson .com), you will find a free "What Should I Do?" series that will walk you through the basic steps. After you've taken some initial steps, you might wish to join the rich and vibrant community of intelligent people who have assembled there, each of whom is working through the specifics of responding in their own ways. I've created a place for people to connect around these ideas that is safe, inviting, mature, and rational. In other words, it's a rare place where one can have a civil, thoughtful discussion about these topics on the Internet.

In the next few chapters, you will find more answers to the question of what you should do. And I hope you will consider joining us online at www.ChrisMartenson.com to explore these issues further.

PART VII
WHAT SHOULD I DO?

CHAPTER 26

THE GOOD NEWS

We Already Have Everything We Need

As daunting as the challenges and predicaments outlined in this book may seem, the good news is that we already have everything we need to create a better future. All of the understanding, resources, technology, ideas, systems, institutions, and thinking are already available, invented, or in place, ready to be deployed in service of a better future; we just need to decide to make use of them. By simply reorienting our priorities, we can simultaneously buy ourselves time and assure that we choose prosperity over growth.

Fundamentally, this book and my work are about exposing the choices and options we have. As dire as things may seem, the future has not yet happened. Hope remains that we can respond intelligently to the current predicaments, and even create something better for ourselves along the way.

Yet it's also true that the stadium is rapidly filling with water and our choices matter very much from here on out. There's a lot less room for error than there was a few decades back, when we had plenty of time to make mistakes and fumble around with our handcuffs. But now that the water is swirling up the bleacher stairs, our choices take on new urgency and matter a great deal. There's no time to waste making wrong choices anymore. History is sitting up straight with pencil poised over notebook, carefully watching to see what we do next and determine how our efforts should be remembered.

TECHNOLOGY

We don't need to develop any new technologies, although it will be nice when they come along. We already know how to build highly efficient

machines and dwellings that use tiny fractions of the energy of those currently in use. We can live extremely comfortable lives using much less
energy than we currently consume by making a few small changes in our
technology choices and daily routines. By doing so, we will preserve some
energy for the future, which will allow us the gift of time. There's nothing
to prevent us from making such a change, except possibly a lack of a coherent vision from our leadership that this is an important thing to do.

It will be fantastic when higher-capacity batteries are developed, but we
don't need them in order to immediately begin using existing technology to
consume less electricity. For example, electricity is still consumed to heat
water for home and commercial use, yet solar hot water panels are a proven, decades-old technology that works and is economically sound even at
current energy prices. Despite this, such panels are relatively rare in some
countries, the United States included. Using fossil fuels to heat water when
the sun can do it efficiently and reliably is a mistake, especially when simple
technology already exists that can be installed quickly and which will save
money and energy over time. Eventually we will collectively come to that
conclusion, but why wait? What is stopping us from making the installation
of solar hot water panels a top priority and beginning immediately? The
limitations that do exist have nothing to do with technology; they are social
and political in nature.

For example, we still beam an enormous amount of electricity into outer
space in the form of stray photons from the area lights that we use in every
city and along major roadways. These could (and should) be replaced with
LED technology that uses a fraction of the electricity of halide and halogen
lamps. Nothing prevents us from doing this today, other than inertia and a
lack of urgency that it needs to be done.

We already know how to build houses that face the sun and use almost
no energy, we know how to build smaller and more fuel-efficient vehicles,
we know how to live, work, and play near where we live, and we have all
the technology we need to live far more sustainably than we currently do.
So what is holding us back? I submit that there's nothing rational or logical
or even economically sensible about our lack of action on these matters; the
cause lies elsewhere.

FOOD

We know that healthy soils produce more and better food than ruined,
nearly biologically sterilized dirt. Reason tells us that flushing vital and irreplaceable nutrients into the sea isn't a good idea. Eventually we're going to

have to find some way of recycling nutrients back to the farms on which our food grows. We understand how to optimize yields for a given area based on the types of soils and the rainfall that exists there. We already know that growing some crops in arid regions is an energetic and biological mistake.

We don't need any more studies, additional insights, or new books to be written. We already know all of these things, and many more besides. We don't need a deeper understanding of what we need to do—we already have the necessary understanding. What we do need is the desire to make such changes a priority and to choose the sustainable path.

Food needs to be grown and consumed locally, and strategies for recycling the nutrients back to the farms need to be implemented. You can help start this process by demanding local foods, which is easy—just start buying them. By supporting local farmers, you help to secure the food that you and your community need in both the short term and the long term. Even better, start growing your own food in a garden, a window box, or even just a pot on the porch. Solutions to the issue of food, though daunting in scale, are easy to conceptualize and are already underway to some extent in virtually every community.

ENERGY

The prescription here is simple: *We need to be as careful and conservative in our use of energy as we can possibly be.* This means s*top wasting energy.* Not stop *using* energy; stop *wasting* it. That is a good first step. Given that fossil fuels are a "one and done" arrangement, sliding as they do down the frictionless entropy slide on their way to becoming lazy heat, we need to develop and nurture a brand-new appreciation for just how valuable energy really is. We really ought to see our fossil energy sources as the one-time, irreplaceable master resources that they are.

Currently, fossil energy sources are "valued" by an abstraction called money, which does an incredibly good job of masking their true worth by concealing the fact that they are limited and depleting. The idea that gasoline, a nonrenewable resource, is only considered to be "worth" a few dollars a gallon, when it capably performs the same amount of work as a human laboring for hundreds of hours, is just silly. Clearly it is worth more to us than its price would indicate. It should be valued more highly, and if it were, I'm confident that it would be used more wisely. If we want to preserve the order and complexity of our economy, and, by extension, of our society, then we need to begin by better appreciating the role of energy in delivering and maintaining both order and complexity.

It is this connection between the economy and energy that's entirely missing from the current practice of mainstream economics. It's almost as if the
current practitioners of economic theory (with relatively few exceptions)[1]
are entirely unaware that the economy would have no form, no function,
and no "life" without energy. This intellectual disconnect explains why
we're so deeply mired in the predicaments in which we find ourselves, and it
explains why I view the risks to our future so seriously.

As Max Planck, the famous physicist, once said, "A new scientific truth
does not triumph by convincing its opponents and making them see the
light, but rather because its opponents eventually die, and a new generation
grows up that is familiar with it."[2] In other words, science advances one
funeral at a time. Historically, new ideas do tend to run into stiff opposition
from the establishment. There are too many economists and other people
in positions of power who seem to have no idea of the connections between
the economy, energy, and the environment. When reality finally convinces
enough of them that it needs to be taken seriously, in what sort of a world
will we be living?

Luckily, we don't have to wait for economists to arrive at the truth
before we begin to act more rationally and use our fossil fuels as if they
were an extremely valuable, nonrenewable, one-time inheritance.

ECONOMY AND MONEY

We can already tell that our debt-based, backed-by-nothing fiat currency is
performing badly, and as its resource props are pulled away, it's likely to
perform even more poorly in the future and eventually wobble and fall.
To counter this, we will need new forms of money, possibly several, that
can operate tolerably well in a world without growth, along with people to
manage them. Fortunately, several new forms of money already exist,
including mutual credit arrangements (such as LET systems),[3] demurrage
money,[4] and various forms of money that are backed by something tangible. If we were to put more of these kinds of currency into play alongside
our current form of money, then we would have a more resilient ecosystem
of money, where if one form gets into difficulty of some sort, there
are others waiting to pick up the slack. If a single currency is like a concrete
channel designed to carry the maximum amount of water, multiple currencies are like wetlands designed to maximize the buffering of the water levels
in times of both drought and flood.

The very first step, however, needs to begin with the idea that you cannot
possibly borrow more than you earn forever. The implication of this is that

the U.S. government will need to cut spending to bring it in line with the actual economic realities that will result from "too much debt" and a looming resource predicament. The entire U.S. society needs to "deleverage"—a fancy word for "cut debt"—and begin to live more carefully within its true earning potential. We already know this; there are dozens of well-constructed models, books, and research papers showing that current spending is unsustainable. But it bears reminding—and begs for action.

POPULATION

We cannot beat around the bush on this "third-rail" topic any longer: We need to stabilize world population at a level that can be sustained. If we don't, then nature will do it for us, and not pleasantly, either. This means stabilizing world population in perpetuity, not only for a little while longer. We may not know what this stable level is just yet, and more study is certainly needed, especially in light of declining energy resources. But we should do everything we can to avoid badly overshooting the number of humans that can be sustainably supported on our planet while carelessly avoiding an examination of the role of petroleum in supporting those populations.

According to the work of professor William Rees, humans are operating well past the Earth's sustainable carrying capacity, which is a function of two things: the number of humans on the earth and their standards of living.[5] According to this work, every organism has an ecological footprint, and humans now require the equivalent of 1.4 Earths to sustain themselves. There are only two ways to solve this problem: reduce the number of people or lower living standards. If those are our options, would we prefer to have fewer people in the world enjoying elevated standards of living, or more people in the world with reduced standards of living? In other words, would we prefer prosperity or growth? Saying "both" is the same thing as saying "growth," because in the battle between growth and prosperity, growth always wins.

KICKING AND SCREAMING

What we need more than anything is to reshape the stories that we tell ourselves. Right now the "growth is essential" story is firmly lodged in our national and global narratives, and so that's what we get—policies and actions that chase growth. If instead we shared a story that placed "long-term prosperity" as our highest goal, then we would hopefully get different actions and results.

But waiting for politicians to arrive at this new story on their own isn't a compelling strategy. As we look back across the long sweep of history and note when the status quo was challenged and changed, we would find that such change was never intended by those in the center to radiate outward. Every single social gain of note—labor rights, civil rights, women's rights, the environmental movement, or any other that you care to think of—began on the periphery of society and was brought, kicking and screaming, to the center.

If it seems as though I'm suggesting that a social movement is needed, it's because I am. The story that I have told in this book needs to be spread far and wide. Others need to tell it in their own way, because we will need many teachers to get the message into every corner and down every side street. We need a tipping point of awareness about the true nature of the predicaments we face.

We each need to be responsible for helping to change the story so that we can have a better future. The alternatives are unacceptable.

THE GOOD NEWS . . .

Again, we don't need anything that we don't already have in order to turn this story around. We know what the issues are, and we know what we have to do. Now we need to make those things a priority.

Eventually we will do so, but with every passing day, our energy surplus shrinks, our other resources deplete, debts continue to climb, our environmental predicaments grow larger, world population continues to swell, and our range of potential reactions become fewer and ever more expensive. Our choice is to decide whether we wish to continue ahead with our foot on the gas pedal and risk hitting the wall at top speed, or give ourselves a sporting chance by applying the brakes now.

What we need is for our leadership to make profound, course-altering decisions, and we should put some effort into ensuring that this happens. But at the same time, it's realistic to recognize that significant changes may not be made in time to prevent some serious disruptions. So call this "good news with an asterisk." Yes, we have everything we need to begin making the right choices, but as a collective whole, it seems quite likely that we won't choose enough of them in time to prevent disruptions from occurring. Read on for more about personal preparation and what you can personally do to make a difference.

CHAPTER 27

What Should I Do?

By now your head may be spinning as you think through the implications of the information contained in this book. The good news is that we can make different and better choices to buy ourselves more time and secure a better future. The bad news is that we probably won't do everything or even most of what is needed at the national or global levels in time to prevent at least a few serious disruptions from occurring.

This possibility leaves you and your community in the position of having to undertake whatever sorts of modifications and preparations you deem appropriate. I've personally undertaken preparations that some might consider extensive and others would feel are wholly insufficient. We each must assess for ourselves what seems prudent and feels right, but we all should be doing *something*, no matter how trivial or insufficient it may seem.

Time to Get a Little Insurance

The purpose of this chapter is to nudge you toward gaining greater control of your future by becoming more resilient and better prepared. If it helps, think of these steps as insurance that you hope you never have to collect on. As a prudent adult, you probably have fire insurance on your house, maybe you have collision insurance on your car, and perhaps you have life insurance on yourself and your spouse because you know life is risky and you want to mitigate what risks you can. The same process applies here.

My philosophy on preparing is simple: *Get started*. Begin by doing whatever is easiest and fastest as a means of taking that first step. It doesn't so much matter what your initial actions are, as long as they demonstrate an alignment between your life and the idea that major changes are on the way. Getting started is the key. Relief from worry is the immediate goal. I should note here that everything I recommend next represents things that I have personally done. I do what I say and I say what I do.

To me, becoming prepared is the act of a selfless, prudent adult seeking to control risk in his or her life, not the act of an antisocial loner or anxious doomer. There are no right or wrong answers or actions, since none of us know precisely what will unfold or when. Instead, we must prepare as if for a trip across open water—right now it seems calm enough, but you never know. Once the waters turn rough, you'll only be able to make use of whatever preparations and training you happen to have brought along—no more and no less.

Becoming Resilient

The point of personal (and community) preparedness can be summed up in a single word: *Resilience*.

We're more resilient when we have multiple sources and systems to supply a needed item, rather than being dependent on a single source. We're more resilient when we have a strong local community with deep connections. We're more resilient when we are in control of how our needs are met and when we can do things for ourselves.

We're more resilient if we can source water from three locations—perhaps from an existing well, a shallow well, and rainwater basins—instead of just one. If we throw in a quality water filter (essential for the rainwater anyway), then just about any source of water becomes potentially drinkable.

We're more resilient if we can grow a little bit more of our own food, rather than rely on a single grocery store. Our community gains food resilience when we demand local food, perhaps by shopping at a farmers market or purchasing a farm produce subscription (also known as "community supported agriculture" or CSA), thereby increasing the number of local farms and food sources.

We're more resilient when our home can be heated by multiple sources and systems, perhaps wood and solar to complement oil or gas.

For me and my family, resilience now stretches well beyond the four walls of our physical home and deep into our local networks and community. But it began with focusing our initial efforts within our household.

Resilience has become the lens through which we filter all of our decisions. It's a great simplifying tool. *Should we buy this, or that, or nothing?* Well, which action will make us more resilient? *Should we invest in developing this new skill?* Well, how will that help us, or our community, become more resilient? *Should we plant these trees or those?* Well, which ones will add the most to the natural diversity and abundance around us so that our environment will be more resilient?

It's really that simple. Instead of finding ourselves overwhelmed by all the things we could or should be doing, we find our lives to be simpler and easier when we increase our resilience.

> *The first concept of becoming prepared is resilience.*

INSUFFICIENT, BUT NECESSARY

We must become the change we wish to see. If we just sit back and wait for a world where people are living with a reduced footprint and in balance with our economic and natural budgets, we will wait forever, and that world will never come. It's up to each of us to inspire others by first inspiring ourselves. The good news is that you are not and never will be alone on this journey.

But let's be perfectly honest: No matter how grand the steps we might take to prepare for a potential environmental, social, or economic disruption, they are almost certain to be insufficient. Yet at the same time, they're still necessary.

They'll be insufficient because being perfectly and completely prepared is infinitely expensive. Even trying to maintain a specific standard of living may become too costly to bear. But actions are still necessary, even if they're inherently insufficient, because they help us align what we do with what we know.

In my experience, when gaps exist between what you know to be true and your actions, anxiety (if not fear) is the result. So while the state of the world may contribute to your sense of anxiety, it's a lack of action that lets it fester.

So we take actions because we must. If we don't, who will? We change the world by changing ourselves. We reduce stress, fear, and anxiety in our lives by aligning our thoughts and our actions, being realistic about what we can preserve, and setting our goals and plans accordingly.

> *The second concept of preparation is that actions are both necessary and insufficient.*

SET TARGETS

When considering preparation, the first question is usually, *How much?* Here I recommend setting a realistic goal, given the amount of money and time you have to devote.

My family's goal has never been to be 100 percent self-sufficient in meeting *any* of our basic needs. Instead, our goal has been to increase our self-sufficiency to something—*anything* —greater than "none." For example, until we got our solar photovoltaic panels, we were 100 percent dependent on the utility grid for our electricity. Now we're just a tiny bit less dependent, perhaps 97 percent, but we can manufacture and deploy our own electricity if necessary, and that's no small feat.

How big is the difference between being zero percent self-reliant and 3 percent? It's huge. With our 3 percent, we can charge batteries, have light at night and, most important, prevent our fully stocked freezer from thawing during a power outage. We have some control over our electricity, the most critical energy source of them all to our daily lives.

Similarly, there's an enormous difference between being zero percent and 10 percent self-sufficient for food production. At zero percent self-sufficiency, you rely entirely on the existing food distribution system. At something over zero percent, you may grow a garden, foster local relationships with farmers, plant fruit trees in the yard, keep a few chickens, and/or maintain a deep pantry, which means you can always meet some of your own food needs. Developing even a limited percentage of your own food sufficiency doesn't take a lot of money, and it requires just a little bit of time. And it allows you and your family to develop skills and connections that will very likely make a huge difference at some point.

So why not set a realistic target that makes sense for you and your family, and then find a way to get there?

> *The third concept of preparation is to set realistic goals.*

BEING IN SERVICE

Reducing my own anxiety was reason enough to prepare, but an equally important objective was to be in a position to serve my community should that need arise in the future. Were a crisis to occur, I would fully expect to find many unprepared people scrambling around in a desperate bid to meet their needs, somewhat paralyzed by the situation and unable to react effectively. I feel it is my duty to reduce (not add to) the confusion and unmet needs and help out as many others as I can.

Some think of personal preparation as a selfish act, perhaps involving such things as guns and bunkers, but that's not at all what this is about; in fact, it is the opposite. My experience in life tells me that being a good community member means putting your own house in order first. If you do, you'll have a stable foundation to utilize, and you'll be in a better position to add valuable resources and skills to community efforts. A strong community begins with strong households. It's like a fractal pattern; the whole is reflected in the parts. A strong community cannot be fashioned from weak households.

My expectation is that communities will rally in the face of a disruption, an act that I have witnessed several times during hurricanes in North Carolina. But some communities will fare better than others, and the difference between them will be determined by the personal resilience of their respective citizen populations. Your challenge here is to first get your own house in order, and then work on ways that you can help to increase the resilience of your local community and personal networks.

You must be the change you wish to see. If it is your wish to live in a resilient community, you must become more resilient yourself. In order to best assist your seatmate, you must put on your oxygen mask first.

> *The fourth concept of preparation is that your community needs you to get yourself prepared.*

STEP ZERO

Many people, when daunted by the potential magnitude of the coming change, immediately jump to some very hard conclusions that prove to be incapacitating. For example, they may have thoughts such as, *I need to go back to school to get an entirely different degree so that I can have a different job!* or *I need to completely relocate to a new area and start over, leaving all of my friends behind!* or *I need to abandon my comfortable home and move to a remote off-grid cabin!* These anxious conclusions may feel so radical that they're quickly abandoned as unfeasible. As a result, nothing gets accomplished. Further, nearly everyone has hidden barriers to action lurking within.

My advice here is crisp and clear: *Find the smallest and easiest thing you can do, and then do it.* It doesn't matter what that first step is. If that thing for you is buying an extra jar of pimentos because you can't imagine life without them, then buy an extra jar next time you're out shopping and put them in the pantry. I'm only halfway joking. I call this "Step Zero" to symbolize something minor that might precede step one. The point is that small steps lead to bigger steps. If you've not yet taken Step One toward personal preparation and resilience, I invite you to consider taking Step Zero first.

Other Step Zero examples might be taking out a small bit of extra cash to store outside of the bank in case of a banking disruption, buying a bit more food each week to slowly deepen your pantry, or going online to learn something more about ways you can increase your resilience around water, food, energy, or anything else you deem important to your future. It doesn't much matter what it is, as long as you take an action that has meaning to you.

The goal of Step Zero is to break the ice now and get things rolling. My motto is, *I'd rather be a year early than a day late.*

> The fifth concept of preparation is to start with small steps.

THE IMPORTANCE OF COMMUNITY

Of all the steps that I've taken, building my community has developed the most important element of my resilience. Whatever the future holds, I'd rather face it surrounded by the people I respect, admire, and love in my local community, people whom I trust and know I can count on. That's my measure of true wealth.

In my case, I joined up with a number of other individuals who were interested in actively preparing for the future. Over the course of a year, we met as a group and went through each and every component of a self-assessment that we designed, covering nine basic areas of our lives. (You can find a free version of this self-assessment on my web site at www .ChrisMartenson.com/self-assessment.) We took a good, hard look at our then-current situations, made plans for preparation and change, and held each other accountable for following through with our plans. The support we shared was, and still is, invaluable.

The rest of my family has become deeply hooked into a wider community of people who are actively engaged in nature awareness, permaculture, native skills, fruit collection, and other pastimes that feel recreational but also offer deeper and more resilient connections to people and nature.

I would recommend working with people you trust or with whom you already share basic values. The closer they live to you geographically, the better. I have no interest in living in fear, and my plan is to live through whatever comes next with a positive attitude and with as much satisfaction and fun as I can possibly muster. So it has always been important to me to be in community with others who share this outlook.

I now count this group as one of the most important elements in my life. I know the people I can talk to about next steps, I know people whom I can count on in an emergency, and I know who will look after my family if I happen to be out of town when something big goes awry. And now that I have experienced the pleasures (and joys and frustrations) of working in a group setting on matters of preparation, I would immediately join or start another group if I happened to move to a different area.

It's incredibly helpful to find people to join forces with as you step through the basics of self-preparation. I encourage you to consider seeking like-minded locals with whom to form such a group, if you haven't already done so, and to encourage others to do the same.

My preparation group is now working outside of our core and exploring ways to help get our larger community into a more resilient position. I'm only as secure as my neighbor is, and we're only as secure as our town, and our town is only as secure as the next town over. But it all begins at the center, like a fractal pattern, with a core of resilient households determining how the future unfolds.

> *The sixth concept of preparation is that community is essential.*

PROTECTING YOUR WEALTH

The time has come to put one foot in front of the other and take responsibility for your own financial future. We've entered some truly treacherous investing waters, where we must question everything and accept nothing, even (and especially) the base assumption that any given currency, be it the U.S. dollar or euro or yen, will retain its value. If you ascribe to the view that our structural predicaments in the economy, energy, and the environment won't lend themselves to easy fixes involving injections of thin-air money and more government deficit spending, then you should take steps to protect your wealth from the likely consequences of those ill-fated efforts.

What follows are the initial steps that I undertook when I first became convinced of the depth and the seriousness of the predicament we're in. Whether you choose to do something similar or very different is entirely up to you. I only offer these suggestions for your edification and consideration, not as specific investment advice.

1. *Get out of personal debt.* This means paying down what you can and taking on no new debt, especially if it won't increase your future cash flows. During the Great Depression, debt was a killer. During the 1990s and 2000s, credit (debt) advanced the living standards of many

and became to be viewed benignly as "something to manage," but the ultimate price was high. Being in debt severely limits your options during good times, and it's a positive destroyer during down times. Less tangibly, being out of debt feels really, really good, as if an invisible weight has been lifted. During stressful times like these, removing a nagging source of worry has a value all its own, which should not be underestimated.

2. *Get some inflation protection.* We can be fairly certain that we'll see inflation over time, especially as resource constraints appear while electronic money presses are working hard to conjure up an economic miracle. But there's another potentially concerning source of inflation in the trillions and trillions of dollars in U.S. debt held by foreign countries that would wreak havoc on the dollar if their holders felt it necessary to cash them in all at once.

So what does it mean to have good "inflation protection"? It means holding non–paper-based assets. Gold, silver, oil, grains, and base metals are a few examples that will suffice to help navigate the first period of transition away from paper and toward things. My personal choice has been to hold gold and silver, but there are many other reasonable vehicles. For those who are interested, there's a short document available on my web site that details the hows and whys of gold/silver purchasing (www.chrismartenson.com/buying_gold).

On a longer-term basis, moving funds out of paper wealth and into productive assets will certainly be the way to go. In this regard, holding titles to productive sources of energy such as gas fields, oil reserves, woodland, and electrical production (such as wind towers and other alternatives) offers the best chance of return, regardless of whether your local currency holds its value or bursts into flames.

3. *Diversify out of U.S. dollars.* Many residents of European countries consider holding all of one's assets in a single currency to be a sign of madness. Of course, Europe has a history of repeatedly and violently supporting the validity of this viewpoint, but you may also want to consider that the highly wealthy in the United States traditionally handle their affairs with assets in multiple currencies and countries. Having a bit of diversification here can be useful, and if you have the opportunity to hold foreign bank accounts, those can offer an important buffer. These opportunities are rapidly dwindling as the IRS and Treasury Department have been extremely active of late in shutting down such avenues for all but the very rich, who can afford the necessary legal teams required to establish foreign accounts.

WHAT TO LOOK FOR IF RELOCATING

After coming to the realization that the future may well be quite different from the past, you may be thinking about whether your current location is where you want to stay. My wife and I picked up our entire family and moved to a place that we judged would provide an excellent quality of life under almost any circumstances. We specifically sought a town or city that would be a fun, enjoyable place during times of both relative abundance and declining energy, and we moved away from an area that struck us as dangerously resistant to new ideas and change.

Community

A detectably functioning community encompassing a healthy spread of ages and skills was a nonnegotiable element for us. The first thing we looked for was a vibrant community where people had already demonstrated an ability to self-organize to create what they wanted. Becca identified the presence of "cooperative grocery stores" (a.k.a. co-ops) as an indicator that the local culture had what we were looking for. Her reasoning was that if people cared enough about their food to organize and sustain their own commercial enterprise around it, then they were the kind of people we wanted to be around.

Once we found an area rich with co-ops, we dug around further looking for other signs of life indicating the local people were actively creating their own opportunities and meeting some of their own needs. Fairs, festivals, and cohesive traditions, such as holiday extravaganzas and block parties, are good indicators that the local population knows how to do more together than accidentally bump into each other at the nearest big-box store.

Next, we looked within each community to see if it was well represented by residents of all ages. We found a few that seemed predominantly inhabited by boomers or retired folks; this is a valuable subset within a community, but we were looking to find a balance that included young families with children along with our middle-aged peers. We also hoped to find a variety of skill sets represented, as having a good mix of tradespeople, business professionals, laborers, artists, thinkers, and doers was important to us.

Population Density

We also wanted to live near enough to other people that we would have ample opportunities to socialize and have fun within our local sphere.

Movies, concerts, events, shows, parties, and so forth all require sufficient population density. So does finding the right kinds of people with which to create a new future. Children need a group of friends and the sense that they are living in the middle of someplace exciting. We didn't want driving to dominate our lives, and we wanted to feel that we really knew our neighbors, so getting the density just right felt very important to us—neither overpopulated nor underpopulated.

Rural with Farmland

Next, we wanted to be in a semirural location with the specific distinction that the local cropland be sufficient to sustainably support the existing population. The area we chose has lots of working farms and some of the best soil in the country. This distinguishes it from places that appear rural but are merely wooded and/or consist of thin, poor soils and are therefore incapable of supporting much in the way of a vibrant, relatively dense local population. Basically, we steered clear of "dirt poor" areas. Yes, you can build soils over time, but starting with thick, healthy soils is a lot easier.

Water

Not much happens without plenty of fresh water, especially predictable crop yields. The area we chose has ample water in the form of rainfall, rivers, and ground water (aquifers), and isn't overly prone to regular droughts. Water was another nonnegotiable element in our equation, and I wouldn't feel at all comfortable living in a place where water availability was questionable. For instance, you couldn't get me to own or invest in property in much of the American southwest, where the dominant source of water is a rapidly depleting aquifer. Definitely consider the available sources of water, both for regular and emergency use, when evaluating your location.

Work

Living and working and playing should ideally happen as close to each other as possible. We looked for an area that did not require significant amounts of driving to address all three of those needs. While many communities will figure out the relocalization details by necessity, we wanted to start in a place where at least some of the details had already been worked out. *Do bike trails exist? Is there navigable water nearby? Does public transportation exist? Do people tend to live close to where they work?*

Some areas don't offer the perfect answers to all three needs, but creative solutions may already exist . . . or perhaps they're waiting for someone like you to implement them.

What Should I Do?

What *should* you do? The list is potentially endless in its details, but simple enough in total: Begin preparing for change. This chapter has offered just a sampling of potential areas of change. I invite you to visit my web site, www.ChrisMartenson.com, for more information on the many subjects that are involved in preparation and to stay abreast of current developments. I have done my best to make this process easier with a free, online preparation guide that addresses the suggestions raised in this chapter in more specific detail (www.ChrisMartenson.com/what-should-i-do).

The sooner you get started, the sooner you'll begin to feel happier, more in control, and ready to face the future with your eyes fixed on the opportunities and options that do inevitably exist.

CHAPTER 28

THE OPPORTUNITIES

The story that I've told here is one of change. In any such story, both challenges and opportunities await. I'm hoping for a favorable, less painful outcome, but I'm also prepared for things to get worse before they get better. One thing that I absolutely don't see happening is a one-way descent into chaos. Yes, there may be dips in the road, and, yes, it may be a long slog toward the light, but even so, we'll pick ourselves up and carry on again. I see enormous opportunities waiting to be claimed, both during the period of adjustment and afterward.

The first opportunity in this story is to take advantage of this information to make changes in your life, investments, and community now, while the options remain abundant, reasonably accessible, and relatively easy. As I shared in the introduction to this book, my family and I have made enormous changes in our lives in response to this information, and we feel strongly that we are better off and enjoy a higher quality of life as a result. No matter how the future turns out, I will enjoy a better outcome because of my actions.

One set of opportunities that the future will not offer is anything that relies upon or requires a simple continuation of the past: an uninterrupted extrapolation of the past trajectory into the wild blue yonder. The energy for such a jaunt will be insufficient, and whether or not that turns out to be a limiting factor (as I believe it will be), the Great Credit Bubble will need to deflate quite a bit more before a renewed bout of debt accumulation can possibly begin again.

Below are the opportunities that I see, based on the understanding that energy and resources will have to be more carefully utilized in the future. Their careful stewardship and higher cultural value will support certain types of jobs, investments, and wealth accumulation, but not others. In most cases, I'm assuming that primary and secondary sources of wealth will triumph over tertiary forms, as we "get back to the basics" for a while.

You may not share my assessment, and that's perfectly all right; nobody has a lock on the future and what it might hold. If anything, I feel I'm more prepared than most to be surprised by how things unfold.

Still, here are a few basic "truths" that I think will shape the future significantly:

1. Net energy has peaked (or will soon), and this is a permanent condition.
2. The global energy allotment available for economic development and the economy itself will decline in lockstep.
3. Without increasing energy flows, the economy will "simplify," which is a euphemism for a massive structural shift that may be incredibly disruptive for a lot of people.
4. Without growth, most tertiary forms of wealth, such as stocks and bonds, will lose an enormous amount of their current value.
5. As with any shift, there will be winners and losers, largely segregated by who sees the changes coming first and adapts most rapidly—and who doesn't.

I reserve the right to change these views, should reliable new information arrive that runs counter to the data that formed these conclusions, and I encourage you to leave space in your thinking for changes based on new information that we may not even be capable of anticipating yet. But the past six years leading up to the writing of this book have seen an almost uninterrupted string of confirmations supporting the ideas and concepts contained herein. With that in mind, here are the opportunities that I see:

Resource Management and Materials Efficiency

In the future, reduce/reuse/recycle will no longer be just a feel-good slogan of environmentalists—it will be an important operating paradigm. Those countries and companies that perform the task of managing their energy and materials streams the most efficiently will fare better than the rest. There will be enormous opportunities in this arena going forward, including everything from point-of-source collection and separation, to recovery and reclamation services for waste streams, to designing more efficient production processes that absolutely minimize waste and loss. New jobs and skills will be required and created in this field. While doing more with less has always been the essence of good business, this field will require a parallel mind-set that can measure and incorporate the intrinsic value of things that simple prices based on money have traditionally overlooked.

If I owned a company that relied upon resource flows, I would seriously consider building up my inventories of those items most critical to value creation. I would trade a few points of profitability gained from cost-effective inventory management for the certainty of knowing that my business had what it needed to continue operating at a time when markets and circumstances might be too turbulent to support my resource requirements.

Part of the new measure of intrinsic value will need to include energy returned on energy invested, or EROEI. Companies and countries alike will need to begin making decisions based on the energy impacts of various factors. For example, should a government support investment in a new high-speed rail system, or the retrofitting of existing structures with additional insulation? Which one would be better for society in the long run? Right now, the decision would be based on cost and political considerations. In the future, the EROEI of the two options should be prominently displayed, like a window tag in a new car revealing the mileage per gallon of the vehicle being considered, so that this information can be weighed alongside other criteria. Developing useful EROEI estimates is not trivial work and will require the services of many bright people.

FOOD

Food is a multihundred-billion-dollar industry, and it will be undergoing a radical transformation over the coming years. Once the energy crunch begins, food will, by necessity, go up in price. The opportunity here, already being seized by communities in all corners of the world, is to get involved in the relocalization of food production, storage, and distribution. As a contrarian investor, when I look at a chart like this, I think that there's only one way for food expenditures as a percent of income to go: up (see Figure 28.1).

Because of the massive energy subsidy provided by petroleum, food expenditures have trended down to all-time lows. When that subsidy is removed, the trend will reverse. One way to combat the trend will be to keep the energy costs of food production as low as possible. That will, in many cases, involve using much less packaging and consuming food much closer to its point of origin (this means no more 1,800-mile Caesar salads).

If you don't have it in you to become a farmer, there are thousands of young people with strong backs and even stronger work ethics who are

Figure 28.1
Food Expenditure as a Percent of Income (U.S. Data)

Source: U.S. Geological Survey.[1]

ready, willing, and able to take on the task but lack the capital to make it happen. If you have the capital, you can facilitate farming by buying a piece of fertile land and developing an agreement with people who will work and improve that land for you as they make a living off of it. It's a win for both parties—your land, a reliable investment, will be steadily improved over time as it's worked in a sustainable fashion, and the tenant farmers will be able to work a more profitable piece of land than if they had taken on debt to buy their own meager parcel.

The next opportunity will be in food storage. Once upon a time, everybody had a means of storing food throughout the winter, either in root cellars or by preserving food. Clearly those features are largely missing from our current landscape and will have to be replicated somehow. While some people will opt to recreate these features for themselves in their own homes, many won't. For those people who won't, engaging a local business to perform the food storage tasks for them may be the preferred option. Very few of these operations currently exist; they will all have to be conceived and constructed. Think of centralized root cellars, where local crops can be stored in idealized conditions under the watchful eye of an experienced person.

People cannot escape the need to eat, and the number of opportunities in this arena are almost too numerous to count.

ENERGY

The big opportunities in energy will be around the areas of efficiency and relocalization. I see a prime area of opportunity in energy retrofits and green energy solutions for existing houses.

When I decided to put solar hot water panels on my house, I began with the usual online research and investigation to determine what the various options and features were. To my surprise, I found only a patchy network of web sites offering very little structured, useful information. When I turned to local installers as a potential source of information, I was quite surprised that not a single one came to my house prepared to type my requirements into a simple spreadsheet and offer a range of quotes based on the two or three key components of the system in a "good"—"better"—"best" configuration. Each quote was laboriously crafted elsewhere, and in each case, materials took several weeks on average to be produced and delivered. When the components finally arrived, they were delivered in a rental truck driven by the proprietor of the retail operation himself from a location over four hours away.

These experiences tell me that the American solar industry is ripe for improvement, and therefore with opportunity. I got the clear sense that if even 1 percent of the people in my region decided to install solar components, the local installation capacity and regional distributors would have been completely swamped and unable to meet the demand.

As energy becomes more expensive—and it will—retrofitting existing structures to make them more energy-efficient will become a very important occupation. Everything from insulating, to air sealing, to subdividing the interiors of oversized McMansions into smaller living units will go through an explosive phase of growth. Many of these retrofits can be marketed and sold as pure investments in which the improved cash flows alone can justify such a project for the homeowner, but we can also almost certainly count on government tax credits and other incentives to continue to play a role in nudging these activities forward.

FINANCIAL SERVICES

It's time to dust off the old valuation books and begin to perform very basic fundamental analysis on individual stocks and bond offerings that will help separate the winners from the losers. Because growth will no longer work as a general, across-the-board concept, index fund investing won't work. To deliver truly superior returns, or any at all, you'll need to know everything about a company—especially its dedication toward energy and materials conservation—and much of this won't appear in the annual report. The opportunity exists for fundamental analysis to regain its footing, and lots of jobs will be created in this area.

The future that I see will require far more nimble and alert money management than ever before. Many clients are going to demand a higher degree of engagement from their financial advisors, and this will open up new avenues for alert professionals in winning and retaining clients. The services to be performed here could include helping people find a qualified investment professional who can operate effectively in the new wealth-generating landscape of the future, or even training financial advisors toward better performance in that new landscape.

Unfortunately for the industry as a whole, I see a coming reduction in the amount of services currently offered. I doubt that the new future will be able to afford having 40 percent of its total profits funneled into the financial industry. But even though I see a lot of shrinkage visiting this industry, I also see plenty of work for those who can shift with the times.

GOVERNMENT EMPLOYMENT

This is one area where I can see only shrinkage. I think government pay, benefits, and total employment have all seen their peaks. In a reduced-energy environment, there's simply no way to afford having one in six workers employed by the government at a far higher total wage package than private workers enjoy.

With that in mind, where's the opportunity here? I think private companies are going to have to fill the void left by shrinking government services, hopefully at a more competitive, cost-effective rate (or the services will be dropped because they won't be worth it). Everything from trash removal, to policing, to sewer, water, and road maintenance will be up for grabs, and many communities have already made the leap to private management in some of these areas.

Whether we think this is the right thing or the wrong thing is beside the point; government services in a time of declining energy are going to be a lot smaller or fewer in number than government services in a time of abundant energy. Yes, there will have to be some trade-offs, and some treasured services may disappear, but not all of them will, and finding the best and most cost-effective way to provide the preserved services will certainly involve a new equilibrium in these areas.

The second opportunity will be for consultants to come in to help make trade-off decisions and provide insights into how to manage the tricky business of doing more with less. I can also envision local politicians needing (or desiring) someone to blame for necessary cuts, and consultants could provide cover for difficult decisions that need to be made.

MONEY

Money is a nonnegotiable element of a rich and complex society. Most people currently rely on others to manage our money for them, which is right and proper, because money is a service and it cannot manage itself. We call those managers "bankers." I see a future that involves different forms of money, offering both competition (which is healthy) and complementary forms of money. There's an enormous risk that our single-currency systems—the dollar or euro or yen or what-have-you—will cease to operate effectively, or at all, in the future. Recognizing this, many communities have decided that having only one currency is both undesirable and entirely too risky. What happens if that one currency fails?

Just as important, every currency enforces some behaviors and punishes others. Debt-based money is very good at motivating people to get out of bed and work extremely hard, but it's not very good at fostering long-range thinking, cooperation, or generational investing. Debt-based money enforces short-range thinking and a perpetual sense of scarcity.

But some communities want to foster long-range thinking and a sense of mutual abundance. The easiest and surest way to do this is to introduce a new money type or system that can operate in parallel with the current system—or perhaps even multiple new types and systems. This way, if the status quo fails for any reason, there will be backups. As I said in Chapter 26 (*The Good News*), these can operate like wetlands during a drought, continuing to feed the river of commerce even if the main tributary has run dry.

My prediction is that enormous opportunities exist for specialists to introduce and operate new money systems for local communities, perhaps even at the municipal, state, or provincial levels. Some of these types of money will be purely electronic, like mutual credit systems, and some may actually be backed by something tangible, such as a commodity like energy, food, or even gold or silver.

It would be a shame to suffer through a damaged economy simply because we relied on a single mismanaged money unit and failed to provide ourselves with an appropriate backup that could facilitate our economic exchanges in a time of need. It's time to recognize that our current money system is no longer serving us; we're serving it. We can both better control our risks and enjoy a future of our own design if we implement new, different, and improved money systems. Bernard Lietaer, one of the world's leading experts on monetary systems and alternative currencies, said this about money:

> While economic textbooks claim that people and corporations are competing for markets and resources, I claim that in reality they are competing for money—using markets and resources to do so. So designing new money systems really amounts to redesigning the target that orients much human effort.
>
> Furthermore, I believe that greed and competition are not a result of immutable human temperament; I've come to the conclusion that greed and fear of scarcity are in fact being continuously created and amplified as a direct result of the kind of money we're using.
>
> For example, we can produce more than enough food to feed everybody, and there's definitely enough work for everybody in the world, but there's clearly not enough money to pay for it all.
>
> The scarcity is in our national currencies. In fact, the job of central banks is to create and maintain that currency scarcity. The direct consequence is that we have to fight with each other in order to survive.[2]

Our current money system is damaged, its chances of survival aren't robust, and we'd do well to build some redundancy and resilience into our experience by introducing and using other forms of money now, while we can. It's my prediction that the difference between communities that merely survive and those that thrive in the future will depend, in part, on which ones have parallel currency systems in place.

CHANGE MANAGEMENT

The enormity of the scope of the changes that I see coming will require whole new skill sets and specialties to be developed and delivered to individuals, companies, and governments alike.

Managing for growth is one skill set; managing for stasis or even shrinkage is a different skill set altogether. Consider the hapless municipal manager who only has experience in growing yearly operational budgets. Every department and function gains a little more in their budget each year. The manager develops skills in negotiating how much goes to each area and keeping everybody reasonably happy with their allotment.

But the reverse of that situation is an entirely different process. Cutting budgets requires knowing which items are essential and which ones aren't. It involves making strategic decisions requiring a view of the future and knowing which services to retain, which to eliminate, and which to outsource. How does one plan for an uncertain future and then budget for it effectively? How does all of this get persuasively communicated to all the various stakeholders? The challenges are numerous, and the skills required to manage successfully here are quite often distinct from those that have been used during periods of active growth. Who will help bring these new skills to all of the municipal and corporate managers?

Reskilling will be important at all levels of the workforce, not just managerial. If my basic ideas hold true, then declining service jobs will be accompanied by a swing back toward manufacturing. Producing more local goods from local materials, especially recycled ones, will require an enormous retraining of a significant proportion of the workforce. In some cases, vital shop skills have been lost and will have to be regained somehow. There will be opportunities in the management and delivery of these reskilling services and lessons. But such dramatic work-life change isn't easy, especially for those past a certain age or who have heavily invested in their prior careers, which means that part of the reskilling services will have to include psychological counseling and management.

Coming to terms with the vast changes is going to be difficult for many and will require the support and participation of individuals who are adept at change management.

THE GREATEST OPPORTUNITY OF THEM ALL

Your greatest opportunity is the chance to rethink everything: your priorities, what you do with your time, and how you relate to others. Great moments of change are opportunities to shift who you are and how you show up in the world. If you feel as though you have been performing in a dress rehearsal rather than living your true life, then perhaps this prospect of change is something to look forward to, not something to be feared.

The opportunity exists here to redefine your life into something with more meaning, greater community connections, and personal fulfillment. The most important thing you can do in the days ahead is to forge stronger community connections, and help your own local community become more aware of and prepared for the changes that are already beginning. For those without either awareness or preparation—and there will be many in every community—the changes are going to feel wrenching, confusing, and possibly overwhelming. You have the chance to help them even as you help yourself. I invite you to trust yourself and make the most of this magnificent opportunity.

Appendix

Figure A.1
Minerals Fully or Partially Imported by the United States

Metal/Element	Percent	Major Import Sources
Arsenic (trioxide)	100	China, Morocco, Hong Kong, Chile
Asbestos	100	Canada
Bauxite (Aluminum)	100	Guinea, Jamaica, Australia, Brazil
Cesium	100	Canada
Fluorspar	100	China, Mexico, South Africa, Mongolia
Graphite (natural)	100	China, Mexico, Canada, Brazil
Indium	100	China, Japan, Canada, Belgium
Manganese	100	South Africa, Gabon, Australia, China
Mica, sheet	100	India, Belgium, China, Brazil
Niobium	100	Brazil, Canada, Estonia, Germany
Quartz Crystal	100	Brazil, Germany, Madagascar, Canada
Rare Earths	100	China, France, Japan, Russia
Rubidium	100	Canada
Strontium	100	Mexico, Germany
Tantalum	100	Australia, Brazil, China, Germany
Thallium	100	Russia, Netherlands, Belgium
Thorium	100	United Kingdom, France
Vanadium	100	Czech Republic, Swaziland, Canada, Austria
Yttrium	100	China, Japan, France, Austria
Gallium	99	China, Ukraine, Japan, Hungary
Gemstones	99	Israel, India, Belgium, South Africa
Bismuth	95	Belgium, Mexico, China, U.K.
Platinum	94	South Africa, U.K., Germany, Canada
Stone (dimension)	90	Italy, Turkey, China, Mexico
Diamond (natural)	88	Botswana, Namibia, Ireland, South Africa
Antimony	86	China, Mexico, Belgium
Rhenium	86	Chile, Germany
Barite	83	China, India
Titanium (natural)	82	South Africa, Australia, Canada, Ukraine
Potash	81	Canada, Belarus, Russia, Germany
Tin	79	Peru, Bolivia, China, Indonesia
Cobalt	78	Norway, Russia, Finland, China
Palladium	73	Russia, South Africa, U.K., Norway
Tungsten	70	China, Canada, Germany, Portugal
Titanium (sponge)	64	Kazakhstan, Japan, Russia, Ukraine
Chromium	62	South Africa, Kazakhstan, Russia, Zimbabwe
Peat	60	Canada

Notes

Chapter 5: Dangerous Exponentials

1. United Nations Population Division, Department of Economic and Social Affairs, "World Population Prospects: The 2008 Revision," *Population Newsletter* 87 (2009): 1.
2. U.S. Census Bureau, "Historical Estimates of World Population," www.census .gov/ipc/www/worldhis.html (accessed November 6, 2010).
3. United Nations Population Division, Department of Economic and Social Affairs, "World Population to 2300," (2004): 179–180. www.un.org/esa/population/ publications/longrange2/WorldPop2300final.pdf (accessed November 6, 2010).
4. Wisdom from Pakistan, "The World's Expected Carrying Capacity in a Post Industrial Agrarian Society," *Oil Drum: Europe*, November 1, 2007. www .theoildrum.com/node/3090 (accessed November 5, 2010).
5. Albert A. Bartlett, "Forgotten Fundamentals of the Energy Crisis," *American Journal of Physics* 46 no. 9 (1978): 876. www.albartlett.org/articles/art_ forgotten_fundamentals_overview.html (accessed November 5, 2010).
6. Albert A. Bartlett, "Arithmetic, Population, and Energy" (video). Last modified June 16, 2007. www.youtube.com/watch?v=F-QA2rkpBSY (accessed November 5, 2010).
7. Grant Smith and Christian Schmollinger, "China Passes U.S. as World's Biggest Energy Consumer, IEA Says," *Bloomberg*, June 20, 2010. www.bloomberg .com/news/2010-07-19/china-passes-u-s-as-biggest-energy-consumer-as-oil- imports-jump-iea-says.html (accessed November 5, 2010).
8. C. Bergsten and others, "Energy Implications of China's Growth," in *China's Rise: Challenges and Opportunities* (Washington, DC: Peterson Institute for International Economics, 2009), 137–168. www.piie.com/publications/ chapters_preview/4174/07iie4174.pdf (accessed September 7, 2010).

Chapter 6: An Inconvenient Lie: The Truth about Growth

1. "Kenneth Boulding," *Wikiquotes*. http://en.wikiquote.org/wiki/Kenneth_Boulding (accessed September 7, 2010).
2. Timothy F. Geithner, "Welcome to the Recovery," *The New York Times*, August 2, 2010. www.nytimes.com/2010/08/03/opinion/03geithner.html (accessed September 7, 2010).

3. Julian L. Simon, "When Will We Run Out of Oil? Never!" *The Ultimate Resource II: People, Materials, Environment,* December 23, 1993. www.juliansimon .com/writings/Ultimate_Resource/TCHAR11.txt (accessed November 4, 2010).

Chapter 7: Our Money System

1. Justin Scheck, "Mackerel Economics in Prison Leads to Appreciation for Oily Fillets," *The Wall Street Journal,* October 2, 2008. http://online.wsj.com/ article/NA_WSJ_PUB:SB122290720439096481.html (accessed September 7, 2010).
2. Larry Richter, "Argentina's Stopgap Cash Gets Some Funny Looks," *The New York Times,* August 26, 2001. www.nytimes.com/2001/08/26/world/ argentina-s-stopgap-cash-gets-some-funny-looks.html?pagewanted=all (accessed November 4, 2010).
3. John Kenneth Galbraith, *Money: Whence It Came, Where It Went* (New York: Houghton Mifflin, 1975), 18.
4. "The Story of the Federal Reserve System," *Federal Reserve Bank of New York.* www.newyorkfed.org/publications/result.cfm?comics=1 (accessed September 7, 2010).
5. "Putting It Simply," *Federal Reserve Bank of Boston,* 1984.

Chapter 8: Problems and Predicaments

1. John Michael Greer, *The Long Descent: The User's Guide to the End of the Industrial Age* (Gabriola Island, British Columbia: New Society, 2008), 22.

Chapter 9: What Is Wealth?: (Hint: It's Not Money)

1. Adam Smith, *The Wealth of Nations* (New York: Classic House Books, 2009), 1.

Chapter 10: Debt

1. Herbert Stein, "Herb Stein's Unfamiliar Quotations," *Slate.* www.slate.com/id/ 2561 (accessed November 5, 2010).
2. Carmen M. Reinhart and Kenneth S. Rogoff, *This Time Is Different: Eight Centuries of Financial Folly* (Princeton: Princeton University Press, 2009).
3. "The Debt to the Penny and Who Holds It," *TreasuryDirect.* www.treasurydirect .gov/NP/BPDLogin?application=np (accessed October 21, 2010).
4. Richard W. Fisher, "The Fed's Response to the Current Economic Challenge (With References to Gershon Bleichröder and Central Bank Independence)," *Federal Reserve Bank of Dallas,* February 9, 2009. www.dallasfed.org/news/ speeches/fisher/2009/fs090209.cfm (accessed October 24, 2010).

Chapter 11: The Great Credit Bubble

1. "Predicting the Housing Future: Los Angeles and Orange Counties. Using the Case-Shiller Index to Find a Bottom," *Dr. Housing Bubble*. www .doctorhousingbubble.com/predicting-the-housing-future-los-angeles-and-orange-counties-using-the-case-shiller-index-to-find-a-bottom (accessed September 7, 2010).
2. "Median Housing Price to Income Ratios For Various Cities," *My Money Blog*. www.mymoneyblog.com/median-housing-price-to-income-ratios-for-various-cities.html (accessed October 24, 2010).
3. "Update: Ratio Median House Price to Median Income," *Calculated Risk*. www.calculatedriskblog.com/2008/06/update-ratio-median-house-price-to.html (accessed September 7, 2010).
4. Nouriel Roubini, "Why Central Banks Should Burst Bubbles," *International Finance* 9 no. 1 (2006): 87–107.
5. "The South Sea Company," *Wikipedia*. http://en.wikipedia.org/wiki/South_Sea_Company (accessed September 7, 2010).
6. Jonathan McCarthy and Richard W. Peach, "Are Home Prices the Next 'Bubble?'" *Economic Policy Review* 10, no. 3 (2004). www.ny.frb.org/research/epr/04v10n3/0412mcca.html (accessed September 7, 2010).
7. Alan Greenspan, "Remarks by Chairman Alan Greenspan—Financial Derivatives—Before the Futures Industry Association, Boca Raton, Florida," *Federal Reserve Board*. www.federalreserve.gov/boarddocs/speeches/1999/19990319 .htm (accessed September 7, 2010).
8. Chris Martenson, "Housing—Simple As That," *ChrisMartenson.com*. www .chrismartenson.com/martensonreport/housing-simple (accessed October 29, 2010).
9. "Flow of Funds Accounts of the United States," *Federal Reserve Statistical Release*. www.federalreserve.gov/releases/z1/ (accessed September 7, 2010).
10. Ludwig von Mises, "Interest, Credit Expansion, and the Trade Cycle: The Monetary or Circulation Credit Theory of the Trade Cycle," *Human Action: The Scholars Edition*. http://mises.org/humanaction/chap20sec8.asp (accessed October 25, 2010).

Chapter 12: Like a Moth to Flame: Our Destructive Tendency to Print

1. Alan Greenspan, "Gold and Economic Freedom," in Ayn Rand, ed., *Capitalism: The Unknown Ideal* (New York: Penguin Group, 1967), 101–108.
2. Carmen M. Reinhart and Kenneth S. Rogoff, *This Time Is Different: Eight Centuries of Financial Folly* (Princeton: Princeton University Press, 2009).

Chapter 13: Fuzzy Numbers

1. Kevin Phillips, "Numbers Racket: Why the Economy Is Worse than We Know." *Harper's Magazine*, May 2008. www.harpers.org/archive/2008/05/0082023 (accessed September 7, 2010).

2. "Fed Luminaries Spar Over U.S. Inflation Target," *The Wall Street Journal*, April 20, 2009. http://online.wsj.com/article/SB124006652812232007.html (accessed October 25, 2010).

3. "Zimbabwean dollar," *Wikipedia*. http://en.wikipedia.org/wiki/Zimbabwean_dollar (accessed September 7, 2010).

4. "Consumer Price Index: December 2007," *Bureau of Labor Statistics*. www.bls.gov/news.release/History/cpi_01162008.txt (accessed October 25, 2010).

5. "Retail Food Prices Up at Beginning of 2008," *American Farm Bureau*, March 27, 2008. www.fb.org/index.php?fuseaction=newsroom.newsfocus&year=2008&file=nr0327.html (accessed September 7, 2010; calculations were done manually by author).

6. Timothy Aeppel, "Accounting for Quality Change," in *Essentials of Economics*, ed. N. Gregory Mankiw (Mason, OH: Cengage Learning, 2008), 350.

7. John Williams, "Alternate Inflation Charts," *Shadow Government Statistics*. www.shadowstats.com/alternate_data/inflation-charts (accessed November 8, 2010).

8. Ibid.

9. Nicole Mayerhauser and Marshall Reinsdorf, "Housing Services in the National Economic Accounts," *Bureau of Economic Analysis*, 1. www.bea.gov/papers/pdf/RIPfactsheet.pdf (accessed September 7, 2010).

10. "Table 7.12. Imputations in the National Income and Product Accounts." *Survey of Current Business*, August 2010. *Bureau of Economic Analysis*, 169, line 133. www.bea.gov/histdata/Releases/GDP_and_PI/2010/Q2/Third_September-30-2010/TP/TPSection7all_xls.xls (accessed October 27, 2010).

11. Ibid., lines 28 and 29.

12. For a rather nice and comprehensive discussion of the role and history behind the utilization of hedonics by the BEA, the reader is directed to a paper by Dave Wasshausen and Brent R. Moulton titled, "The Role of Hedonic Methods in Measuring Real GDP in the United States." www.bea.gov/papers/pdf/hedonicGDP.pdf (accessed October 15, 2010).

13. Mike Shedlock, "Grossly Distorted Procedures," *Mish's Global Economic Analysis*, May 11, 2005. http://globaleconomicanalysis.blogspot.com/2005/05/grossly-distorted-procedures.html (accessed November 4, 2010).

14. Phillips, "Numbers Racket."

Chapter 14: Starting the Race with Our Shoes Tied Together

1. "Crumbling Nation? U.S. Infrastructure Gets a 'D,'" *MSNBC.com Staff and News Service Reports*, March 9, 2005. www.msnbc.msn.com/id/7137552/ (accessed September 7, 2010).

2. "Personal Savings Drop to a 73-Year Low," *Associated Press*, January 1, 2007. www.msnbc.msn.com/id/16922582/ (accessed September 7, 2010).

3. "Eurozone household savings rate in December 2009 was 15.1% compared with US at 3.6% and Japan just above 2.0%," *Finfacts Ireland*, April 30, 2010. www.finfacts.ie/irishfinancenews/article_1019587.shtml (accessed October 27, 2010).

4. Aart Kraay, "Household Saving in China," *World Bank Economic Review*, September 2000. www-wds.worldbank.org/external/default/WDSContentServer/IW3P/IB/2001/02/10/000094946_0101300532131/Rendered/PDF/multi_page.pdf (accessed October 27, 2010).

5. "Plutarch." *BrainyQuote.com*, *Xplore Inc*, 2010. www.brainyquote.com/quotes/quotes/p/plutarch109440.html (accessed October 27, 2010).

6. "Dire Outcomes Predicted for Municipal Pension Systems." *Kellogg School of Management*. www.kellogg.northwestern.edu/News_Articles/2010/municipal-pension-systems.aspx (accessed October 27, 2010).

7. Steven Greenhut, "Vallejo's Painful Lessons in Municipal Bankruptcy," *The Wall Street Journal*, March 26, 2010. http://online.wsj.com/article/SB100014240527 4870362530457511555157876200 6.html (accessed September 7, 2010).

8. Jonathan Stempel, "Corporate America Faces Big Pension Shortfalls." *Reuters*, January 8, 2009. www.reuters.com/article/idUSN0854172520090108 (accessed September 7, 2010).

9. Laurence Kotlikoff, "U.S. Is Bankrupt and We Don't Even Know It." *Bloomberg News*, August 10, 2010. www.bloomberg.com/news/2010-08-11/u-s-is-bankrupt-and-we-don-t-even-know-commentary-by-laurence-kotlikoff.html (accessed September 7, 2010).

10. Ibid.

Chapter 15: Energy and the Economy

1. Eric Beinhocker, *Origin of Wealth: Evolution, Complexity, and the Radical Remaking of Economics* (Boston: Harvard Business School Press, 2006), 68.

2. Ibid., 9 and 11.

3. Mark Buchanan, *Ubiquity: Why Catastrophes Happen* (New York: Three Rivers Press, 2001).

4. Brad DeLong, "Estimating World GDP," May 24, 1998. www.j-bradford-delong.net/TCEH/1998_Draft/World_GDP/Estimating_World_GDP.html (accessed November 3, 2010).

5. Thom Hartmann, *Last Hours of Ancient Sunlight, Revised and Updated: The Fate of the World and What We Can Do Before It's Too Late* (New York: Three Rivers Press, 2004): 12–13.

6. Ibid.

7. C.J. Cleveland, "Net Energy from Oil and Gas Extraction in the United States, 1954–1997," *Energy* 30 (2005): 769–782.

8. "Salazar Reforms Oil Shale Program—Department of Interior News Release," *Department of the Interior Bureau of Land Management*, October 20, 2009. www.blm.gov/wo/st/en/prog/energy/oilshale_2.html (accessed October 27, 2010).

9. Nate Hagens, "Unconventional Oil: Tar Sands and Shale Oil—EROI on the Web, Part 3 of 6." *Oil Drum*, April 15, 2008. www.theoildrum.com/node/3839 (accessed November 8, 2010).

10. Cutler J. Cleveland and Peter O'Connor, "An Assessment of the Energy Return on Investment (EROI) of Oil Shale," *Western Resource Advocates*.

www.westernresourceadvocates.org/land/pdf/oseroireport.pdf (accessed September 7, 2010).

11. Cutler J. Cleveland, et al., "Energy and the U.S. Economy: A Biophysical Perspective," *Science* (New Series) 225:4665 (Aug. 31, 1984), 890–897.

12. Daniela Russi, "An Integrated Assessment of a Large-Scale Biodiesel Production in Italy: Killing Several Birds with One Stone?" *Energy Policy* 36 (2008): 1169–1180.

13. H. Shapouri, et al., "The 2001 Net Energy Balance of Corn Ethanol," *USDA Office of the Chief Economist*, July 14, 2004. www.brdisolutions.com/Site%20Docs/Net_Energy_Balance_of_Corn_Ethanol_Shapouri.pdf. (accessed November 8, 2010).

14. D. Pimentel and Tad Patzek, "Ethanol Production Using Corn, Switchgrass, and Wood; Biodiesel Production Using Soybean and Sunflower," *Natural Resources Research*, 14:1 (March 2005): 65–76.

15. Robert Rapier, "Understanding EROEI," *R-Squared Energy Blog*. http://robertrapier.wordpress.com/2008/03/05/understanding-eroei/ (accessed November 4, 2010).

16. Ida Kubiszewski, et al., Meta-Analysis of Net Energy Return for Wind Power Systems, *Renewable Energy* 35 (2010): 218–225.

17. 1 Gallon of Gas = 124,262 BTUs
Source: www.eia.doe.gov/kids/energy.cfm?page=about_energy_conversion_calculator-basics.
3,412 BTUs = 1 KWh
Source: U.S. Department of Energy, Bonneville Power Mgt.
1 Gallon of Gas = 36.4 KWh
(124,262 BTUs in a gallon of gas divided by 3,412 BTUs in 1 KWh)
Human work (sustained): 74 Watts/Hour (agricultural work) to 100 Watts/hour (very fit individual)
Therefore, 1 Gallon of Gas = 492 hours to 364 hours of human work output

18. David Pimentel and Mario Giampietro, "Food, Land, Population and the U.S. Economy," *Carrying Capacity Network*, November 21, 1994. http://dieoff.org/page40.htm (accessed November 4, 2010).

Chapter 16: Peak Oil

1. Richard Heinberg, *The Party's Over*, 2nd ed. (Gabriola Island, British Columbia: New Society Publishers, 2005); Thom Hartmann, *The Last Hours of Ancient Sunlight* (New York: Three Rivers Press, 2004); James Howard Kunstler, *The Long Emergency* (New York: Atlantic Monthly Press, 2005); Matthew Simmons, *Twilight in the Desert* (Hoboken, NJ: John Wiley & Sons, Inc., 2005); Richard Heinberg, *Power Down* (New York: Oxford University Press, 2009); Kenneth S. Deffeyes, *Beyond Oil: The View from Hubbert's Peak* (New York: Hill and Wang, 2005).

2. Praveen Ghanta, "Is Peak Oil Real? A List of Countries Past Peak," *Oil Drum*. www.theoildrum.com/node/5576 (accessed October 28, 2010).

3. Kevin Morrison and Steve Johnson, "UK Net Oil Importer for First Time in Decade," *Energy Bulletin—Post Carbon Institute,* August 11, 2004. www .energybulletin.net/node/1604 (accessed September 7, 2010).

4. Andrew McNamara, "Highway of Diamonds," *ASPO Australia*, March 4, 2008. www.aspo-australia.org.au/general/highway-of-diamonds.html (accessed September 7, 2010).

5. "The World Factbook," *Central Intelligence Agency.* www.cia.gov/library/ publications/the-world-factbook/geos/xx.html (accessed November 6, 2010).

6. "Table 11.5 World Crude Oil Production 1960–2009," Energy Information Administration. www.eia.doe.gov/aer/txt/ptb1105.html (accessed November 8, 2010).

7. International Energy Agency, "Demand," *Oil Market Report,* March 13, 2009. http://omrpublic.iea.org/omrarchive/13mar09dem.pdf (accessed November 4, 2010).

8. "World Energy Outlook 2008: Executive Summary," *International Energy Agency.* November 2008, 6. www.worldenergyoutlook.org/weo2008/ WEO2008_es_english.pdf (accessed November 4, 2010).

9. "Export Land Model," Wikipedia. http://en.wikipedia.org/wiki/Export_Land_ Model (accessed November 5, 2010).

Chapter 17: Alternatives: Necessary but Insufficient

1. Julian Simon, "When Will We Run Out of Oil? Never!" *The Ultimate Resource II: People, Materials and Environment.* www.juliansimon.com/writings/ Ultimate_Resource/TCHAR11.txt (accessed October 30, 2010).

2. "Energy Units," *Bioenergy Feedstock Information Network.* http://bioenergy .ornl.gov/papers/misc/energy_conv.html (accessed October 30, 2010).

3. U.S. Energy Information Administration, "Petroleum (Oil) Production," *International Petroleum Monthly*, September 2010, Table 4.4. www.eia.doe.gov/ ipm/supply.html (accessed October 28, 2010).

4. Author's own calculations relying on various information sources from the EIA, World Bank, and existing solar installations and biofuels production.

5. "International Energy Outlook 2010," *Energy Information Administration*, July 27, 2010. www.eia.gov/oiaf/ieo/index.html (accessed November 4, 2010).

6. "World Wind Energy Report 2009," *World Wind Energy Association*, March 2010. www.wwindea.org/home/images/stories/worldwindenergyreport 2009_s.pdf (accessed October 30, 2010).

7. Vaclav Smil, *Energy Transitions: History, Requirements, Prospects* (Westport, CT: Praeger, 2010.)

8. National Research Council Committee on Assessment of Resource Needs for Fuel Cell and Hydrogen Technologies, "Plug-In Hybrid Vehicle Costs Likely to Remain High, Benefits Modest for Decades," *Transitions to Alternative Transportation Technologies—Plug-in Hybrid Electric Vehicles,* (The National Academies Press, December 2009). www8.nationalacademies.org/onpinews/ newsitem.aspx?RecordID=12826 (accessed October 30, 2010).

9. Robert Bryce, *Gusher of Lies: The Dangerous Delusions of Energy Independence* (New York: Public Affairs, 2008), 206.

10. "Plans For New Reactors Worldwide," *World Nuclear Association*, August 2010. www.world-nuclear.org/info/inf17.html (accessed October 30, 2010); and "Nuclear Power Plants, World-Wide," *European Nuclear Society*. www.euronuclear.org/info/encyclopedia/n/nuclear-power-plant-world-wide.htm (accessed October 30, 2010).

11. Wang Ying and John Duce, "Uranium Bottoming as China Boosts Stockpiles," *Bloomberg News*, July 12, 2010. www.bloomberg.com/news/2010-07-11/uranium-bottoming-as-china-boosts-stockpiles-with-10-000-tons-from-cameco.html (accessed September 7, 2010).

12. "Uranium Mining," *Wikipedia*. http://en.wikipedia.org/wiki/Uranium_mining (accessed October 30, 2010).

13. "Uranium Resources and Nuclear Energy," *Energy Watch Group*, December 2006, 9. www.energywatchgroup.org/fileadmin/global/pdf/EWG_Report_Uranium_3-12-2006ms.pdf (accessed October 30, 2010).

14. Ibid, 10.

15. "Military Warheads as a Source of Nuclear Fuel," *World Nuclear Association*, October 2009. www.world-nuclear.org/info/inf13.html (accessed October 30, 2010).

16. "Megatons to Megawatts," *USEC, Inc.* www.usec.com/megatonstomegawatts.htm (accessed September 7, 2010).

17. Thomas B. Cochrane, et al., "Fast Breeder Reactor Programs: History and Status," *International Panel on Fissile Materials*, February 2010, 1. http://brc.gov/pdfFiles/May2010_Meeting/IPFM%20Research%20Report%208%20Breeders,%20Web.pdf,%20Web.pdf (accessed October 30, 2010).

18. Ibid, 2.

19. "Clean Coal or Dirty Coal?" Alternative Energy Blog. http://alt-e.blogspot.com/2006_10_01_archive.html (accessed September 7, 2010).

20. Smil, *Energy Transitions*, appendix 1.

21. Bartlett, "Arithmetic, Population and Energy."

22. "Annual Energy Review." *U.S. Energy Information Administration*, August 19, 2010. www.eia.doe.gov/emeu/aer/coal.html (accessed September 7, 2010).

23. T.W. Patzek and G.D. Croft, "A Global Coal Production Forecast with Multi-Hubbert Cycle Analysis," *Energy*, 35:3109–3122.

24. Alternative Energy Outlook 2006 with Projections to 2030," *U.S. Energy Information Administration*, December 2005. eia.gov/oiaf/archive/aeo06/excel/figure102_data.xls (accessed September 7, 2010).

25. Peter Fairley, "China's Coal Future," *Technology Review*, January 1, 2007. www.technologyreview.com/energy/18069/ (accessed September 7, 2010).

26. Euan Mearns, "The Chinese Coal Monster," *Energy Bulletin*, July 12, 2010. www.energybulletin.net/node/53411 (accessed September 7, 2010).

27. C. Lowell Miller, "Coal Conversion—Pathway to Alternate Fuels," *Office of Fossil Energy, U.S. Department of Energy*. January 19, 2007, 15. www.futurecoalfuels.org/documents/011907_miller.pdf (accessed November 5, 2010).

28. "Simmons Oil Monthly—Solar Energy Overview," *Simmons & Company International*, February 16, 2006, 1.

29. Dennis Avery, "Biofuels, Food or Wildlife? The Massive Land Costs of U.S. Ethanol," *Competitive Enterprise Institute*, September 21, 2006. cei.org/gencon/025,05532.cfm (accessed September 7, 2010).

30. "How the Palm Oil Industry Is Cooking the Climate," *Greenpeace International*, 2007. www.greenpeace.org/raw/content/international/press/reports/palm-oil-cooking-the-climate.pdf (accessed September 7, 2010).

31. Suzanne Goldenberg, "US Navy Completes Successful Test on Boat Powered by Algae," *The Guardian*, October 27, 2010. www.guardian.co.uk/environment/2010/oct/27/us-navy-biofuel-gunboat (accessed October 28, 2010).

32. "2016 Levelized Cost of New Generation Resources from the Annual Energy Outlook 2010," *U.S. Energy Information Association*, January 12, 2010. www.eia.doe.gov/oiaf/aeo/electricity_generation.html (accessed October 30, 2010).

33. Personal conversation with David Murphy, an EROEI researcher.

Chapter 18: Why Technology Can't Fix This

1. Robert Hirsch et al, "Peaking of World Oil Production: Impacts, Mitigation and Risk Management," *Energy Bulletin*, March 6, 2005. www.energybulletin.net/node/4638 (accessed November 8, 2010).

Chapter 19: Minerals: Gone with the Wind

1. "Cleopatra: (Late 69 BC–August 12, 30 BC)," *Wikipedia*. http://en.wikipedia.org/wiki/Cleopatra_VII (accessed November 5, 2010); "Cheops Pyramid: 2589–2566 BC," *Oracle Thinkquest*. http://library.thinkquest.org/J002037F/cheops_pyramid.htm (accessed November 5, 2010); "Space Shuttle Columbia," *Wikipedia*. http://en.wikipedia.org/wiki/Space_Shuttle_Columbia (accessed November 8, 2010).

2. Christine McLelland, "What Earth Materials Are in My Subaru?," *American Geological Society*. www.geosociety.org/educate/LessonPlans/Earth_Materials_in_Subaru.pdf (accessed November 6, 2010).

3. "Table 1.11: Number of U.S. Aircraft, Vehicles, Vessels and Other Conveyances," *Research and Innovation Technology Administration Bureau of Transportation Statistics*. www.bts.gov/publications/national_transportation_statistics/html/table_01_11.html (accessed November 8, 2010).

4. A.M. Diederen, "Metal Minerals Scarcity and the Elements of Hope," *The Oil Drum: Europe*, March 10, 2009. http://europe.theoildrum.com/node/5559 (accessed November 8, 2010).

Chapter 20: Soil: Thin, Thinner, Gone

1. "How to Feed the World in 2050," *Food and Agriculture Association of the United Nations*, October 2009, 8. www.fao.org/fileadmin/templates/wsfs/docs/expert_paper/How_to_Feed_the_World_in_2050.pdf (accessed October 30, 2010).

2. Rob Avis, "The Story of Soil," *Permaculture Research Institute*, June 17, 2010. http://permaculture.org.au/2010/06/17/the-story-of-soil (accessed September 7, 2010).
3. W.M. Stewart, "Fertilizer Contributions to Crop Yield," *News and Views: Potash and Phosphate Institute and Potash and Phosphate Institute of Canada,* May 2002. www.ipni.net/ppiweb/ppinews.nsf/$webcontents/7DE814BEC3A5 A6EF85256BD80067B43C/$file/Crop+Yield.pdf (accessed October 30, 2010).
4. Cheryl Long, "Industrial Farming Is Giving Us Less Nutritious Food," *Mother Earth News,* June/July 2009. www.motherearthnews.com/Sustainable-Farming/ Nutrient-Decline-Industrial-Farming.aspx (accessed November 4, 2010).
5. Euan Rocha, "Potash Corp Rejects BHP Billiton's $39 Bln Bid," *Reuters,* August 17, 2010. www.reuters.com/article/idUSTRE67G1R620100817 (accessed October 30, 2010).
6. James Elser and Stuart White, "Peak Phosphorous," *Foreign Policy*, April 20, 2010. www.foreignpolicy.com/articles/2010/04/20/peak_phosphorus (accessed October 30, 2010).
7. Timothy Egan, *The Worst Hard Times* (New York: Mariner Books, 2006), 8.

Chapter 21: Parched: The Coming Water Wars

1. Lester R. Brown, *Plan B 4.0: Mobilizing to Save Civilization* (NY: W.W. Norton), 2009.
2. Brown, *Plan B*; and Sandra Postel, *Pillar of Sand: Can the Irrigation Miracle Last?* (New York: W.W. Norton) 1999.
3. Brown, *Plan B*.
4. Brown, *Plan B*.
5. David Seckler, et al., "Water Scarcity in the Twenty First Century," Water Brief 1 (Colombo, Sri Lanka: International Water Management Institute, 1999).
6. Dale Allen Pfeiffer , "Eating Fossil Fuels," *The Wilderness Publications*, October 3, 2003. www.organicconsumers.org/corp/fossil-fuels.cfm (accessed October 30, 2010).
7. P. Torcellini, N. Long, and R. Judkoff, "Consumptive Water Use for U.S. Power Production," *National Renewable Energy Laboratory*, December 2003. www .nrel.gov/docs/fy04osti/33905.pdf (accessed October 30, 2010).

Chapter 22: All Fished Out

1. Myers, Ransom and Worm, Boris. "Rapid Worldwide Depletion of Predatory Fish Communities." *Nature* 423 (2003): 280–283. www.nature.com/nature/ journal/v423/n6937/full/nature01610.html (accessed October 30, 2010).
2. Lester R. Brown, *Plan B 3.0: Mobilizing to Save Civilization* (NY: W.W. Norton), 2003.
3. Arthur Max, "Toxins Found in Whales Bode Ill for Humans," *ABC News*, June 24, 2010. http://abcnews.go.com/Technology/wireStory?id=11003954 (accessed October 30, 2010).

4. John Roach, "Source of Half Earth's Oxygen Gets Little Credit," *National Geographic News*, June 7, 2004. http://news.nationalgeographic.com/news/2004/06/0607_040607_phytoplankton.html (accessed November 4, 2010).

5. Steve Connor, "The Dead Sea: Global Warming Blamed for 40 Percent Decline in the Ocean's Phytoplankton," *The Independent*, July 29, 2010. www.independent.co.uk/environment/climate-change/the-dead-sea-global-warming-blamed-for-40-per-cent-decline-in-the-oceans-phytoplankton-2038074.html (accessed November 4, 2010).

6. Watson W. Gregg and Margarita E. Conkright, "Decadal Changes in Global Ocean Chlorophyll," *Geophysical Research Letters* (2002) 29:15. http://gmao.gsfc.nasa.gov/research/oceanbiology/reprints/greggconkright_GRL2002.pdf (accessed November 4, 2010).

7. David Perlman, "Decline in Oceans' Phytoplankton Alarms Scientists," SFGate.com, October 6, 2003. http://articles.sfgate.com/2003-10-06/news/17513683_1_plankton-ocean-plants-carbon-dioxide (accessed November 4, 2010).

Chapter 23: Convergence

1. "Paulson Says U.S. Was 'Very Close' to Financial Collapse: Video," *Bloomberg*, February 2, 2010. www.bloomberg.com/news/2010-02-02/paulson-says-u-s-was-very-close-to-financial-collapse-video.html (accessed October 30, 2010); and "Bank of England's Mervyn King Says HBOS and RBS Came within Hours of Collapse," *Telegraph*, September 24, 2009, www.telegraph.co.uk/finance/newsbysector/banksandfinance/6226238/Bank-of-Englands-Mervyn-King-says-HBOS-and-RBS-came-within-hours-of-collapse.html (accessed October 30, 2010).

2. Donella Meadows, *Limits to Growth* (New York: Signet) 1972.

Chapter 25: Future Scenarios

1. "Saving Oil in a Hurry," *International Energy Administration*. www.iea.org/textbase/nppdf/free/2005/SavingOil.pdf (accessed November 5, 2010).

2. "Reserve Currency," *Wikipedia*. http://en.wikipedia.org/wiki/Reserve_currency (accessed October 30, 2010).

Chapter 26: The Good News

1. H. E. Daly, *Steady-State Economics: The Economics of Biophysical Equilibrium and Moral Growth.* (San Francisco: W. H. Freeman) 1977.

2. *Wissenschaftliche Selbstbiographie. Mit einem Bildnis und der von Max von Laue gehaltenen Traueransprache.*, Johann Ambrosius Barth Verlag, (Leipzig 1948), p. 22, as translated in Max Planck, *Scientific Autobiography and Other Papers,* trans. F. Gaynor (New York: Philosophical Library, 1949), pp.33–34 (as cited in T.S. Kuhn, *The Structure of Scientific Revolutions.* (Chicago: University of Chicago Press, 1962).

3. "Local Exchange Trading Systems," *Wikipedia*. http://en.wikipedia.org/wiki/Local_Exchange_Trading_Systems (accessed November 4, 2010).

4. "Demurrage (currency)," *Wikipedia*. http://en.wikipedia.org/wiki/Demurrage_%
28currency%29 (accessed November 7, 2010).
5. "Ecological Footprint," *Wikipedia*. http://en.wikipedia.org/wiki/Ecological_
footprint (accessed November 4, 2010).

Chapter 28: The Opportunities

1. "The US Geological Survey Mineral Resource Program Five-Year Plan,
2006–2010," *U.S. Department of the Interior, U.S. Geological Survey.*
http://minerals.usgs.gov/plan/2006-2010/mrp-plan-2006-2010.pdf (accessed
November 8, 2010), 3.
2. Bernard Lietaer, "Beyond Greed and Scarcity," *Yes!*, June 30, 1997. www.yes
magazine.org/issues/money-print-your-own/beyond-greed-and-scarcity (accessed
October 30, 2010).

INDEX